W9-ASB-012

WITHDRAWN

WITHDRAWN

Masterworks of the British Cinema

63443

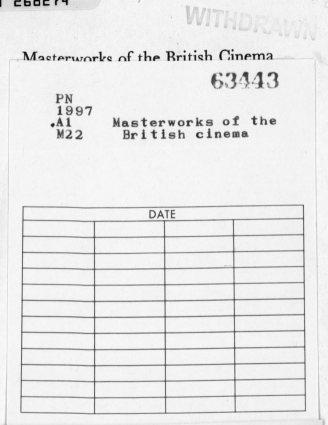

DATE			

© THE BAKER & TAYLOR CO.

Masterworks of the British Cinema

Introduction by John Russell Taylor

Brief Encounter
The Third Man
Kind Hearts and Coronets
Saturday Night and Sunday
Morning

Icon Editions

Harper & Row, Publishers

New York, Evanston, San Francisco, London

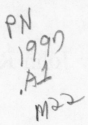

PN
1997
.A1
M22

FIRST US EDITION

ISBN: 0-06-438614-7 (cloth) 0-06-430060-9 (paper)

LIBRARY OF CONGRESS CATALOG CARD NUMBER: 74-11709

CONTENTS

ACKNOWLEDGEMENTS

The publishers wish to thank the following individuals and organizations for their help in the preparation of this volume: The British Film Institute, for the provision of viewing facilities; Anglo-EMI Distributors, for providing stills from *Kind Hearts and Coronets*; Mr Joel Finler, for the loan of stills; Dr Roger Manvell, for permission to reprint an extract from his book *The Film and The Public;* Faber and Faber Ltd, for permission to reprint an extract from *A Mirror for England* by Raymond Durgnat; *Film Heritage*, for permission to reprint an article on *The Third Man* by Joseph A. Gomez; *Films and Filming*, for permission to reprint extracts from an article on *Kind Hearts and Coronets* by Alan Stanbrook; Mr. Boleslaw Sulik, for permission to reprint his article on *Saturday Night and Sunday Morning*.

INTRODUCTION

by John Russell Taylor

The two great legends about the British cinema are that it has no auteurs and that its finest works are product of the team spirit. The precise relationship of these two ideas is not very clear. Possibly teamwork predominates because there are no outstanding individual creators to take over the film-making process completely and compel it the way they want it to go; possibly self-effacement in the cause of teamwork and group identity is the decent, sensible, British thing which those awkward, temperamental, unreliable foreigners have never been disciplined enough to understand and practise. But either way, somehow a tone of awful self-congratulation usually manages to creep in: even if we are aesthetically poorer, at least we are in some idefinable way morally richer.

Such an implication, of course, enables us conveniently to side-step the essential issues: is this reading of the British cinema true, and if it is, can we really take it as anything but a crippling statement of limitation? It is not necessary, after all, to hold closely and literally to the theoretical basis of the auteur theory as propounded by the young French critics in the heyday of *Cahiers du Cinéma* in order to look for and appreciate the qualities in film which they regarded as the distinguishing features of an auteur's work. Any national cinema would be poorly off if it lacked completely films which had the quality of personal artistic statements, which seemed somehow to reflect the style and concerns of one individual rather than the combined efforts of a group of skilled craftsmen or the impersonal efficiency of a machine.

Such films, it must be confessed, have not been exactly the strong point of British cinema. True, in the 1930s there was Hitchcock, but otherwise most of what one remembers was in the lavish house-style of Korda productions. In the 1940s there were the exceptions like Thorold Dickinson's period films, *Gaslight* and *Queen of Spades*, or Laurence Olivier's first two Shakespeare films, but the rule was something more along the lines of Michael Balcon's production programme at Ealing, with the company's brand-image paramount and the individual personalities (if any) of the various directors who worked there kept very much in abeyance.

And yet, just as we would expect, what really worked, even in those areas most completely, dogmatically dedicated to the team spirit, were the films of the great unaccountable individualists who somehow managed to slip through the net: among Grierson's documentarists in the GPO Film Unit and its successors, it is the surrealist poet-painter Humphrey Jennings who stands out today; among Michael Balcon's young men at Ealing it is Robert Hamer, sophisticate among the whimsical fantasticks, fastidious stylist among the rosy realists, acid intelligence among mild-mannered devotees of the quaint. Hamer, of course, was a writer as well as a director, and moreover made his most famous film, *Kind Hearts and Coronets*, dangerously far afield from the cosy communal criticism sessions of Ealing mornings, among the alien corn of Pinewood.

Kind Hearts and Coronets is undoubtedly Hamer's masterpiece, and one of the relatively few films of the 1940s which survive unfaded. Before it, Hamer had graduated from editing to writing, and from writing to directing one episode of Ealing's composite ghost-film *Dead of Night* — the sequence involving a haunted mirror. Between that and *Kind Hearts and Coronets* in 1949 he had directed two features, *Pink String and Sealing Wax* and *It Always Rains on Sunday*, the latter also scripted by him. From these previous films, with hindsight, one might gather together a collection of qualities which were to come together with dazzling effect in *Kind Hearts and Coronets*: a vivid sense of period and a particular feeling for the raffish underside of the English social scene in *Pink String and Sealing Wax*, an unexpectedly strong grasp of character, a sometimes mordent sense of humour and something very like a social conscience embodied in *It Always Rains on Sunday*'s downbeat story of born losers, dreaming of escape but trapped for life in a dreary London suburb.

But *Kind Hearts and Coronets* combined and transformed all these qualities into something very different, something which spoke clearly in an unmistakably personal tone. The precise form that this utterance took was more than a trifle unexpected. The film is a high comedy, more readily comparable with Wilde and Congreve than

8

with anything else in the cinema. Hamer's screenplay is based on a novel called *Israel Rank* (the title is mentioned nowhere on or in connection with the film, perhaps tactfully in a film distributed by the Rank Organization), written in the 1900s by Roy Horniman, a lesser follower of Wilde in his Dorian Gray mode. The novel, which is self-consciously decadent and rather strident in its social criticism, actually provided little more than the germ of the script — the notion of the despised offspring of an aristocratic lady who married beneath her, wreaking his revenge by murdering his way cold-bloodedly through his entire family to fortune and a title. Horniman's hero does it with a lot of Ninetyish posturing about his role as a Nietzschean superman above mere human morality; he betrays his subservience to conventional morality by the fuss he makes about rejecting it out-of-hand.

Not so Hamer's hero Louis Mazzini. Admittedly Hamer gave as the third of the possibilities which turned him on to the subject ' that of making a picture which paid no regard whatever to established, although not practised, moral convention '. But the way he went about realizing this possibility had much more to do with the other two cited, ' that of making a film not noticeably similar to any previously made in the English language ', and ' that of using this English language, which I love, in a more varied and, to me, more interesting way than I had previously had the chance of doing in a film '. The language, as so seldom in films, creates the tone and stance of the film. The dialogue is conceived in a lapidary, epigrammatic style which Wilde would not have disdained. And the cool elegance of speech is the prerogative particularly of Louis, a dandy with words as he becomes, when he has the means, with clothes. He does not attitudinize about his actions, except, perhaps, for the affectation of permanent cool, of not caring, of living and, if necessary dying, as though it is all a game for gentlemen to while away the time.

The verbal style, therefore, is functional in a way it seldom is in Wilde, except for *The Importance of Being Earnest*, where all is refined into a comedy of language. But though the language of the script is used as an essential tool in directing our attitude to character, the film is not literary in its conception to the exclusion or even the serious harm of what are taken to be more strictly cinematic qualities. The film is in some ways like an experimental demonstration of the different levels at which the spoken word can collaborate fruitfully with the image in cinema. At the time of the film's appearance, some exception was taken, on rather antiquatedly theoretical grounds, to the use of a first-person narration: why do we need to be told what we can see for ourselves, and if it tells us something we cannot see for ourselves, is it not automatically branding itself as a ' literary ', un-cinematic device?

But, of course, things are seldom as simple as that, and certainly they are not in this film. Even when the visuals and the words on the soundtrack seem to be doing the same thing (and there are times when they are ironically divergent), the effect is never one of enfeebling duplication. Even the simplest jokes, like Louis' observation as he disposes of his aunt Agatha in the midst of a balloon flight to distribute suffragette literature:

I shot an arrow in the air
She fell to earth in Berkeley Square . . .

has the value of governing our responses to the happening, placing it safely (but not too safely) on the level of artificial comedy. The visual style of the film complements this: the images have a fastidious elegance and airiness suggestive of Tissot's social scenes on the one hand and, in their wispy, understated 1940ish romanticism, of Felix Kelly's wan paintings of country houses on the other. Well though the script of the film reads divorced from the images, it remains, curiously enough, the film out of the four in this volume which yields least to anything less than the total experience of seeing the film complete as it left its creator's hands.

Two of the other scripts here collected show high-powered, established writers collaborating in a pretty ambitious fashion with directors almost equally high-powered, or well on their way to being so. *Brief Encounter* was David Lean's fourth collaboration with Noël Coward, and the one, understandably, where the creative responsibility for the film as a whole is most evenly divided between the two of them. *The Third Man* is Carol Reed's second collaboration with Graham Greene, distinguished from its predecessor, *Fallen Idol*, in that it is an original screenplay worked out from the earliest stages in collaboration, or at least in close consultation, with the director.

Brief Encounter, indeed, constitutes almost a declaration of independence on Lean's part from his fruitful but by 1945 no doubt increasingly constricting association with Coward's writing. On his first film, *In Which We Serve,* he had been brought in as co-director with Coward, taking care of the technical end in a sort of one-man-band operation, featuring Coward as author of the original screenplay, director, star and composer of the music. The next two films, *This Happy Breed* and *Blithe Spirit,* were smooth, easy, essentially faithful adaptations of recent Coward stage successes. *Brief Encounter* is something rather different. Though it takes as its starting-point *Still Life,* a one-act play from Coward's 1936 collection, *Tonight at 8.30,* the screenplay elaborates considerably to fill in the background of the two principal characters' ' brief encounter ' in a railway station buffet. And it is not just the conventional ' opening-out ' process by which snatches of dialogue and whole scenes from the stage play are arbitrarily scattered in a variety of improbable locales in the cause of Cinema. The whole thing is radically rethought in terms of the screen and its possibilities, to such an extent that it becomes more or less an original screenplay on the same theme as the stage play.

The play is a classic essay in British understatement and the good old stiff upper-lip. Two sublimely improbable people, married, settled, middle-aged, find themselves embarrassingly involved in a great romantic passion that they can do nothing about. People like them don't do things like that, and the only possible answer is the decent, dutiful one: they must part for good. The film, by telling us a lot more about them, about their background, about the circumstances of their meetings and their parting, intensifies our understanding of and belief in both their passionate feelings for each other, and the very real problems that they have of squaring these with their normal codes of duty, their natural desire not to hurt people they also love, if not quite with the same intensity.

The film, in fact, becomes a far more emotional, far more romantic statement than the play. Partly this is the effect of a very simple device: that of making Laura the narrator, and telling the whole story from her point of view after the parting, when her despair has reached and just passed its moment of maximum intensity. The narration provides us ready-made with an emotional colouring, an attitude to the story we are being told — and again, like the narration in *Kind Hearts and Coronets,* came in for criticism at the time because this was felt to be somehow not playing fair, not doing things the 'cinematic' way. However, the device does work, despite occasional moments of weakening duplication: as a rule what Laura tells us about what is going on inside her, complements the visuals without overwhelming or replacing them.

Much of the effect of the film, though, resides in the way David Lean directs it (something which could not really be said of his three previous films). Throughout his career Lean seems to be rather a cold director, a brilliant technician who steers clear of leaving any personal mark on his subjects and appears, if anything, to be positively embarrassed by any overt displays of emotionalism. *Brief Encounter* might, therefore, depending which way one looks at it, be the ideal subject for him, matching his reticence with its own, or a disaster, encouraging him to cool down to freezing point something which was already pretty chilly and undemonstrative. As it turned out, the first pattern seems to be that which prevailed: the film has, unlike any of Lean's other films, the feeling that intense emotions are there, underneath, made all the more intense by the iron control under which they are held.

Partly this is effected by the moody, chiaroscuro camerawork, which makes the most of rain-washed night streets, clouds of smoke and steam from the steam trains that still rumble or roar through Milford station. Occasionally the camera takes over on its own, as in the once-renowned sequence of Laura's temptation to suicide, in which the angles become more and more extreme until after the express has rushed through (its presence made palpable by the soundtrack and the flashing lights on Laura's anguished face) and our viewpoint is gradually returned to the everyday horizontal, as Laura goes back sensibly to the buffet she just precipitately left.

But most of all the mood of the film, its emotional temperature, is created by one stroke of something like genius: the use of Rachmaninov's Second Piano Concerto on the soundtrack (the practical motivation for this being that the work in question is being played on the radio as Laura starts her reverie). Again, maybe the use of this very highly charged, emotional music is not quite playing fair, at any rate by conventional canons of cinema. But it works, triumphantly, by giving at once an extra dimension to the most prosaic, seemingly unemotional exchanges, making us aware that we are in the presence of Harold Pinter's second silence: ' below the words spoken, is the thing known and unspoken. . . .'

At this distance of time *Brief Encounter* assumes another, rather surprising quality — that of a documentary insight into a vanished scene, a vanished way of life. This time-capsule element it shares with *The Third Man*, another film which hardly suggests itself at first glance as offering a documentary insight on anything. But the most extraordinary part of Carol Reed's achievement in bringing Graham Greene's script to the screen is his hauntingly concrete recreation of a place — war-torn Vienna; and an atmosphere — the sort of tired, disillusioned melancholy of a world worn out by war and hopelessly daunted by the immense task of peacetime reconstruction. If one were to look for something: a novel, a poem, a painting, a play, a film, to sum up just how it felt to be there, how it was to live through that time, it would be hard to better *The Third Man*.

And yet the effect is clearly something very consciously created, not in any sense merely found. Though the ruins of Vienna are there palpably enough, they are used largely as elements in the creation of a highly artificial, theatrical decor. Much of the film takes place at night; in wet streets bizarrely lit and photographed from consistently outré angles. The overall gesture of the film is baroque, yet at points it can be astonishingly simple. Well, admittedly the famous final shot, in which, when all the talk is over, Anna walks down the long avenue and right past the waiting Holly Martins, out of frame, is simple in a way so theatrical as to constitute a flamboyant gesture of its own. But the scene on the ferris wheel, in which really Holly Martins and Harry Lime (particularly the latter) just talk, is handled very simply and straightforwardly: when the point of a scene lies primarily in what is said, Reed does not hesitate to efface himself and leave it up to Greene.

But equally Greene has chosen to trust the film medium, and especially Reed's ability to handle it. If one compares the final screenplay with the original treatment, published as one of Greene's ' entertainments ' though written specifically as a starting-point for the film, there are some radical differences. The immediate temptation is to suggest that in making his story into a screenplay, Greene decided (perforce?) to simplify. Were one to judge the screenplay strictly as a literary artifact, this would not be an entirely unfair judgment. But that would be to leave out of account the various modes of discourse available to the film, beyond those that can be readily rendered on the printed page. Greene obviously appreciates this — as well he should after his extensive experience as a film writer and film critic — and writes for the screen accordingly.

To begin with, there are the obvious differences between any literary form and any dramatic form. The very casting of actors in roles, for instance, can tell us or make us feel immediately things about the characters they are playing, which the author of a novel would have to work long and hard to achieve. The charismatic presence of Orson Welles in the very small role of Harry Lime, makes it difficult to believe that he is on screen for so little time. It radically alters the balance of our interests and sympathies within the film, by making Harry into a big bad character instead of a little villain. Mistakenly idolised by one of the other characters, he becomes, in fact, more of a satanic hero to whom Anna's line 'A man doesn't alter because you find out more about him' (spoken out of ignorance in the story, sad experience in the film) applies with rich ironic ambiguity.

But then all the characters take on stronger outlines in the script (hence the superficial impression that they have been simplified) whilst assuming also greater complexity and ambiguity because of the way they are cast and played; because the narration in the book (Calloway's), with its exterior, cut-and-dried view of the story, is eliminated and instead we follow the happenings more or less through the slowly opening eyes of Holly Martins; and because the film has forsaken the crisp, linear narrative of the story for an approach much more devious, glancing, incidental, playing heavily on our associations, our imaginative participation. The zither music of Anton Karas, with its ubiquitous Harry Lime theme, permeates the film with his largely unseen presence.

And always, in the background, the ruins of Vienna — the reality which, Greene has said, was merely the setting for a fairy-tale in the story. But if the story was fantasy, validated by a businesslike dose of reality, the film is about the conflict between fantasy and reality, or between different kinds of reality. Curiously enough, the film, through the collaboration of director, photographer, composer, actors, has come out more purely, essentially Greene in its total statement than the story which was his own unaided work: the story belongs completely in Greene's slightly derogatory 'entertainment' class among his writings; the film has taken on the subtlety and density of one of his major novels.

Saturday Night and Sunday Morning is the only example in this collection of what has hopefully been called the New Cinema in Britain. Which is to say that it came in the wake of the New Drama introduced by John Osborne's *Look Back in Anger* in 1956, and is based on a novel by one of the new generation of working-class, decidedly non-metropolitan novelists. It is directed (a first feature film) by one of the younger directors who first achieved attention in the context of the National Film Theatre's Free Cinema programmes (1956); and uses actors, notably Albert Finney, who were not yet stars and diverged widely from the gentlemanly, upper-middle-class image of the traditional English leading man.

Despite this, the film does not at this distance of time seem so much like the leader of a revolution as one might expect. True, its procedures are less stuffy and academic than those by which the other famous working-class novel of the period, *Room at the Top*, was brought to the screen. But still, the main novelty of the film lies in its subject-matter and milieu — a novelty which can now be appreciated only by an exercise of the historical imagination — and otherwise it is not so different in kind from *Brief Encounter* or *The Third Man*. It is certainly no more (and no less) realistic than either of them; gritty, unvarnished reality it is not. It just chooses to get romantic about slightly different things. But the hero, for all his roughness and provincial uncouthness, extracts himself from a punch-up in which he is obviously outweighed and outnumbered with all the aplomb of a Bulldog Drummond.

There are other elements of the film which, fresh then, have since become clichés — in particular the visit to a fairground, amusement arcade, deriving perhaps from Lindsay Anderson's famous short *O Dreamland*, which gives *Saturday Night and Sunday Morning* one of its showier scenes and then, for a while, became an absolutely obligatory part of any British New Cinema film. So did a number of images and ideas first put effectively into circulation in this film. Suddenly life, to be accepted as real and earnest in a British film, had to be set in a grimy working-class area. Possibly in some hitherto uncelebrated area of south London, like Clapham Junction, but preferably in the industrial Midlands or the mysterious North. There people were close to the harsh realities, old folk incessantly disapproved and prophesied doom while the young swilled beer and dressed up for Saturday night. If they were men they had affairs with married women and got girls into trouble, if they were girls they were duly got into trouble and ended in abortion or at the altar of a forced, loveless marriage.

If this is a less than fair picture of *Saturday Night and Sunday Morning*, that is not because it is seriously inaccurate. But rather that the conventions have not yet hardened in this film; that Alan Sillitoe's screenplay carries over, from the book it quite faithfully adapts, a gift for the unexpected, enlivening detail, a wry, self-deflating humour; and that Karel Reisz, being, with his Czech background, still something of a stranger here himself, does coolly and critically re-examine all the neo-Lawrentian myths associated with his subject. He handles it with no seeming sense of doing anything more extraordinary than, or essentially different from, what David Lean was doing with his picture of another slice of English society in *Brief Encounter*. Peculiarly enough, it is just because the director himself seems unimpressed with the supposed novelty of what he is doing that the film transcends its particular moment, and takes on in retrospect an almost classic quality.

Also, if we compare the finished film with the screenplay (and for that matter the original novel), we can feel a certain change of emphasis which is no doubt the joint contribution of Karel Reisz and Albert Finney. Sillitoe's hero is much more clearly heroic than the film finally makes him out to be — and much more normal-seeming. Reisz has shown, throughout his subsequent films, a pre-occupation with characters living on the borderline between sanity and madness (one of the more memorable instances being also played by Albert Finney, in *Night Must Fall*). And he sees Arthur Seaton as a character whose intermittent rebelliousness and sheer bloody-mindedness carries him up to, and sometimes over, the line of sane behaviour. This reading of the character gives the film an extra dimension of sheer extravagance and oddity, which distinguishes it from the sort of semi-documentary realism which is the keynote of such superficially similar films as John Schlesinger's *A Kind of Loving*. And just as the real significance of John Osborne's drama was misunderstood on its first appearance (it was expected to lead the way to a new drama of proletarian realism and social protest), so *Saturday Night and Sunday Morning* was too unthinkingly taken by critics of the time to herald a new wave of social-realist cinema

16

in Britain. Actually it marked — more excitingly — the emergence of a strikingly individual film-maker with a distinctive personal vision. Which, as it happens, was happily symptomatic of the way the British cinema was going to develop in the succeeding years.

Almost all of this is the director's contribution in the *way* the film is made, as apart from what can be read in the screenplay. Indeed, it is curious that of the four screenplays in this book it is the newest, the one which should by rights demonstrate a new freedom, a new creative spirit in the British cinema, which sticks closest to and is most dependent on a literary original. After all, the literary emphasis of British cinema has been something constantly held against it, as a recurrent fault we were supposed to be getting out of. And so, to an extent, we have. While films never entirely escape the temptations of the ' pre-sold property ', the more recent films of Lindsay Anderson, like *If* . . . and *Oh Lucky Man*, not to mention films as different as Mike Leigh's *Bleak Moments*, Mike Hodges' *Get Carter*, Stephen Frears' *Gumshoe*, Philip Trevelyan's *The Moon and the Sledgehammer*, Bill Douglas's *My Childhood*, or even the eccentric creations of Ken Russell (on the subject of which grown men have been known to come to blows), seem to show a decisive move away from the safely literary. But then the most exciting films in the British cinema have nearly always shown a similar happy independence or transcendence of literature, and it is one of the uses of the three earlier scripts included here that they all, in various ways, help to remind us of this.

CREDITS:

In Charge of Production	Anthony Havelock-Allan
	Ronald Neame
Producer	Noël Coward
Director	David Lean
Screenplay	Noël Coward
Director of Photography	Robert Krasker
Art Director	L. P. Williams
Editor	Jack Harris
Sound Editor	Harry Miller
Sound Recordists	Stanley Lambourne
	Desmond Dew
Production Manager	E. Holding
Assistant Director	George Pollock
Camera Operator	B. Francke

CAST:

Laura Jesson	Celia Johnson
Alec Harvey	Trevor Howard
Albert Godby	Stanley Holloway
Myrtle Bagot	Joyce Carey
Fred Jesson	Cyril Raymond
Dolly Messiter	Everley Gregg
Beryl Waters	Margaret Barton
Stanley	Dennis Harkin
Stephen Lynn	Valentine Dyall
Mary Norton	Marjorie Mars
Mrs Rolandson	Nuna Davey
Woman Organist	Irene Handl
Bill	Edward Hodge
Johnnie	Sydney Bromley
Policeman	Wilfrid Babbage
Waitress	Avis Scutt
Margaret	Henrietta Vincent
Bobbie	Richard Thomas
Clergyman	George V. Sheldon

The action of this film takes place during the winter of 1938-39. It is early evening. A local train is pulling into platform Number 1 of Milford Junction Station, as a voice over the loudspeaker announces:

LOUDSPEAKER: *Milford Junction — Milford Junction.*

The train comes closer and closer, and a great cloud of steam is hissed out from the engine. The screen becomes completely white as the main titles appear. With the last title the steam disperses, revealing again the engine, which starts to pull out of the station. ALBERT GODBY is at the ticket barrier. He is somewhere between 30 and 40 years old. His accent is north country. He collects the last few tickets from the passengers of the departing train and moves towards the edge of the platform. An express train is approaching from the distance. ALBERT jumps down from platform Number 1 onto the track, and waits for the express to pass. It roars by, practically blotting out the view. ALBERT watches the train pass, as the lights from the carriage windows flash across his face. From his waistcoat pocket he takes out a watch and chain, and checks the time of the train. The watch reads 5.35. By the look of satisfaction on his face we know that the train is punctual. He puts the watch back and the lights cease flashing on his face. The train has passed, and ALBERT follows it with his eyes as it roars into the tunnel. He crosses the line over which the express has just gone by, jumps onto platform Number 2, and moves towards the refreshment room.

Inside the refreshment room he crosses to the counter, behind which stand MYRTLE BAGOT and her assistant BERYL WATERS. MYRTLE is a buxom and imposing widow. Her hair is piled high, and her expression is reasonably jaunty except on those occasions when a strong sense of refinement gets the better of her. BERYL is pretty but dimmed, not only by MYRTLE's personal effulgence, but by her firm authority.

ALBERT: *Hullo! — Hullo! — Hullo!*

MYRTLE: *Quite a stranger, aren't you?*

ALBERT: *I couldn't get in yesterday.*

MYRTLE bridling: *I wondered what happened to you.*

ALBERT: *I 'ad a bit of a dust-up.*

MYRTLE preparing his tea: *What about?*

ALBERT: *Saw a chap getting out of a first-class compartment, and when he comes to give up 'is ticket it was third-class, and I told 'im he'd have to pay excess, and then he turned a bit nasty and I 'ad to send for Mr Saunders.*

MYRTLE: *Fat lot of good he'd be.*

ALBERT: *He ticked him off proper.*

MYRTLE: *Seein's believing. . . .*

In the far end of the refreshment room, seated at a table, are ALEC HARVEY and LAURA JESSON. He is about 35 and wears a mackintosh and squash hat. She is an attractive woman in her thirties. Her clothes are not smart, but obviously chosen with taste. They are in earnest conversation, but we do not hear what they are saying.

ALBERT off: *I tell you, he ticked 'im off proper — 'You pay the balance at once,' he said, ' or I'll 'and you over to the police.' You should 'ave seen the chap's face at the mention of the word ' police '. Changed his tune then 'e did — paid up quick as lightning.*

MYRTLE off: *That's just what I mean. He hadn't got the courage to handle it himself. He had to call in the police.*

ALBERT off: *Who said he called in the police?*

MYRTLE off: *You did, of course.*

ALBERT off: *I didn't do any such thing. I merely said he mentioned the police, which is quite a different thing from calling them in. He's not a bad lot, Mr Saunders. After all, you can't expect much spirit from a man who's only got one lung and a wife with diabetes.*

MYRTLE off: *I thought something must be wrong when you didn't come.*

Close shot of ALBERT and MYRTLE. BERYL is in the background. Close shots of ALBERT and MYRTLE individually, as they are speaking.

ALBERT: *I'd have popped in to explain, but I had a date, and 'ad to run for it the moment I went off.*

MYRTLE frigidly: *Oh, indeed!*

ALBERT: *A chap I know's getting married.*

MYRTLE: *Very interesting, I'm sure.*

ALBERT: *What's up with you, anyway?*

MYRTLE: *I'm sure I don't know to what you're referring.*

ALBERT: *You're a bit unfriendly all of a sudden.*

MYRTLE ignoring him: *Beryl, hurry up — put some coal in the stove while you're at it.*

BERYL: *Yes, Mrs Bagot.*

MYRTLE: *I'm afraid I really can't stand here wasting my time in idle gossip, Mr Godby.*

ALBERT: *Aren't you going to offer me another cup?*

MYRTLE: *You can 'ave another cup and welcome when you've finished that one. Beryl 'll give it to you — I've got my accounts to do.*

ALBERT: *I'd rather you gave it to me.*

MYRTLE: *Time and tide wait for no man, Mr Godby.*

ALBERT: *I don't know what you're huffy about, but whatever it is I'm very sorry.*

> DOLLY is seen at the counter. Forgetting her tea, she hurries across the room to join LAURA and ALEC.

DOLLY: *Laura! What a lovely surprise!*

LAURA dazed: *Oh, Dolly!*

DOLLY: *My dear, I've shopped until I'm dropping! My feet are nearly falling off, and my throat's parched. I thought of having tea in Spindle's but I was terrified of losing the train. I'm always missing trains, and being late for meals, and Bob gets disagreeable for days at a time — he's been getting those dreadful headaches you know — I've been trying to make him see a doctor, but he won't.* Flopping down at their table: *Oh, dear.*

LAURA: *This is Doctor Harvey.*

ALEC rising: *How do you do!*

DOLLY shaking hands: *How do you do. Would you be a perfect dear and get me my cup of tea? I don't think I could drag my poor old bones back to the counter again. I must get some chocolates for Tony, too, but I can do that afterwards.*

> She offers him money.

ALEC waving it away: *No, please. . . .*

> He goes drearily out of frame towards the counter.

> Close shot of DOLLY and LAURA.

DOLLY: *My dear — what a nice-looking man. Who on earth is he?*

Really, you're quite a dark horse. I shall telephone Fred in the morning and make mischief — this is a bit of luck. I haven't seen you for ages, and I've been meaning to pop in, but Tony's had measles, you know, and I had all that awful fuss about Phyllis —
LAURA with an effort: *Oh, how dreadful!*

At the counter, ALEC is standing next to ALBERT, who is finishing his cup of tea. ALBERT leaves and MYRTLE hands ALEC the change for DOLLY's cup of tea.

DOLLY off: *Mind you, I never cared for her much, but still Tony did. Tony adored her, and — but never mind, I'll tell you all about that in the train.*

ALEC picks up DOLLY's tea and moves back to the table. He sits down again.

DOLLY: *Thank you so very much. They've certainly put enough milk in it — but still, it'll be refreshing.* She sips it. *Oh, dear — no sugar.*
ALEC: *It's in the spoon.*

DOLLY: *Oh, of course — what a fool I am — Laura, you look frightfully well. I do wish I'd known you were coming in today, we could have come together and lunched and had a good gossip. I loathe shopping by myself anyway.*

There is the sound of a bell on the platform, and a loudspeaker voice announces the arrival of the Churley train.

LAURA: *There's your train.*
ALEC: *Yes, I know.*
DOLLY: *Aren't you coming with us?*
ALEC: *No, I go in the opposite direction. My practice is in Churley.*
DOLLY: *Oh, I see.*
ALEC: *I'm a general practitioner at the moment.*
LAURA dully: *Doctor Harvey is going out to Africa next week.*
DOLLY: *Oh, how thrilling.*

There is the sound of ALEC's train approaching.

ALEC: *I must go.*
LAURA: *Yes, you must.*
ALEC: *Good-bye.*
DOLLY: *Good-bye.*

ALEC shakes hands with DOLLY, looks at LAURA swiftly once, and gives her shoulder a little squeeze. The train is heard rumbling into the station. He goes over to the door and out onto the platform.

LAURA is gazing at the door through which ALEC has just passed. She seems unaware of the chattering DOLLY at her side, who proceeds to fumble in her handbag for lipstick and a mirror. Close shot of LAURA.

DOLLY: *He'll have to run or he'll miss it — he's got to get right over to the other platform. Talking of missing trains reminds me of that awful bridge at Broadham Junction — you have to go traipsing all up one side, along the top and down the other! Well, last week I'd been over to see Bob's solicitor about renewing the lease of the house — and I arrived at the station with exactly half a minute to spare. . . .*

Close shot of DOLLY, who is applying lipstick to her chattering mouth and watching the operation in her little hand-mirror.

DOLLY: *. . . My dear, I flew — I had Tony with me, and like a fool, I'd brought a new shade for the lamp in the drawing-room — I could just as easily have got it here in Milford.*

Close shot of LAURA.

DOLLY off: *. . . It was the most enormous thing and I could hardly see over it — I've never been in such a frizz in my life — I nearly knocked a woman down.*

The door onto the platform is seen from LAURA's point of view.

DOLLY off: *. . . Of course, by the time I got it home it was battered to bits.*

There is the sound of a bell on the platform as we resume on LAURA and DOLLY.

DOLLY: *Is that a train?*

She addresses MYRTLE.

DOLLY: *Can you tell me, is that the Ketchworth train?*

MYRTLE off: *No, that's the express.*

LAURA: *The boat-train.*

DOLLY: *Oh, yes — that doesn't stop, does it?*

She gets up and crosses to MYRTLE at the counter.

DOLLY: *Express trains are Tony's passion in life — I want some chocolate, please.*

MYRTLE: *Milk or plain?*

DOLLY: *Plain, I think — or no, perhaps milk would be nicer. Have you any with nuts in it?*

The express is heard in the distance.

MYRTLE: *Nestle's nut-milk — shilling or sixpence?*

DOLLY: *Give me one plain and one nut-milk.*

The noise of the express sounds louder. The express roars through the station as DOLLY finishes buying and paying for her chocolate. She turns to see that LAURA is no longer at the table.

DOLLY: *Oh, where is she?*

MYRTLE looking over the counter: *I never noticed her go.*

There is the sound of a door opening and they both look up. LAURA comes in through the door from Number 2 platform, looking very white and shaky. She shuts the door and leans back against it. DOLLY enters frame.

DOLLY: *My dear, I couldn't think where you'd disappeared to.*

LAURA: *I just wanted to see the express go through.*

DOLLY: *What on earth's the matter? Do you feel ill?*

LAURA: *I feel a little sick.*

LAURA goes slowly over to the table, where DOLLY helps her into a chair. The platform bell goes and the loudspeaker announces the arrival of the Ketchworth train.

LAURA: *That's our train.*

DOLLY goes out of shot towards the counter.

DOLLY off: *Have you any brandy?*

MYRTLE off: *I'm afraid it's out of hours.*

DOLLY off: *Surely — if someone's feeling ill. . . .*

LAURA: *I'm all right really.*

Close shot of DOLLY and MYRTLE.

DOLLY: *Just a sip of brandy will buck you up.* To MYRTLE: *Please. . . .*

MYRTLE: *Very well. . . .*

She pours out some brandy as the train is heard approaching the station.

DOLLY: *How much?*

MYRTLE: *Tenpence, please.*

Resume on LAURA at the table.

DOLLY off: *There!*

The train is heard rumbling into the station. DOLLY moves into frame with the brandy.

DOLLY: *Here you are, dear.* (*Still*)

LAURA taking it: *Thank you.*

She gulps down the brandy as DOLLY proceeds to gather up her parcels. They hurry across the refreshment room and out of the door leading to Number 3 platform.

Outside they cross the platform to the train. A porter opens the door of a third-class compartment. There is the sound of the door slamming, off. Through the carriage window at the far end can be seen platform Number 4. LAURA sits down and DOLLY bustles over to the corner seat opposite her.

DOLLY: *Well, this is a bit of luck, I must say. . . .*

The carriage gives a jolt and the train starts to pull out of the station.

DOLLY: *. . . This train is generally packed.*

DOLLY, having placed her various packages on the seat beside her, leans forward to talk to LAURA.

DOLLY: *I really am worried about you, dear — you look terribly peaky.*

Close shot of LAURA over DOLLY's shoulder.

LAURA: *I'm all right — really I am — I just felt faint for a minute, that's all. It often happens to me you know — I once did it in the middle of Bobbie's school concert! I don't think he's ever forgiven me.*

She gives a little smile. It is obviously an effort, but she succeeds reasonably well.

Close shot of DOLLY over LAURA's shoulder.

DOLLY after a slight pause: *He was certainly very nice-looking.*

LAURA: *Who?*

DOLLY: *Your friend — that Doctor whatever his name was.*

Resume on LAURA, over DOLLY's shoulder.

LAURA: *Yes. He's a nice creature.*

DOLLY: *Have you known him long?*

LAURA: *No, not very long.*

LAURA smiles again, quite casually, but her eyes remain miserable.

LAURA: *I hardly know him at all, really. . . .*

DOLLY off: *Well, my dear, I've always had a passion for doctors. I can well understand how it is that women get neurotic. Of course some of them go too far. I'll never forget that time Mary Norton had jaundice. The way she behaved with that doctor of hers was absolutely scandalous. Her husband was furious and said he would. . . .*

25

DOLLY's words fade away. LAURA's mouth remains closed, but we hear her thoughts.

LAURA'S VOICE: *I wish I could trust you. I wish you were a wise, kind friend, instead of just a gossiping acquaintance that I've known for years casually and never particularly cared for. . . . I wish. . . . I wish. . . .*

Close shot of DOLLY over LAURA's shoulder.

DOLLY: *Fancy him going all the way to South Africa. Is he married?*

LAURA: *Yes.*

DOLLY: *Any children?*

Close shot of LAURA.

LAURA: *Yes — two boys. He's very proud of them.*

DOLLY off: *Is he taking them with him, his wife and children?*

LAURA: *Yes — yes, he is.*

Close shot of DOLLY.

DOLLY: *I suppose it's sensible in a way — rushing off to start life anew in the wide open spaces, and all that sort of thing, but I must say wild horses wouldn't drag me away from England. . . .*

Resume on LAURA.

DOLLY off: *. . . and home and all the things I'm used to — I mean, one has one's roots after all, hasn't one?*

LAURA: *Yes, one has one's roots.*

Close shot of DOLLY's mouth.

DOLLY: *A girl I knew years ago went out to Africa you know — her husband had something to do with engineering or something, and my dear. . . .*

Close shot of LAURA.

DOLLY off: *She really had the most dreadful time — she got some awful kind of germ through going out on a picnic and she was ill for months and months. . . .*

DOLLY's voice has gradually faded away, and we hear LAURA's thoughts — her lips do not move.

LAURA'S VOICE: *I wish you'd stop talking — I wish you'd stop prying and trying to find out things — I wish you were dead! No — I don't mean that — that was unkind and silly — but I wish you'd stop talking. . . .*

DOLLY's voice fades in again.

DOLLY off: *. . . all her hair came out and she said the social life*

26

was quite, quite horrid — provincial, you know, and very nouveau riche. . . .

LAURA wearily: *Oh, Dolly. . . .*

Close shot of DOLLY over LAURA's shoulder.

DOLLY: *What's the matter, dear — are you feeling ill again?*

LAURA: *No, not really ill, but a bit dizzy — I think I'll close my eyes for a little.*

DOLLY: *Poor darling — what a shame and here am I talking away nineteen to the dozen. I won't say another word and if you drop off I'll wake you just as we get to the level crossing. That'll give you time to pull yourself together and powder your nose before we get out.*

Close shot of LAURA.

LAURA: *Thanks, Dolly.*

She leans her head back and closes her eyes. The background of the railway compartment darkens and becomes a misty movement. The noise of the train fades away and music takes its place.

LAURA's VOICE: *This can't last — this misery can't last — I must remember that and try to control myself. Nothing lasts really — neither happiness nor despair — not even life lasts very long — there will come a time in the future when I shan't mind about this any more — when I can look back and say quite peacefully and cheerfully ' How silly I was ' — No, no, — I don't want that time to come ever — I want to remember every minute — always — always — to the end of my days. . . .*

LAURA's head gives a sudden jerk as the train comes to a standstill.

DOLLY off: *Wake up, Laura! We're here!*

Simultaneously the background of the compartment comes back to normal. Station lights flash past onto LAURA's face.

The music stops, and the screech of brakes takes its place.

A porter's voice is heard calling:

PORTER off: *Ketchworth — Ketchworth — Ketchworth!*

Dissolve to Ketchworth Station. It is night. LAURA and DOLLY walk along the platform. The lights from the stationary train illuminate their faces.

DOLLY: *I could come to the house with you quite easily, you know — it really isn't very much out of my way — all I have to do is to*

27

cut through Elmore Lane — past the Grammar School and I shall be home in two minutes.

LAURA: *It's sweet of you, Dolly, but I really feel perfectly all right now. That little nap in the train did wonders.*

DOLLY: *You're quite sure?*

LAURA: *Absolutely positive.*

LAURA and DOLLY pass the barrier, where they give up their tickets. A whistle blows and the train can be heard leaving the station. They stop in the station yard beyond.

LAURA: *Thank you for being so kind.*

DOLLY: *Nonsense, dear. Well — I shall telephone in the morning to see if you've had a relapse.*

LAURA: *I shall disappoint you.* She kisses DOLLY. *Good night.*

DOLLY: *Good night — give my love to Fred and the children.*

Dissolve to the exterior of LAURA's house. LAURA is seen approaching the gate of a solid, comfortable-looking house. As she enters the gate, she feels in her handbag for her latch-key, finds it, opens the front door and goes inside.

Seen from the hallway, LAURA enters the front door, glances around, shuts the door quietly and moves out of shot towards the stairs.

The foreground of the shot is framed by a man's hat and coat on a hat-stand. Beyond is the stairway and an open door leading to the sitting-room. LAURA enters frame and starts to go up the stairs.

FRED off, from the sitting-room: *Is that you, Laura?*

LAURA stopping on the stairs: *Yes, dear.*

FRED off: *Thank goodness you're back, the house has been in an uproar.*

LAURA: *Why — what's the matter?*

FRED off: *Bobbie and Margaret have been fighting again, and they won't go to sleep until you go in and talk to them about it.*

MARGARET off: *Mummy — Mummy! Is that you, Mummy?*

LAURA: *Yes, dear.*

BOBBIE off, from upstairs: *Come upstairs at once, Mummy — I want to talk to you.*

LAURA on the way upstairs again: *All right. I'm coming — but you're both very naughty. You should be fast asleep by now.*

28

On the upstairs landing, LAURA crosses to the half-open door of the children's night nursery.

Inside the night nursery, the foreground is framed by two small twin beds. The room is in darkness and LAURA is silhouetted in the doorway.

LAURA: *Now what is it, you two?*

BOBBIE: *Well, Mummy, tomorrow's my birthday and I want to go to the circus, and tomorrow's not Margaret's birthday, and she wants to go to the pantomime, and I don't think it's fair.*

MARGARET: *I don't see why we've got to do everything Bobbie wants, just because it's his silly old birthday. Besides, my birthday is in June, and there aren't any pantomimes in June.*

BOBBIE persuasively: *Mummy, why don't you come and sit down on my bed?*

MARGARET: *No, Bobbie, Mummy's going to sit on my bed. She sat with you last night.*

LAURA: *I'm not going to sit with either of you. In fact I'm not going to come into the room. It's far too late to discuss it tonight, and if you don't go to sleep at once I shall tell Daddy not to let you go to either.*

BOBBIE and MARGARET together: *Oh, Mummy!*

Dissolve to the interior of the dining room. Close shot of LAURA and her husband FRED, who is a pleasant-looking man in his forties. They are seated at a round dining-room table and are just finishing their meal. LAURA is officiating at the Cona machine. (*Still*) The dining room is furnished comfortably without being in anyway spectacular.

FRED: *Why not take them to both? One in the afternoon and one in the evening?*

LAURA: *You know that's impossible. We shouldn't get home to bed until all hours — and they'd be tired and fractious.*

FRED: *One on one day, then, and the other on the other.*

LAURA handing him a cup of coffee: *Here you are, dear. You're always accusing me of spoiling the children. Their characters would be ruined in a month if I left them to your over-tender mercies.*

FRED cheerfully: *All right — have it your own way.*

Close shot of LAURA.

LAURA: *Circus or pantomime?*

FRED off: *Neither. We'll thrash them both soundly and lock them in the attic, and go to the cinema ourselves.*

LAURA's eyes suddenly fill with tears.

LAURA: *Oh, Fred!*

Close shot of FRED.

FRED: *What on earth's the matter?*

LAURA frantically dabbing her eyes: *Nothing — really it's nothing.*

FRED rises and crosses over to her. He puts his arms round her.

Close shot of FRED and LAURA.

FRED: *Darling — what's wrong? Please tell me. . . .*

LAURA: *Really and truly it's nothing — I'm just a little run-down. I had a sort of fainting spell in the refreshment room at Milford — wasn't it idiotic? Dolly Messiter was with me and talked and talked and talked until I wanted to strangle her — but still she meant to be kind — isn't it awful about people meaning to be kind? . . .*

FRED gently: *Would you like to go up to bed?*

LAURA: *No, Fred — really. . . .*

FRED: *Come and sit by the fire in the library and relax — you can help me with The Times crossword.*

LAURA forcing a smile: *You have the most peculiar ideas of relaxation.*

FRED: *That's better.*

LAURA rises with his arms still round her.

Dissolve to the interior of the library. FRED and LAURA are sitting on either side of the fire. FRED is in the foreground; on his lap is The Times, opened at the crossword puzzle. (*Still*) He holds a pencil in his hand. LAURA has some sewing to do. The library is cosy and intimate.

Close shots of LAURA and FRED individually, as they speak.

FRED: *But why a fainting spell? I can't understand it.*

LAURA: *Don't be so silly, darling — I've often had fainting spells and you know it. Don't you remember Bobbie's school concert and Eileen's wedding, and that time you insisted on taking me to that Symphony Concert in the Town Hall?*

FRED: *That was a nose bleed.*

LAURA: *I suppose I must just be that type of woman. It's very humiliating.*

FRED: *I still maintain that there'd be no harm in you seeing Doctor Graves.*

LAURA a little tremulously: *It would be a waste of time.*

FRED looks at her.

LAURA: *Do shut up about it, dear — you're making a fuss about nothing. I'd been shopping and I was tired and the refreshment room was very hot and I suddenly felt sick. Nothing more than that — really nothing more than that. Now get on with your old puzzle and leave me in peace.*

FRED: *All right — have it your own way.* After a pause: *You're a poetry addict — help me over this — it's Keats — ' When I behold upon the night starred face, huge cloudy symbols of a high' — something — in seven letters.*

LAURA with an effort: *Romance, I think — yes, I'm almost sure it is. ' Huge cloudy symbols of a high romance ' — It'll be in the Oxford Book of English Verse.*

FRED: *No that's right, I'm certain — it fits in with ' delirium ' and ' Baluchistan '.*

LAURA: *Will some music throw you off your stride?*

FRED: *No, dear — I'd like it.*

LAURA crosses the room, turns on the radio and returns to her chair. She has tuned in to the opening movement of the Rachmaninoff Concerto in C minor.

Close shot of LAURA. She takes up her sewing, then puts it down again and looks at her husband.

Close shot of FRED. He is concentrating hard and scratching his head thoughtfully with the pencil.

Close shot of LAURA, as her eyes fill with tears again. Her mouth remains closed but we hear her thoughts. . . .

LAURA'S VOICE: *Fred — Fred — dear Fred. There's so much that I want to say to you. You are the only one in the world with enough wisdom and gentleness to understand — if only it were somebody else's story and not mine. As it is you are the only one in the world that I can never tell — never — never — because even if I waited until we were old, old people, and told you then, you would be bound to look back over the years . . . and be hurt and oh, my dear, I don't want you to be hurt. You see, we are a happily married couple, and must never forget that. This is my home. . . .*

A shot of FRED over LAURA's shoulder. He is engrossed in his crossword puzzle.

LAURA'S VOICE: *. . . you are my husband — and my children are upstairs in bed. I am a happily married woman — or rather, I was,*

until a few weeks ago. This is my whole world and it is enough —
or rather, it was, until a few weeks ago.

Close shot of LAURA.

LAURA'S VOICE: *. . . But, oh, Fred, I've been so foolish. I've fallen*
in love! I'm an ordinary woman — I didn't think such violent things
could happen to ordinary people.

Again a shot of FRED over LAURA's shoulder.

LAURA'S VOICE: *It all started on an ordinary day, in the most ordin-*
ary place in the world.

The scene, with the exception of LAURA, slowly starts to dim
out. LAURA remains a solid figure in the foreground. As the room
fades away, the station refreshment room takes its place. LAURA,
as well as being in the foreground of the picture, is also seated
on one of the tables in the refreshment room, thus giving the
impression that she is watching herself. Dissolve.

It is now night time, about 5.30 p.m. The scene takes place in
the refreshment room at the Milford Junction Station. There
are only two or three other people in the room. MYRTLE and
BERYL are behind the counter, against which ALBERT is lolling,
sipping a cup of tea.

LAURA'S VOICE: *. . . the refreshment room at Milford Junction. I*
was having a cup of tea and reading a book that I'd got that morn-
ing from Boots — my train wasn't due for ten minutes. . . . I looked
up and saw a man come in from the platform. He had on an ordinary
mac with a belt. His hat was turned down, and I didn't even see his
face. He got his tea at the counter and turned — then I did see his
face. It was rather a nice face. He passed my table on the way to his.
The woman at the counter was going on as usual. You know, I told
you about her the other day — the one with the refined voice. . . .

Cut to MYRTLE, BERYL and ALBERT at the counter.

BERYL: *Minnie hasn't touched her milk.*

MYRTLE: *Did you put it down for her?*

BERYL: *Yes, but she never came in for it.*

ALBERT conversationally: *Fond of animals?*

MYRTLE: *In their place.*

ALBERT: *My landlady's got a positive mania for animals — she's*
got two cats, one Manx and one ordinary; three rabbits in a hutch
in the kitchen, they belong to her little boy by rights; and one of

them foolish-looking dogs with hair over his eyes.

MYRTLE: *I don't know to what breed you refer.*

ALBERT: *I don't think it knows itself. . . .*

Cut to LAURA, as she glances at the clock, and collects her parcels in a leisurely manner.

MYRTLE off: *Go and clean off Number Three, Beryl, I can see the crumbs on it from here.*

LAURA walks over to the door leading to Number 2 platform.

ALBERT off: *What about my other cup? I shall have to be moving — the five-forty will be in in a minute.*

MYRTLE off: *Who's on the gate?*

ALBERT off: *Young William.*

Outside, the express roars into Milford Junction Station.

LAURA is standing on the platform with the windows of the refreshment room behind her. The lights from the express flash across her face as it streaks through Number 2 platform. She suddenly puts her hand to her face as a piece of grit gets into her eye. She takes out a handkerchief and rubs her eye for a few moments, then turns and walks back into the refreshment room.

MYRTLE is in the foreground of the shot. LAURA enters through the door, comes over to the counter and stands beside ALBERT, who is drinking his second cup of tea. She rubs her eye. (*Still*)

LAURA: *Please, could you give me a glass of water? I've got some-thing in my eye and I want to bathe it.*

MYRTLE: *Would you like me to have a look?*

LAURA: *Please don't trouble. I think the water will do it.*

MYRTLE handing her a glass of water: *Here.*

MYRTLE and ALBERT watch in silence as LAURA bathes her eye.

ALBERT: *Bit of coal-dust, I expect.*

MYRTLE: *A man I knew lost the sight of one eye through getting a bit of grit in it.*

ALBERT: *Nasty thing — very nasty.*

MYRTLE as LAURA lifts her head: *Better?*

LAURA obviously in pain: *I'm afraid not — oh!*

ALEC comes in.

ALEC: *Can I help?*

LAURA: *Oh, no please — it's only something in my eye.*

MYRTLE: *Try pulling down your eyelid as far as it'll go.*

41

ALBERT: *And then blow your nose.*

ALEC: *Please let me look. I happen to be a doctor.*

LAURA: *It's very kind of you.*

ALEC: *Turn round to the light, please.*

Close shot of LAURA and ALEC.

ALEC: *Now — look up — now look down — I can see it. Keep still. . . .*

He twists up the corner of his handkerchief and rapidly operates with it.

ALEC: *There. . . .*

LAURA blinking: *Oh, dear — what a relief — it was agonizing.*

ALEC: *It looks like a bit of grit.*

LAURA: *It was when the express went through. Thank you very much indeed.*

ALEC: *Not at all.*

There is the sound of a bell on the platform.

ALBERT off: *There we go — I must run.*

LAURA: *How lucky for me that you happened to be here.*

ALEC: *Anybody could have done it.*

LAURA: *Never mind, you did, and I'm most grateful.*

ALEC: *There's my train — good-bye.*

ALEC leaves the buffet and goes out of the door to Number 3 platform.

Outside, he comes out of the refreshment room and hurries along the platform and down the subway.

LAURA also comes out of the refreshment room door on to Number 4 platform. She idly glances across at the opposite platform and sees ALEC.

He emerges from the subway entrance, walks a few steps. His train pulls into the station and he is hidden from view.

Close-up of LAURA. She watches the train as it draws to a standstill.

LAURA'S VOICE: *. . . That's how it all began — just through me getting a little piece of grit in my eye.*

LAURA looks up as she hears her own train approaching.

A shot of Number 3 and 4 platforms. The engine of ALEC's train is in the background. LAURA's train steams into Number 3 platform, hiding it from view.

From outside the window of LAURA's compartment, we see

LAURA sitting down, opening her book and starting to read.

LAURA'S VOICE: *I completely forgot the whole incident — it didn't mean anything to me at all, at least I didn't think it did.*

There is the sound of a guard's whistle and the train starts to move off. Fade out.

As the screen goes black, we hear LAURA's voice.

LAURA'S VOICE: *The next Thursday I went into Milford again as usual. . . .*

Fade in on Milford High Street where LAURA walks along, carrying a shopping basket. She checks the contents of the basket with a shopping list and, having decided on her next port of call, she quickens her step. Dissolve.

We are inside Boots Chemist. LAURA is walking away from the library section and goes over to a counter with soaps, toothbrushes, etc.

LAURA'S VOICE: *I changed my books at Boots — Miss Lewis had at last managed to get the new Kate O'Brien for me — I believe she'd kept it hidden under the counter for two days! On the way out I bought two new toothbrushes for the children — I like the smell of a chemist's better than any other shop — it's such a mixture of nice things — herbs and scent and soap. . . .*

Close shot of MRS LEFTWICH at the end of the counter.

LAURA'S VOICE: *. . . that awful Mrs Leftwich was at the other end of the counter, wearing one of the silliest hats I've ever seen.*

Cut to LAURA placing the toothbrushes in her shopping bag and leaving the counter.

LAURA'S VOICE: *. . . fortunately she didn't look up, so I got out without her buttonholing me. Just as I stepped out on to the pavement. . . .*

Dissolve to LAURA as she comes out of Boots. ALEC comes by walking rather quickly. He is wearing a turned-down hat. He recognizes her, stops, and raises his hat.

ALEC: *Good morning.*

LAURA jumping slightly: *Oh — good morning.*

ALEC: *How's the eye?* (*Still*)

LAURA: *Perfectly all right. How kind it was of you to take so much trouble.*

ALEC: *It was no trouble at all.*

43

After a slight pause.

ALEC: *It's clearing up, I think.*

LAURA: *Yes — the sky looks much lighter, doesn't it?*

ALEC: *Well, I must be getting along to the hospital.*

LAURA: *And I must be getting along to the grocer's.*

ALEC with a smile: *What exciting lives we lead, don't we? Good-bye.*

Dissolve to the interior of the subway. It is night time. LAURA is walking along, a little out of breath.

LAURA'S VOICE: *That afternoon I had been to the Palladium as usual, but it was a terribly long film, and when I came out I had had to run nearly all the way to the station.*

LAURA starts to go up the steps leading to Number 3 platform. She comes up the subway on to the platform.

LAURA'S VOICE: *As I came up on to the platform the Churley train was just puffing out.*

Cut to the train leaving Number 4 platform.

Close shot of LAURA, watching the Churley train.

LAURA'S VOICE: *I looked up idly as the windows of the carriages went by, wondering if he was there. . . . I remember this crossing my mind but it was quite unimportant — I was really thinking of other things — the present for your birthday was worrying me rather. It was terribly expensive, but I knew you wanted it, and I'd sort of half taken the plunge and left a deposit on it at Spink and Robson's until the next Thursday. The next Thursday. . . .*

Dissolve to the interior of Spink and Robson. Close-up of a travelling clock with a barometer and dates, all in one. It is standing on a glass show case.

LAURA is looking down at it admiringly.

LAURA'S VOICE: *. . . Well — I squared my conscience by thinking how pleased you would be, and bought it — it was wildly extravagant, I know, but having committed the crime, I suddenly felt reckless and gay. . . . .*

Dissolve to Milford High Street. LAURA walks along the street, carrying a small parcel in her hand. It is a sunny day and she is smiling. A barrel organ is playing.

LAURA'S VOICE: *The sun was out and everybody in the street looked more cheerful than usual — and there was a barrel organ at the corner by Harris's, and you know how I love barrel organs — it was playing 'Let the Great Big World Keep Turning', and I gave the man sixpence and went to the Kardomah for lunch.*

Dissolve to inside of a Kardomah Café. LAURA is sitting at an alcove table. A waitress is just finishing taking her order.

LAURA'S VOICE: *It was very full, but two people had got up from the table just as I had come in — that was a bit of luck, wasn't it? Or was it? Just after I had given my order, I saw him come in. He looked a little tired, I thought, and there was nowhere for him to sit, so I smiled and said . . .*

LAURA: *Good morning.*

Close-up of ALEC.

ALEC: *Good morning. Are you alone?*

Resume on LAURA and ALEC.

LAURA: *Yes, I am.*

ALEC: *Would you mind very much if I shared your table — it's very full and there doesn't seem to be anywhere else?*

LAURA moving a couple of parcels and her bag: *Of course not.*

ALEC hangs up his hat and mackintosh and sits down next to her.

ALEC: *I'm afraid we haven't been properly introduced — my name's Alec Harvey.*

LAURA shaking hands: *How do you do — mine's Laura Jesson.*

ALEC: *Mrs or Miss?*

LAURA: *Mrs. You're a doctor, aren't you? I remember you said you were that day in the refreshment room.*

ALEC: *Yes — not a very interesting doctor — just an ordinary G.P. My practice is in Churley.*

A waitress comes to the table.

WAITRESS: *Can I take your order?*

ALEC to LAURA: *What did you plump for?*

LAURA: *The soup and the fried sole.*

ALEC to WAITRESS: *The same for me, please.*

WAITRESS: *Anything to drink?*

ALEC: *No, thank you.*

ALEC pauses and looks at LAURA.

ALEC: *That is — would you like anything to drink?*

LAURA: *No, thank you — just plain water.*

ALEC to WAITRESS: *Plain water, please.*

45

As the WAITRESS goes away, a Ladies Orchestra starts to play very loudly. LAURA jumps.

Cut to a view of the Ladies Orchestra. They are playing with enthusiasm.

Close shot of LAURA and ALEC. They both laugh. ALEC catches LAURA's eye and nods towards the cellist.

Close shot of the cellist. She is a particularly industrious member of the orchestra.

LAURA'S VOICE: *I'd seen that woman playing the cello hundreds of times, but I've never noticed before how funny she looked.*

Close shot of LAURA and ALEC.

LAURA: *It really is dreadful, isn't it — but we shouldn't laugh — they might see us.*

ALEC: *There should be a society for the prevention of cruelty to musical instruments — you don't play the piano, I hope?*

LAURA: *I was forced to as a child.*

ALEC: *You haven't kept it up?*

LAURA smiling: *No — my husband isn't musical at all.*

ALEC: *Bless him!*

LAURA: *For all you know, I might have a tremendous, burning professional talent.*

ALEC shaking his head: *Oh dear, no.*

LAURA: *Why are you so sure?*

ALEC: *You're too sane — and uncomplicated!*

LAURA fishing in her bag for her powder puff: *I suppose it's a good thing to be so uncomplicated — but it does sound a little dull.*

ALEC: *You could never be dull.*

LAURA: *Do you come here every Thursday?*

ALEC: *Yes, to spend a day in the hospital. Stephen Lynn — he's the chief physician here — graduated with me. I take over from him once a week — it gives him a chance to go up to London and me a chance to study the hospital patients.*

LAURA: *I see.*

ALEC: *Do you?*

LAURA: *Do I what?*

ALEC: *Come here every Thursday?*

LAURA: *Yes — I do the week's shopping, change my library book, have a little lunch, and generally go to the pictures. Not a very exciting routine, really, but it makes a change.*

ALEC: *Are you going to the pictures this afternoon?*

LAURA: *Yes.*

ALEC: *How extraordinary — so am I.*

LAURA: *But I thought you had to work all day in the hospital.*

ALEC: *Well, between ourselves, I killed two patients this morning by accident and the Matron's very displeased with me. I simply daren't go back. . . .*

LAURA: *How can you be so silly. . . .*

ALEC: *Seriously — I really did get through most of my work this morning — it won't matter a bit if I play truant. Would you mind very much if I came to the pictures with you?*

LAURA hesitatingly: *Well — I. . . .*

ALEC: *I could sit downstairs and you could sit upstairs.*

LAURA: *Upstairs is too expensive.*

She smiles. The orchestra stops playing.

LAURA'S VOICE: *The orchestra stopped as abruptly as it had started, and we began to laugh again, and I suddenly realized that I was enjoying myself so very much.*

The WAITRESS arrives back with the soup.

LAURA'S VOICE: *I had no premonitions although I suppose I should have had. It all seemed so natural — and so — so innocent.*

Close-up of ALEC over LAURA's shoulder, followed quickly by a close-up of LAURA over ALEC's shoulder.

Dissolve to close shot of the luncheon bill on a plate. ALEC's hand comes into view and picks it up. LAURA's hand tries to take it from him.

LAURA'S VOICE: *We finished lunch, and the idiot of a waitress had put the bill all on one.*

Close shot of LAURA and ALEC.

ALEC: *I really must insist.*

LAURA: *I couldn't possibly.*

ALEC: *Having forced my company on you, it's only fair that I should pay through the nose for it!*

LAURA: *Please don't insist — I would so much rather we halved it, really I would — please.*

ALEC: *I shall give in gracefully.*

LAURA'S VOICE: *We halved it meticulously — we even halved the tip.*

LAURA and ALEC get up from the table and the orchestra plays

47

again. They start laughing as they leave the restaurant.

Dissolve to Milford High Street. The camera tracks with LAURA and ALEC as they are walking along.

LAURA: *We have two choices — ' The Loves of Cardinal Richelieu ' at the Palace, and ' Love in a Mist ' at the Palladium.*

ALEC: *You're very knowledgeable.*

LAURA: *There must be no argument about buying the tickets — we each pay for ourselves.*

ALEC: *You must think me a very poor doctor if I can't afford a couple of one and ninepennies!*

LAURA: *I insist.*

ALEC: *I had* hoped *that you were going to treat me!*

LAURA: *Which is it to be — Palace or Palladium?*

ALEC with decision: *Palladium, I was once very sick on a channel steamer called ' Cardinal Richelieu '.*

Dissolve to inside of the cinema where we see the Palladium Proscenium. On the screen a trailer is being shown, advertising a coming attraction. Superimposed over four spectacular shots in ever increasing sizes, are the following words, which zoom up towards the audience:

STUPENDOUS! COLOSSAL!!
GIGANTIC!!! EPOCH-MAKING!!!!

A burst of flame appears, followed by the title of the picture ' Flame of Passion ' coming shortly. The trailer ends abruptly and the first of a series of advertisements is flashed on the screen. It is a drawing of a pram with the words:

BUY YOUR PRAM AT BURTONS
22, MILFORD HIGH STREET.

Close shot of LAURA and ALEC who are seated in the middle of the front row of the circle. A beam of light from the projector forms the background of the scene.

LAURA leaning forward over the edge of the circle: *I feel awfully grand perched up here — it was very extravagant of you.*

ALEC: *It was a famous victory.*

LAURA: *Do you feel guilty at all? I do.*

ALEC: *Guilty?*

LAURA: *You ought to more than me really — you neglected your*

48

work this afternoon.

ALEC: *I worked this morning — a little relaxation never did any harm to anyone. Why should either of us feel guilty?*

LAURA: *I don't know.*

ALEC: *How awfully nice you are.*

There is a deafening peal of organ music.

With ALEC and LAURA in the foreground, a woman organist rises from the depths of the orchestra pit, organ and all, playing away as though her life depended on it.

Close shot of LAURA and ALEC, as they are watching the organist. A surprised look appears on both their faces. They look at each other, then lean forward to get a better view of the organist.

Close shot of the organist, acknowledging the applause from the audience. She is the woman that plays the cello at the Kardomah Café.

Close shot of LAURA and ALEC.

LAURA: *It can't be.*

ALEC: *It is.*

They both roar with laughter.

Dissolve to Milford Junction Station, showing the yard and booking hall. It is night time. The camera tracks with LAURA and ALEC, who are walking across the station yard.

LAURA'S VOICE: *We walked back to the station. Just as we were approaching the barrier he put his hand under my arm. I didn't notice it then, but I remember it now.*

LAURA: *What's she like, your wife?*

ALEC: *Madeleine? Oh — small, dark, rather delicate —*

LAURA: *How funny — I should have thought she would be fair.*

ALEC: *And your husband — what's he like?*

They enter the lighted booking hall.

LAURA: *Medium height, brown hair, kindly, unemotional, and not delicate at all.*

ALEC: *You said that proudly.*

LAURA: *Did I?*

They pass the ticket barrier, where ALBERT is on duty, and out on to Number 1 platform.

LAURA: *We've just got time for a cup of tea before our trains go.*

Dissolve to the refreshment room. From behind the counter,

MYRTLE and BERYL are seen gossiping in the foreground, while ALEC and LAURA enter through the door. LAURA goes over to a table out of shot. ALEC comes forward to the counter.

MYRTLE: *And for the third time in one week he brought that common man and his wife to the house without so much as by your leave.* To ALEC: *Yes?*

ALEC: *Two teas, please.*

MYRTLE: *Cakes or pastry?*

LAURA off: *No, thank you.*

ALEC: *Are those Bath buns fresh?*

MYRTLE: *Certainly they are — made this morning.*

ALEC: *Two, please.*

MYRTLE puts two Bath buns on a plate. Meanwhile BERYL has drawn two cups of tea.

MYRTLE: *That'll be sevenpence.*

ALEC: *All right.*

He pays her.

MYRTLE: *Take the tea to the table, Beryl.*

ALEC: *I'll carry the buns.*

LAURA has now seated herself at a table. BERYL brings the tea while ALEC follows with the buns.

ALEC: *You must eat one of these — fresh this morning.*

LAURA: *Very fattening.*

ALEC: *I don't hold with such foolishness.*

BERYL goes out of view towards the counter.

BERYL off: *What happened then, Mrs Bagot?*

LAURA gives ALEC a nudge to draw his attention to MYRTLE and BERYL.

Close shot of MYRTLE and BERYL behind the counter.

MYRTLE slightly relaxed in manner: *Well — it's all very faine, I said, expecting me to do this, that and the other, but what do I get out of it? You can't expect me to be a cook-housekeeper and char rolled into one during the day, and a loving wife in the evening, just because you feel like it. Oh, dear, no. There are just as good fish in the sea, I said, as ever came out of it, and I packed my boxes then and there and left him.*

BERYL: *Didn't you never go back?*

MYRTLE: *Never, I went to my sister's place at Folkestone for a bit, and then I went in with a friend of mine and we opened a tea-shop*

50

in Hythe.

BERYL: *And what happened to him?*

MYRTLE: *Dead as a doornail inside three years.*

BERYL: *Well, I never.*

Close shot of LAURA and ALEC.

LAURA: *Is tea bad for one? Worse than coffee, I mean?*

ALEC: *If this is a professional interview my fee is a guinea.*

LAURA: *Why did you become a doctor?*

ALEC: *That's a long story. Perhaps because I'm a bit of an idealist.*

LAURA: *I suppose all doctors ought to have ideals, really — otherwise I should think their work would be unbearable.*

ALEC: *Surely you're not encouraging me to talk shop?*

LAURA: *Why shouldn't you talk shop? It's what interests you most, isn't it?*

ALEC: *Yes — it is. I'm terribly ambitious really — not ambitious for myself so much as for my special pigeon.*

LAURA: *What is your special pigeon?*

ALEC: *Preventative medicine.*

LAURA: *Oh, I see.*

ALEC laughing: *I'm afraid you don't.*

LAURA: *I was trying to be intelligent.*

ALEC: *Most good doctors, especially when they're young, have private dreams — that's the best part of them; sometimes, though, those get over-professionalized and strangulated and — am I boring you?*

LAURA: *No — I don't quite understand — but you're not boring me.*

ALEC: *What I mean is this — all good doctors must be primarily enthusiastic. They must have, like writers and painters and priests, a sense of vocation — a deep-rooted, unsentimental desire to do good.*

LAURA: *Yes — I see that.*

ALEC: *Well, obviously one way of preventing disease is worth fifty ways of curing it — that's where my ideal comes in — preventative medicine isn't anything to do with medicine at all, really — it's concerned with conditions, living conditions and common sense and hygiene. For instance, my speciality is pneumoconiosis.*

LAURA: *Oh, dear!*

ALEC: *Don't be alarmed, it's simpler than it sounds — it's nothing but a slow process of fibrosis of the lung due to the inhalation of particles of dust. In the hospital here there are splendid opportunities for observing cures and making notes, because of the coalmines.*

LAURA: *You suddenly look much younger.*

ALEC brought up short: *Do I?*

LAURA: *Almost like a little boy.*

ALEC: *What made you say that?*

LAURA staring at him: *I don't know — yes, I do.*

ALEC gently: *Tell me.*

LAURA with panic in her voice: *Oh, no — I couldn't really. You were saying about the coal-mines.*

ALEC looking into her eyes: *Yes — the inhalation of coal-dust — that's one specific form of the disease — it's called anthracosis.*

LAURA hypnotized: *What are the others?*

ALEC: *Chalicosis — that comes from metal-dust — steel-works, you know. . . .*

LAURA: *Yes, of course. Steel-works.*

ALEC: *And silicosis — stone-dust — that's gold-mines.*

LAURA almost in a whisper: *I see.*

There is the sound of a bell.

LAURA: *That's your train.*

ALEC looking down: *Yes.*

LAURA: *You mustn't miss it.*

ALEC: *No.*

LAURA again with panic in her voice: *What's the matter?*

ALEC with an effort: *Nothing — nothing at all.*

LAURA socially: *It's been so very nice — I've enjoyed my afternoon enormously.*

ALEC: *I'm so glad — so have I. I apologize for boring you with those long medical words.*

LAURA: *I feel dull and stupid, not to be able to understand more.*

ALEC: *Shall I see you again?*

There is the sound of a train approaching.

LAURA: *It's the other platform, isn't it? You'll have to run. Don't worry about me — mine's due in a few minutes.*

ALEC: *Shall I see you again?*

LAURA: *Of course — perhaps you could come over to Ketchworth one Sunday. It's rather far, I know, but we should be delighted to see you.*

ALEC intensely: *Please — please. . . .*

The train is heard drawing to a standstill. . . .

LAURA: *What is it?*

ALEC: *Next Thursday — the same time.*

LAURA: *No — I can't possibly — I. . . .*

ALEC: *Please — I ask you most humbly. . . .*

LAURA: *You'll miss your train!*

ALEC: *All right.*

He gets up.

LAURA: *Run. . . .*

ALEC taking her hand: *Good-bye.*

LAURA breathlessly: *I'll be there.*

ALEC: *Thank you, my dear.*

He leaves LAURA, and the camera tracks into a big close shot to hold her, smiling with joy.

LAURA collects her shopping basket and goes towards the door to Number 3 platform.

She comes out of the refreshment room on to the platform. She looks up past camera at ALEC's train, which can be heard pulling out of the station.

A shot of ALEC, from LAURA's view-point. He is leaning out of a carriage window, and waves to her as the train starts to pull out of the station.

Close-up of LAURA. She waves back, and her eyes follow the departing train.

LAURA's VOICE: *I stood there and watched his train draw out of the station. I stared after it until its little red tail light had vanished into the darkness. I imagined him arriving at Churley and giving up his ticket and walking through the streets, and letting himself into his house with his latchkey. Madeleine, his wife, would probably be in the hall to meet him — or perhaps upstairs in her room — not feeling very well — small, dark and rather delicate — I wondered if he'd say ' I met such a nice woman in the Kardomah — we had lunch and went to the pictures ' — then suddenly I knew that he wouldn't — I knew beyond a shadow of doubt that he wouldn't say a word, and at that moment the first awful feeling of danger swept over me.*

A cloud of steam from an incoming engine blows across the screen, almost obscuring LAURA. The grinding of brakes and hiss of steam as her train draws to a standstill, interrupts her thoughts. She walks out of view towards the train.

Through the clearing steam we see her enter a third-class compartment, crowded with people.

She sits down between two other passengers, and glances around the carriage.

LAURA'S VOICE: *I looked hurriedly around the carriage to see if anyone was looking at me.*

The camera pans along the passengers seated on the opposite side of the carriage.

LAURA'S VOICE: *. . . as though they could read my secret thoughts. Nobody was looking at me except a clergyman in the opposite corner.*

The clergyman catches her eye and turns his head away.

Close-up of LAURA as she opens her library book.

LAURA'S VOICE: *I felt myself blushing and opened my library book and pretended to read.*

The train gives a jerk as it starts to move off.

Dissolve to Ketchworth Station, where LAURA walks along the platform towards the barrier. There are several other passengers around her.

LAURA'S VOICE: *By the time we got to Ketchworth, I had made up my mind definitely that I wouldn't see Alec any more.*

A WOMAN'S VOICE: *Good evening, Mrs Jesson.*

LAURA does not hear.

LAURA'S VOICE: *It was silly and undignified flirting like that with a complete stranger.*

She walks on a pace or two, then turns.

LAURA: *Oh — oh — good evening.*

Dissolve to LAURA's house. She walks up the path to the front door.

LAURA'S VOICE: *I walked up to the house quite briskly and cheerfully. I had been behaving like an idiot admittedly, but after all no harm had been done.*

LAURA opens the front door.

She enters the hall, and looks up towards the stairs.

LAURA'S VOICE: *You met me in the hall. Your face was strained and worried and my heart sank.*

LAURA: *Fred, what's the matter?*

Cut to FRED, who walks down the stairs into the hall.

FRED: *It's all right, old girl, but you've got to keep calm and not be upset.*

LAURA: *What is it? What's wrong?*

FRED: *It's Bobbie — he was knocked down by a car on the way home from school. . . .*

LAURA gives a little cry.

FRED: *It's not serious — he was just grazed by the mudguard but it knocked him against the kerb and he's got slight concussion — the doctor's upstairs with him now. . . .*

LAURA flings down her parcels and book and goes upstairs at a run, tearing off her coat as she goes. FRED follows.

Through the open door of the night nursery we see LAURA arrive on the landing and hurry towards the room. She stops in the doorway as she sees the doctor standing beside BOBBIE's bed. BOBBIE is lying with his eyes shut, and his head and right arm bandaged. The doctor puts his fingers to his lips.

DOCTOR: *It's all right, Mrs Jesson — nothing to worry about — he'll be as right as rain in a few hours.*

LAURA goes across the room and kneels at the side of BOBBIE's bed. The DOCTOR now becomes an unimportant part of the scene; his legs only being visible.

LAURA whispering: *You're sure — you're sure it's not serious?*

DOCTOR smiling: *Quite sure — but it was certainly a very lucky escape.*

The DOCTOR moves off out of view.

DOCTOR off: *I've given him a little sedative, and I should advise keeping him at home for a couple of days. It must have been a bit of a shock and his right arm is rather badly bruised.*

The DOCTOR's voice gradually fades away.

LAURA's VOICE: *I felt so dreadful, Fred — looking at him lying there with that bandage round his head. I tried not to show it, but I was quite hysterical inside as though the whole thing were my fault — a sort of punishment — an awful, sinister warning.*

Dissolve to LAURA and BOBBIE. She is seated on his bed, as the maid comes into view and hands BOBBIE a plate of bread and milk.

LAURA's VOICE: *An hour or two later, of course, everything became quite normal again. He began to enjoy the whole thing thoroughly,*

55

and revelled in the fact that he was the centre of attraction. Do you
remember how we spent the whole evening planning his future?

Dissolve to FRED and LAURA in the library. They are seated on
either side of the fire. FRED is on the sofa with a crossword
puzzle and LAURA is smoking a cigarette.

LAURA: *But he's much too young to decide really.*

FRED: *It's a good life — and if the boy has a feeling for it. . . .*

LAURA: *How can we possibly really know that he has a feeling for it?*
He'll probably want to be an engine driver next week.

FRED: *It was last week that he wanted to be an engine driver.*

LAURA: *But it seems so final somehow, entering a child of that age*
for the Navy.

FRED: *It's a healthy life.*

LAURA with slight exasperation: *I know it's a good life, dear, and I*
know that he'll be able to see the world, and have a wife in every
port and keep on calling everybody ' sir ' — but what about us?

FRED: *How do you mean? ' What about us? '*

LAURA: *We shall hardly ever see him. . . .*

FRED: *Nonsense.*

LAURA: *It isn't nonsense. He'll be sent away to sea as a smooth-faced*
boy, and the next thing we know he'll be walking in with a long
beard and a parrot.

FRED: *I think you take rather a Victorian view of the Navy, my dear.*

LAURA: *He's our only son and I should like to be there while he's*
growing up.

FRED: *All right, old girl. We'll put him into an office and you can*
see him off on the eight-fifty every morning.

LAURA crushing her cigarette out: *You really are very annoying —*
you know perfectly well that I should hate that.

LAURA rises and goes round to the sofa table, behind FRED. On
the table is a work basket, out of which she starts to take some
wool, etc.

FRED: *All right — all right, have it your own way.*

After a pause we resume on close-ups of FRED and LAURA,
individually.

LAURA suddenly: *Fred. . . .*

FRED busily counting spaces: *Yes —*

LAURA: *I had lunch with a strange man to-day and he took me to*
the movies.

56

FRED: *Good for you.*

LAURA: *He's awfully nice — he's a doctor. . . .*

FRED rather abstractedly filling in a word: *A — very — noble — profession. . . .*

LAURA helplessly: *Oh dear!*

FRED: *It was Richard the Third who said ' My kingdom for a horse ', wasn't it?*

LAURA: *Yes, dear.*

FRED: *Well, all I can say is that I wish he hadn't — it ruins everything.*

LAURA: *I thought perhaps we might ask him over to dine one evening. . . .*

FRED: *By all means.* He looks up. *Who?*

LAURA: *Doctor Harvey. The one I was telling you about.*

FRED: *Must it be dinner?*

LAURA: *You're never at home for lunch.*

FRED: *Exactly.*

LAURA leaves the table and goes over to sit beside FRED.

LAURA starting to laugh, almost hysterically: *Oh, Fred!*

Close shot of FRED and LAURA.

FRED looking up: *What on earth's the matter?*

LAURA laughing more: *It's nothing — it's only that. . . .*

She breaks off and goes on laughing helplessly until she has to wipe her eyes.

LAURA: *Oh, Fred. . . .*

FRED: *I really don't see what's so terribly funny.*

LAURA: *I do — it's all right, darling, I'm not laughing at you — I'm laughing at me, I'm the one that's funny — I'm an absolute idiot — worrying myself about things that don't really exist — making mountains out of molehills. . . .*

FRED: *I told you when you came in that it wasn't anything serious — there was no need for you to get into such a state. . . .*

LAURA: *No — I see that now — I really do. . . .*

She goes on laughing.

Dissolve to interior of the Kardomah Café. LAURA is sitting at the same table; she is alone. The Ladies Orchestra is playing away as usual.

LAURA'S VOICE: *I went to the Kardomah and managed to get the*

same table. I waited a bit but he didn't come. . . . The ladies'
orchestra was playing away as usual — I looked at the cellist — she
had seemed to be so funny last week, but to-day didn't seem funny
any more — she looked pathetic, poor thing.

Dissolve to LAURA, who is walking past the hospital.

LAURA'S VOICE: *After lunch I happened to pass by the hospital —*
I remember looking up at the windows and wondering if he were
there, and whether something awful had happened to prevent him
turning up.

Dissolve to the refreshment room. It is night time. LAURA is
leaving the counter, carrying a cup of tea, which MYRTLE has
just poured out for her. She walks over to a table and sits down.

LAURA'S VOICE: *I got to the station earlier than usual. I hadn't*
enjoyed the pictures much — it was one of those noisy musical
things and I'm so sick of them — I had come out before it was over.

MYRTLE comes over to the stove in the centre of the room.
She bends down to put more coal into it. ALBERT GODBY enters
and perceiving her slightly vulnerable position he tiptoes
towards her.

LAURA is watching ALBERT. After a moment there is a loud
smack, off. LAURA smiles.

MYRTLE springs to an upright position.

MYRTLE: *Albert Godby, how dare you?*

ALBERT: *I couldn't resist it.*

MYRTLE: *I'll trouble you to keep your hands to yourself.*

MYRTLE walks out of view towards the counter.

ALBERT: *You're blushing — you look wonderful when you're angry*
— like an avenging angel.

ALBERT follows her.

At the counter we see individual close-ups of MYRTLE and
ALBERT.

MYRTLE: *I'll give you avenging angel — coming in here taking*
liberties. . . .

ALBERT: *I didn't think after what you said last Monday you'd*
object to a friendly little slap.

MYRTLE: *Never you mind about last Monday — I'm on duty now.*
A nice thing if Mr Saunders had happened to be looking through
the window.

ALBERT: *If Mr Saunders is in the 'abit of looking through windows,*

it's time he saw something worth looking at.
MYRTLE: *You ought to be ashamed of yourself!*
ALBERT: *It's just high spirits — don't be mad at me.*
MYRTLE: *High spirits indeed! Here, take your tea and be quiet.*
ALBERT: *It's all your fault, anyway.*
MYRTLE: *I don't know what you're referring to, I'm sure.*
ALBERT: *I was thinking of to-night.*
MYRTLE: *If you don't learn to behave yourself there won't be a to-night — or any other night, either. . . .*
ALBERT: *Give us a kiss.*
MYRTLE: *I'll do no such thing. The lady might see us.*
ALBERT: *Just a quick one — across the counter.*
    He grabs her arm across the counter.
MYRTLE: *Albert, stop it!*
ALBERT: *Come on — there's a love.*
MYRTLE: *Let go of me this minute.*
ALBERT: *Come on, just one. . . .*
    They scuffle for a moment, upsetting a neat pile of cakes on to the floor.
MYRTLE: *Now look at me Banburys — all over the floor.*
    ALBERT bends down to pick them up.
    Cut to STANLEY as he enters the door.
STANLEY: *Just in time or born in the vestry.*
    LAURA glances up at the clock, takes up her shopping basket, and during the following dialogue, the camera pans with her to the door which leads to Number 3 platform.
MYRTLE off: *You shut your mouth and help Mr Godby pick up them cakes. Come along, what are you standing there gaping at?*
    LAURA comes out of the refreshment room door on to Number 3 platform.
LAURA'S VOICE: *As I left the refreshment room I saw a train coming in — his train. He wasn't on the platform, and I suddenly felt panic-stricken at the thought of not seeing him again.*
    Dissolve to the subway entrance to Number 2 and 3 platforms.
    ALEC dashes up the steps on to the platform, and runs towards LAURA.
ALEC breathlessly: *Oh, my dear, I'm so sorry — so terribly sorry.*
LAURA: *Quick — your train — you'll miss it.*
    They both rush along the platform towards the subway.

ALEC as they go: *I'd no way of letting you know — the house surgeon had to operate suddenly — it wasn't anything really serious, but I had to stand by as it was one of my special patients.*

Inside the subway LAURA and ALEC are running down the steps.

ALEC: *. . . You do understand, don't you?*

LAURA now rather breathless: *Of course — it doesn't matter a bit.*
They turn the corner at the foot of the steps, and the camera tracks with them as they run along the subway towards Number 4 platform.

ALEC: *I thought of sending a note to the Kardomah, but I thought they would probably never find you, or keep on shouting your name out and embarrass you, and I. . . .*
They start running up the steps leading to Number 4 platform.

LAURA: *Please don't say any more — I really do understand. . . .*
A whistle blows as LAURA and ALEC hurry on to the platform.

LAURA: *Quickly — oh, quickly. The whistle's gone.*
They hurry to the waiting train. ALEC opens the door of a third-class compartment and turns to LAURA.

ALEC: *I'm so relieved that I had a chance to explain — I didn't think I would ever see you again.*

LAURA: *How absurd of you.*
The train starts to move off.

LAURA: *Quickly — quickly. . . .*
ALEC jumps into the train, and leans out of the window.
LAURA walks along a few paces with the train.

ALEC: *Next Thursday.*

LAURA: *Yes. Next Thursday.*
The train gradually gains on LAURA, and ALEC goes out of view.
LAURA watches ALEC's departing train, waves after it and stands quite still until the sound of it has died away in the distance.
A strident voice from the loudspeaker breaks in:

LOUDSPEAKER: *The train for Ketchworth is standing at Number 3 platform.*
LAURA suddenly realizes that she is about to miss her own train, and she makes a dash for the subway steps.

Dissolve to a close shot of LAURA and ALEC sitting in the front row of the circle at the Palladium Cinema. They are both laughing and are obviously very happy. The lights go up.

ALEC: *The stars can change in their courses, the universe go up in flames and the world crash around us, but there'll always be Donald Duck.*

LAURA: *I do love him so, his dreadful energy, his blind frustrated rages. . . .*

The lights begin to dim.

ALEC: *It's the big picture now — here we go — no more laughter — prepare for tears.*

Dissolve to the main title of the big picture, flashed on to the screen. It is the film advertised in the trailer of two weeks ago, ' Flame of Passion '.

LAURA'S VOICE: *It was a terribly bad picture.*

Dissolve to LAURA and ALEC walking up the last few steps of the circle towards the exit. The back of an usherette forms the foreground of the shot.

LAURA'S VOICE: *We crept out before the end, rather furtively, as though we were committing a crime. The usherette at the door looked at us with stony contempt.*

Dissolve to a medium shot of LAURA and ALEC coming out of the cinema. ALEC takes LAURA's arm, as they walk along the street.

LAURA'S VOICE: *It really was a lovely afternoon, and it was a relief to be in the fresh air. Do you know, I believe we should all behave quite differently if we lived in a warm, sunny climate all the time. We shouldn't be so withdrawn and shy and difficult.*

Dissolve to a picturesque shot of ALEC and LAURA as they walk along by the side of a lake.

LAURA'S VOICE: *Oh, Fred, it really was a lovely afternoon. There were some little boys sailing their boats — one of them looked awfully like Bobbie — that should have given me a pang of conscience I know, but it didn't! . . .*

After a few moments ALEC stops walking and turns to LAURA.

LAURA'S VOICE: *Alec suddenly said that he was sick of staring at the water and that he wanted to be on it.*

The foreground of the scene is now composed of one or two rowing boats, which have been covered up for the winter. On the landing stage in the background, a boatman is pushing ALEC and LAURA away from the shore.

LAURA'S VOICE: *All the boats were covered up but we managed to persuade the old man to let us have one.*

Close shot of the boatman.

LAURA'S VOICE: *He thought we were raving mad. Perhaps he was right.*

The boat is in the water, with the boatman in the foreground.

LAURA'S VOICE: *. . . Alec rowed off at a great rate, and I trailed my hand in the water — it was very cold but a lovely feeling.*

ALEC and LAURA are in the boat. LAURA is in the foreground of the shot. ALEC catches a crab and an oar slips out of its rowlock.

LAURA: *You don't row very well, do you?*

ALEC putting the oar back in the rowlock: *I'm going to be perfectly honest with you. I don't row at all, and unless you want to go round in ever narrowing circles, you had better start steering.* (*Still*)

LAURA laughs and picks up the steering ropes. They start off again.

The boat is following a somewhat erratic course.

LAURA'S VOICE: *We had such fun, Fred. I felt gay and happy and sort of released — that's what's so shameful about it all — that's what would hurt you so much if you knew — that I could feel as intensely as that — away from you — with a stranger.*

The camera is tracking with the boat. LAURA is in the foreground of the shot. They are approaching a very low bridge.

LAURA: *Oh, look out . . . we shan't get through.*

ALEC glancing behind: *Pull on your left.*

As the bridge looms nearer and nearer, ALEC rises to his feet. LAURA pulls the wrong rope and looks up inquiringly at ALEC. There is a crash and a shudder as the boat hits the bridge.

LAURA'S VOICE: *I never could tell left from right.*

The boat rocks violently and there is a loud splash. LAURA looks towards the water and begins to laugh.

ALEC is standing in the lake. The water only comes up to his knees. He is very wet.

Close-up of LAURA, who is roaring with laughter.

Dissolve to the interior of the boathouse. ALEC's trousers are hanging over a line in front of an open ' Ideal ' boiler. ALEC himself is seated on an upturned dinghy. He is wearing an overcoat, which is obviously not his own, and is smoking a cigarette. He looks at LAURA.

She is kneeling by the boiler, laying out ALEC's shoes and socks to dry.

She gets up and goes over to a carpenter's bench, where a kettle is boiling on a gas ring. Beside the ring is a bottle of milk and two cups. In the background of the shot are a collection of punts, boats, oars, etc. LAURA starts to make tea.

LAURA: *The British have always been nice to mad people. That boatman thinks we are quite dotty, but just look how sweet he has been: overcoat, tea, milk — even sugar.*

Close shot of ALEC as he watches her prepare the tea. After a moment we hear the sound of LAURA walking across the boathouse towards ALEC. He follows her with his eyes. Her hand comes into view and gives him a cup of tea.

ALEC: *Thank you.*

LAURA sits down on an old wooden chair, and they both begin to stir their tea.

ALEC quietly: *You know what's happened, don't you?*

LAURA: *Yes — yes, I do.*

ALEC: *I've fallen in love with you.*

LAURA: *Yes — I know.*

ALEC: *Tell me honestly — my dear — please tell me honestly if what I believe is true. . . .*

LAURA in a whisper: *What do you believe?* (Still)

ALEC: *That it's the same with you — that you've fallen in love too.*

LAURA near tears: *It sounds so silly.*

ALEC: *Why?*

LAURA: *I know you so little.*

ALEC: *It is true, though — isn't it?*

LAURA with a sigh: *Yes — it's true.*

ALEC making a slight movement towards her: *Laura. . . .*

LAURA: *No please . . . we must be sensible — please help me to be sensible — we mustn't behave like this — we must forget that we've said what we've said.*

ALEC: *Not yet — not quite yet.*

LAURA panic in her voice: *But we must — don't you see!*

ALEC leaning forward and taking her hand: *Listen — it's too late now to be as sensible as all that — it's too late to forget what we've said — and anyway, whether we'd said it or not couldn't have mattered — we know — we've both of us known for a long time.*

LAURA: *How can you say that — I've only known you for four weeks — we only talked for the first time last Thursday week.*

ALEC: *Last Thursday week. Hadn't it been a long time since then — for you? Answer me truly.*

LAURA: *Yes.*

ALEC: *How often did you decide that you were never going to see me again?*

LAURA: *Several times a day.*

ALEC: *So did I.*

LAURA: *Oh, Alec.*

ALEC: *I love you — I love your wide eyes and the way you smile and your shyness, and the way you laugh at my jokes.*

LAURA: *Please don't. . . .*

ALEC: *I love you — I love you — you love me too — it's no use pretending that it hasn't happened because it has.*

LAURA with tremendous effort: *Yes it has. I don't want to pretend anything either to you or to anyone else . . . but from now on I shall have to. That's what's wrong — don't you see? That's what spoils everything. That's why we must stop here and now talking like this. We are neither of us free to love each other, there is too much in the way. There's still time, if we control ourselves and behave like sensible human beings, there's still time to — to. . . .*

She puts her head down and bursts into tears.

ALEC: *There's no time at all.*

ALEC goes over to her, takes her in his arms and kisses her. Cut to close-up of the station bell, ringing loudly at Milford Junction Station. It is night time.

LAURA and ALEC come on to Number 1 platform from the booking hall.

LAURA: *There's your train.*

ALEC: *Yes.*

LAURA: *I'll come with you — over to the other platform.*

They walk along the platform and down the subway steps. In the subway ALEC stops and takes her in his arms. She struggles a little.

LAURA: *No dear — please . . . not here — someone will see.*

ALEC kissing her: *I love you so.*

They are interrupted by the sound of feet coming down the subway steps. A shadow appears on the wall behind them. They hurry off through the subway.

In the foreground of the shot, the dim outline of LAURA can be seen. She is watching herself and ALEC as they walk along the subway towards Number 4 platform. The sound of an express train roaring overhead, becomes the sound of loud music. FRED's voice is heard.

FRED's VOICE: *Don't you think we might have that down a bit, darling?*

After a slight pause.

FRED's VOICE: *Hoi — Laura!*

Dissolve to a shot over LAURA's shoulder. The subway has suddenly disappeared, and FRED and the library have taken its place.

LAURA jumping: *Yes, dear?*

FRED: *You were miles away.*

LAURA: *Was I? Yes, I suppose I was.*

FRED rising: *Do you mind if I turn it down a little — it really is deafening. . . .*

He goes towards the radio.

LAURA with an effort: *Of course not.*

She bends down and starts sewing. FRED turns down the radio, and returns to his place.

FRED: *I shan't be long over this, and then we'll go up to bed. You look a bit tired, you know. . . .*

LAURA: *Don't hurry — I'm perfectly happy.*

She continues her sewing for a moment or two, then she looks up again. FRED's head is down, concentrating on the paper.

LAURA passes her hand across her forehead wearily.

LAURA's VOICE: *How can I possibly say that? ' Don't hurry, I'm perfectly happy.' If only it were true. Not, I suppose, that anybody is perfectly happy really, but just to be ordinarily contented — to be at peace. It's such a little while ago really, but it seems an eternity since that train went out of the station — taking him away into the darkness.*

Dissolve to LAURA walking in the subway. The sound of her train is heard pulling in overhead.

LAURA's VOICE: *I went over to the other platform and got into my train as usual.*

Close shot of LAURA in the railway compartment. She is seated in a corner.

LAURA'S VOICE: *This time I didn't attempt to read — even to pretend to read — I didn't care whether people were looking at me or not. I had to think. I should have been utterly wretched and ashamed — I know I should but I wasn't — I felt suddenly quite wildly happy — like a romantic schoolgirl, like a romantic fool! You see he had said he loved me, and I had said I loved him, and it was true — it was true! I imagined him holding me in his arms — I imagined being with him in all sorts of glamorous circumstances. It was one of those absurd fantasies — just like one has when one is a girl — being wooed and married by the ideal of one's dreams — generally a rich and handsome Duke.*

As LAURA turns to look out of the window, the camera tracks and pans slowly forward until the darkened countryside fills the screen.

LAURA'S VOICE: *I stared out of the railway carriage window into the dark and watched the dim trees and the telegraph posts slipping by, and through them I saw Alec and me.*

The countryside fades away and ALEC and LAURA are seen, dancing a gay waltz. The noise of the train recedes, and is replaced by music.

LAURA'S VOICE: *Alec and me — perhaps a little younger than we are now, but just as much in love, and with nothing in the way.*

The sound of the train returns for a moment and the dancing figures fade away. The train noise dies away again, and is replaced by the sound of an orchestra tuning up, as the passing countryside changes to a picture of ALEC and LAURA in a theatre box. ALEC gently takes a beautiful evening cloak from her shoulders and hands her a programme and opera glasses.

LAURA'S VOICE: *I saw us in Paris, in a box at the Opera. The orchestra was tuning up. Then we were in Venice — drifting along the Grand Canal in a gondola.*

LAURA and ALEC are reclining in a gondola. There is the sound of lovely tenor voices and mandolins coming over the water. The scene changes to one of ALEC and LAURA in a car. They are driving through beautiful countryside, and the wind blowing LAURA's hair accentuates the feeling of speed.

LAURA's VOICE: *I saw us travelling far away together; all the places I have always longed to go.*

We now see the rushing wake of a ship; then a ship's rail.

LAURA's VOICE: *I saw us leaning on the rail of a ship looking at the sea and the stars — standing on some tropical beach in the moon-light with the palm trees sighing above us. Then the palm trees changed into those pollarded willows by the canal just before the level crossing. . . .*

The camera pulls back from the window of the railway compartment and pans to include LAURA.

LAURA's VOICE: *. . . and all the silly dreams disappeared, and I got out at Ketchworth and gave up my ticket. . . .*

Dissolve to the booking hall and station yard of Ketchworth Station. LAURA gives up her ticket and walks away across the station yard.

LAURA's VOICE: *. . . and walked home as usual — quite soberly and without any wings at all.*

Dissolve to the interior of LAURA's bedroom. It is night time. LAURA is seated at her dressing table. The camera shoots on to the mirror of the dressing table.

LAURA's VOICE: *When I had changed for dinner and was doing my face a bit — do you remember? I don't suppose you do, but I do — you see you don't know that that was the first time in our life together that I had ever lied to you — it started then, the shame of the whole thing, the guiltiness, the fear. . . .*

The reflection of FRED can be seen coming into the bedroom. He comes forward and kisses LAURA lightly.

FRED: *Good evening, Mrs Jesson.*

LAURA: *Hullo, dear.*

FRED: *Had a good day?*

LAURA: *Yes, lovely.*

FRED: *What did you do?*

LAURA: *Well — I shopped — and had lunch — and went to the pictures.*

FRED moving away: *All by yourself?*

LAURA in sudden panic: *Yes — no — that is, not exactly.*

FRED cheerfully: *How do you mean, not exactly?*

LAURA with a rush: *Well I went to the pictures by myself, but I had lunch with Mary Norton at the Kardomah — she couldn't come to the pictures because she had to go and see her in-laws — you know, they live just outside Milford — so I walked with her to the bus and then went off on my own.*

FRED: *I haven't seen Mary Norton for ages. How was she looking?*

LAURA: *She was looking very well really — a little fatter, I think. . . .*

FRED: *Hurry up with all this beautifying — I want my dinner.*

LAURA gaily: *Go on down — I shan't be five minutes. . . .*

> FRED goes out. LAURA sits staring at herself in the glass. She puts her hand to her throat as if she were suffocating.
>
> Dissolve to a close shot of LAURA at the telephone.

LAURA on the telephone: *Is Mrs Norton there, please? Yes, I'll hold on. Hallo, is that you Mary — no — I know — I haven't seen you for ages. Listen, my dear, will you be a saint and back me up in the most appalling domestic lie?* She laughs forcedly. *Yes— my life depends on it. Yesterday I went into Milford as usual to do my shopping with the special intention of buying a far too expensive present for Fred's birthday.*

> MARY NORTON is at the other end of the telephone, as she stands in the hallway of her house. She is plump and rather blousy.

LAURA off: *Well, Spink and Robson's hadn't got what I wanted which was one of those travelling clocks with the barometer, and everything in one, but they rang up their branch in Broadham, and said that there was one there — so I hopped on to the one-thirty train and went to get it.*

> Resume on LAURA, back in her bedroom.

LAURA: *Now then, this is where the black lie comes in — Fred asked me last night if I had had a good day in Milford, and I said yes, and you and I had lunched together at the Kardomah, and that you had gone off to see your in-laws, and I had gone to the pictures, so if by any chance you should run into him — don't let me down. All right?* She laughs again. *Yes, dear, I promise I'll do the same for you. Yes, that would be lovely. No I can't on Thursday, that's my Milford day. What about Friday? Very well — perfect — Good-bye.*

> She hangs up the telephone and the social smile on her face fades.
>
> Dissolve to FRED and LAURA's bedroom. The lights are out and she is awake, while FRED is asleep.

LAURA's VOICE: *That week was misery. I went through it in a sort of trance — how odd of you not to have noticed that you were living with a stranger in the house.*

Dissolve to the exterior of the hospital. It is day time. LAURA is walking up and down outside. (*Still*)

LAURA's VOICE: *Thursday came at last — I had arranged to meet Alec outside the hospital at twelve-thirty.*

ALEC comes out of the main doors of the hospital and down the steps in the background. He sees LAURA and comes up to her.

ALEC almost breathlessly: *Hullo. . . .*

LAURA with a strained smile: *Hullo. . . .*

ALEC: *I thought you wouldn't come — I've been thinking all the week that you wouldn't come.*

LAURA: *I didn't mean to really — but here I am. . . .*

He takes her arm, they turn and walk away together along the road. The camera follows them, shooting on to their backs from a low angle. The background of the scene is composed of roof-tops and trees.

Dissolve to the Royal Hotel restaurant where LAURA and ALEC are seated at a corner table. A wine waiter is standing beside ALEC, who is examining the wine list. LAURA is looking around the room.

LAURA's VOICE: *Do you know, I hadn't been inside the Royal since Violet's wedding reception? It all seemed very grand.*

The wine waiter leaves the table.

LAURA's VOICE: *He actually ordered a bottle of champagne! And when I protested he said that we were only middle-aged once! We were very gay during lunch and talked about quite ordinary things.*

Close shot of ALEC over LAURA's shoulder.

LAURA's VOICE: *Oh, Fred, he really was charming — I know you would have liked him if only things had been different.*

Dissolve to the hotel entrance lounge. ALEC and LAURA come into view through the door leading from the restaurant.

LAURA's VOICE: *As we were going out he said that he had a surprise for me, and that if I would wait in the lounge for five minutes he'd show me what it was.*

ALEC runs down some steps towards the main entrance.

LAURA'S VOICE: *He went out and down the steps at a run — more like an excited schoolboy than a respectable doctor.*

LAURA watches ALEC as he leaves the hotel. She turns and the camera focuses on the restaurant doorway out of which are emerging MARY NORTON and MRS ROLANDSON. MARY NORTON'S clothes are reasonably good but carelessly worn. MRS ROLANDSON is over smartly dressed; her hat is too young for her, and she gives the impression of being meticulously enamelled. They both recognize LAURA.

LAURA smiles with agonized amiability.

MARY: *Laura, it was you after all! Hermione said it was you but you know how shortsighted I am — I peered and peered and couldn't be sure.*

LAURA, with a bright fixed expression, shakes hands with them both.

LAURA: *I never saw you at all — how dreadful of me — I expect it was the champagne — I'm not used to champagne at lunch — or for dinner either for the matter of that — but Alec insisted. . . .*

MARY: *Alec who, dear?*

LAURA with a gay little laugh: *Alec Harvey of course. Surely you remember the Harveys — I've known them for years.*

MARY: *I don't think I ever. . . .*

LAURA: *He'll be back in a minute — you'll probably recognize him when you peer at him closely. . . .*

MRS ROLANDSON: *He certainly looked very charming and very attentive!*

LAURA: *He's a dear — one of the nicest people in the world and a wonderful doctor.*

ALEC comes bounding back up the steps, and joins the group.

LAURA flashes him one anguished look and then introduces him.

LAURA: *Alec — you remember Mrs Norton, don't you?*

ALEC politely shaking hands: *I . . . er . . . I'm afraid I. . . .*

MARY: *It's no use Laura — we've never met before in our lives — I'm sure we haven't. . . .*

LAURA: *How absurd — I made certain that he and Madeleine were there when you dined with us just before Christmas — Alec — this is Mrs Rolandson.*

MRS ROLANDSON: *How do you do.*

They shake hands. There is a pause.

70

MRS ROLANDSON: *What horrid weather, isn't it?*

ALEC: *Yes.*

MRS ROLANDSON: *Still, I suppose we can't expect spring at this time of the year, can we?*

ALEC: *No.*

There is another pause.

MARY: *Well, we really must be going — I'm taking Hermione with me to see the in-laws — to give moral support — Good-bye, Doctor Harvey.*

ALEC: *Good-bye.*

They shake hands. (*Still*)

MRS ROLANDSON bowing: *Good-bye. Good-bye, Mrs Jesson.*

LAURA: *Good-bye.*

She smiles pleasantly.

MARY to LAURA: *Good-bye, my dear. I do so envy you and your champagne.*

MARY NORTON and MRS ROLANDSON go out of view towards the steps.

LAURA putting her hands over her face: *That was awful — awful. . . .*

ALEC: *Never mind.*

LAURA: *They had been watching us all through lunch — oh dear. . . .*

ALEC with an attempt at brightness: *Forget it — come out and look at the surprise.*

Dissolve to the exterior of the Royal Hotel. In the foreground of the scene is a small two-seater car, which is parked outside the hotel entrance. ALEC and LAURA come out of the hotel and get into the car.

LAURA'S VOICE: *There at the foot of the steps was a little two-seater car. Alec had borrowed it from Stephen Lynn for the afternoon. We got in in silence and drove away.*

Dissolve to the car driving through the outskirts of Milford.

It pulls up near a small bridge over a stream.

LAURA'S VOICE: *When we were out in the real country — I think it was a few miles beyond Brayfield — we stopped the car just outside a village and got out. There was a little bridge and a stream and the sun was making an effort to come out but really not succeeding very well. We leaned on the parapet of the bridge and looked down into the water. I shivered and Alec put his arm around me.*

LAURA and ALEC are leaning on the bridge, looking down into

71

the water.

ALEC: *Cold?*

LAURA: *No — not really.*

ALEC: *Happy?*

LAURA: *No — not really.*

ALEC: *I know what you're going to say — that it isn't worth it — that the furtiveness and the necessary lying outweigh the happiness we might have together — wasn't that it?*

LAURA: *Yes. Something like that.*

ALEC: *I want to ask you something — just to reassure myself.*

LAURA her eyes filling with tears: *What is it?*

ALEC: *It is true for you, isn't it? This overwhelming feeling that we have for each other — it is as true for you as it is for me — isn't it?*

LAURA: *Yes — it's true.*

> She bursts into tears and ALEC puts his arms closer around her. They stand in silence for a moment and then kiss each other passionately.

> Dissolve to another shot of LAURA and ALEC. They are now again leaning on the bridge.

LAURA'S VOICE: *I don't remember how long we stayed on that bridge or what we said. I only remember feeling that I was on the edge of a precipice, terrified yet wanting desperately to throw myself over.*

> ALEC and LAURA start to move towards the car.

LAURA'S VOICE: *Finally we got back into the car and arrived at Stephen Lynn's garage just as it was getting dark.*

> Dissolve to the inside of a small lock-up garage. The camera is shooting towards the entrance. The car drives into the garage towards the camera and stops. The headlights are turned off and ALEC and LAURA get out. They are silhouetted against the entrance, behind which are the lighted windows of the block of flats.

LAURA'S VOICE: *We put the car away and Alec said he had to leave the keys of the car in Stephen Lynn's flat, and suggested that I came up with him. I refused rather too vehemently. Alec reminded me that Stephen wasn't coming back till late, but I still refused.*

> ALEC shuts the garage doors.

> Dissolve to the exterior of station approach. LAURA and ALEC are walking along towards the camera. In the background of the scene is a signal box and railway lines. An express can be

heard approaching in the distance.

ALEC stopping: *I'm going to miss my train. I'm going back.*

LAURA: *Back where?*

ALEC: *To Stephen's flat.*

LAURA: *Oh, Alec.*

They look at each other as the noise of the express rises to a thundering crescendo out of which emerges the scream of the train whistle.

The express hurtles into the tunnel.

LAURA and ALEC are in each other's arms.

LAURA pushing him away in panic: *I must go now. I really must go home.*

She runs off out of view. ALEC stands watching her.

We see LAURA entering the booking hall, from ALEC's viewpoint.

ALEC turns and walks away.

In the refreshment room LAURA takes a cup of tea over to her usual table.

LAURA'S VOICE: *I got my cup of tea at the counter, and went over to our usual table. Two soldiers came in and started to make a scene at the counter.*

LAURA sits at the table, sipping her tea. Her face looks strained and exhausted.

Cut to MYRTLE, BERYL and the two soldiers, BILL and JOHNNIE, who have just arrived at the counter.

BILL: *Afternoon, lady.*

MYRTLE grandly: *Good afternoon.*

BILL: *A couple of splashes, please.*

MYRTLE: *Very sorry, it's out of hours.*

BILL: *Just sneak us a couple under cover of them poor old sandwiches.*

MYRTLE: *Them sandwiches were fresh this morning, and I shall do no such thing.*

BILL: *Come on, be a sport. You could pop it into a couple of teacups.*

MYRTLE: *You can have as much as you want after six o'clock.*

JOHNNIE: *My throat's like a parrot's cage — listen!*

He makes a crackling noise with his throat.

73

of flats. LAURA comes in from the street. It is raining. She pauses for a moment to examine a board on which are listed the names of the tenants and their flat numbers. She walks up the stairs to the door of Stephen Lynn's flat on the second floor, and rings the bell. ALEC opens the door, and she goes quickly past him into the hall almost without looking at him.

ALEC softly: *Oh, darling, I didn't dare to hope.*

ALEC leads her gently through to the sitting room. It is rather a bleak little room. The furniture looks impersonal. He has lit the fire, but it hasn't had time to get under way and is smoking. They stand quite still for a moment, looking at each other.

LAURA: *It's raining.*

ALEC his eyes never moving from her face: *Is it?*

LAURA: *It started just as I turned out of the High Street.*

ALEC: *You had no umbrella and your coat's wet. . . .*

He gently helps her off with her coat.

ALEC: *You mustn't catch cold — that would never do.*

LAURA looking at herself in the glass over the mantelpiece, and slowly taking off her hat: *I look an absolute fright.*

ALEC taking her hat and her scarf: *Let me put these down.*

LAURA: *Thank you.*

ALEC putting them on a chair near the writing desk with the coat: *I hope the fire will perk up in a few minutes. . . .*

LAURA: *I expect the wood was damp.*

ALEC ruefully: *Yes — I expect it was.*

There is silence.

ALEC: *Do sit down, darling. . . .*

LAURA sits down on the sofa.

LAURA with an attempt at gaiety: *I got right into the train and then got out again — wasn't that idiotic?*

ALEC sitting down next to her and taking her in his arms: *We're both very foolish.*

He kisses her.

LAURA weakly: *Alec — I can't stay you know — really, I can't.*

ALEC: *Just a little while — just a little while. . . .*

There is the sound of the lift gates clanging. They both break apart and look up.

From their view-point we see the flat hallway. There is the sound of a step outside on the landing, and then the sound of

76

a key fitted into the front door.

LAURA and ALEC jump to their feet.

LAURA in a frantic whisper: *Quickly — quickly — I must go.* . . .

ALEC snatches up her hat and coat and pushes them into her hand.

ALEC: *Here — through the kitchen — there's a tradesmen's staircase.* . . .

They rush into the small kitchen where there is a door opening on to the fire escape. ALEC tears it open. LAURA runs through it on to a metal staircase, without even looking back. She disappears down the stairs. ALEC shuts the door quietly after her and leans against it for a moment with his eyes closed.

A MAN'S VOICE from the sitting room: *Is that you, Alec?*

ALEC as casually as he can: *Yes.*

He starts to walk back into the sitting room.

STEPHEN LYNN is standing by the entrance to the hall. He is a thin, rather ascetic-looking man. ALEC walks towards him.

ALEC: *You are back early.*

STEPHEN: *I felt a cold coming on so I denied myself the always questionable pleasure of dining with that arch arguer Roger Hinchley, and decided to come back to bed.* Walking to the chair by the writing desk: *Inflamed membranes are unsympathetic to dialectic —*

ALEC: *What will you do about food?*

STEPHEN smiling: *I can ring down to the restaurant later on if I want anything — we live in a modern age and this is a service flat.*

ALEC with a forced laugh: *Yes — Yes — I know.*

STEPHEN still smiling: *It caters for all tastes.*

He lightly flicks LAURA's scarf off the chair and hands it to ALEC.

STEPHEN: *You know, Alec, my dear, you have hidden depths that I never even suspected.*

ALEC: *Look here, Stephen, I really.* . . .

STEPHEN holding up his hand: *For heaven's sake, Alec, no explanations or apologies — I am the one who should apologize for having returned so inopportunely — it is quite obvious to me that you were interviewing a patient privately — women are frequently neurotic creatures, and the hospital atmosphere upsets them. From the rather undignified scuffling I heard when I came into the hall, I gather that she beat a hurried retreat down the backstairs. I'm surprised at this farcical streak in your nature, Alec — such carryings on were quite unnecessary — after all, we have known each other for years and I am the most broad-minded of men.*

ALEC stiffly: *I'm really very sorry, Stephen. I'm sure that the whole situation must seem inexpressibly vulgar to you. Actually it isn't in the least. However, you are perfectly right — explanations are unnecessary — particularly between old friends. I must go now.*

STEPHEN still smiling: *Very well.*

ALEC: *I'll collect my hat and coat in the hall. Good-bye.*

STEPHEN: *Perhaps you'd let me have my latch key back? I only have two and I'm so afraid of losing them — you know how absent-minded I am.*

ALEC giving him the key: *You're very angry, aren't you? (Still)*

STEPHEN: *No, Alec — not angry — just disappointed.*

ALEC goes out without another word.

In the street outside, the camera is tracking on a close shot of LAURA's legs and feet. She is running fast along the pavement. It is pouring with rain.

Close-up of LAURA, who is still running. The background of the scene is composed of the tops of houses. As she approaches a lamp post, the light increases on her face and dies away quickly as she passes it.

The camera tracks to the pavement from LAURA's angle. Her shadow becomes large and elongated as she moves further away from the lamp post.

Resume on LAURA as she approaches another lamp post. She is out of breath and slows down to a walk.

LAURA's VOICE: *I ran until I couldn't run any longer — I leant against a lamp post to try to get my breath — I was in one of those side-roads that lead out of the High Street. I know it was stupid to run, but I couldn't help myself.*

Close shot of LAURA as she leans against the lamp post.

LAURA's VOICE: *I felt so utterly humiliated and defeated and so dreadfully, dreadfully ashamed. After a moment or two I pulled myself together, and walked on in the direction of the station.*

The camera starts to track with her along the street.

LAURA's VOICE: *It was still raining but not very much. I suddenly realized that I couldn't go home, not until I had got myself under*

more control, and had a little time to think. Then I thought of you
waiting at home for me, and the dinner being spoilt.

LAURA is now at the telephone in a tobacconist's shop. She
looks pale and bedraggled.

LAURA'S VOICE: *So I went into the High Street and found a tobac-*
conist and telephoned to you — do you remember — ?

LAURA at the telephone (*Still*): *Fred — is that you?* With a tremendous effort she makes her voice sound ordinary: *Yes, dear — it's*
me — Laura — Yes — of course everything's perfectly all right, but I
shan't be home to dinner — I'm with Miss Lewis, dear — the
librarian at Boots I told you about — I can't explain in any detail
now because she's just outside the telephone box — but I met her
a little while ago in the High Street in the most awful state — her
mother has just been taken ill, and I've promised to stay with her
until the doctor comes — Yes, dear, I know, but she's always been
tremendously kind to me and I'm desperately sorry for her — No —
I'll get a sandwich — tell Ethel to leave a little soup for me in a
saucepan in the kitchen — Yes, of course — as soon as I can. Good-
bye.

She hangs up the telephone.

LAURA'S VOICE: *It's awfully easy to lie — when you know that you're*
trusted implicitly — so very easy, and so very degrading.

She walks slowly out of the telephone box.

The camera is shooting from a high angle on to a road leading
off the High Street. It has stopped raining but the pavement is
still wet and glistening. LAURA is slowly walking towards the
camera.

LAURA'S VOICE: *I started walking without much purpose — I turned*
out of the High Street almost immediately — I was terrified that I
might run into Alec — I was pretty certain that he'd come after me
to the station.

The camera is shooting down on to another street. LAURA is
still walking.

LAURA'S VOICE: *I walked for a long while. . . .*

Dissolve to a shot of the war memorial. The foreground of the
shot is composed of part of the war memorial statue: a soldier's
hand gripping a bayoneted service rifle. Beyond it LAURA is seen
as a tiny figure walking towards a seat near the base of the
memorial.

LAURA'S VOICE: *Finally, I found myself at the war memorial — you know it's right at the other side of the town. It had stopped raining altogether, and I felt stiflingly hot so I sat down on one of the seats.*

Close shot of LAURA on the seat.

LAURA'S VOICE: *There was nobody about, and I lit a cigarette (Still) — I know how you disapprove of women smoking in the street — I do too, really — but I wanted to calm my nerves and I thought it might help.*

She is now in profile to the camera, and has finished her cigarette.

LAURA'S VOICE: *I sat there for ages — I don't know how long — then I noticed a policeman walking up and down a little way off — he was looking at me rather suspiciously. Presently he came up to me.*

The POLICEMAN walks up into a shot over LAURA's shoulder.

POLICEMAN: *Feeling all right, Miss?*

LAURA faintly: *Yes, thank you.*

POLICEMAN: *Waiting for someone?*

LAURA: *No — I'm not waiting for anyone.*

POLICEMAN: *You don't want to go and catch cold you know — that would never do. It's a damp night to be sitting about on seats, you know.*

LAURA rising: *I'm going now anyhow — I have a train to catch.*

Close shot of LAURA and the POLICEMAN.

POLICEMAN: *You're sure you feel quite all right?*

LAURA: *Yes — quite sure — good night.*

POLICEMAN: *Good night, Miss.*

As LAURA walks off the camera pans and tracks with her, shooting at her back.

LAURA'S VOICE: *I walked away — trying to look casual — knowing that he was watching me. I felt like a criminal. I walked rather quickly back in the direction of the High Street.*

Dissolve to Milford Junction Station. The clock on platforms 2 and 3 forms the foreground of shot. The time is six minutes to ten. LAURA comes up out of the subway in the background and walks along the platform. The station is not very well lit, and there is hardly anyone about.

LAURA'S VOICE: *I got to the station fifteen minutes before the last train to Ketchworth, and then I realized that I had been wandering about for over three hours, but it didn't seem to be any time at all.*

LAURA comes into the refreshment room.

It is nearly closing time, and the room is half-lighted. There is the melancholy noise of a goods train chugging through the station. BERYL is draping the things on the counter with muslin cloths while STANLEY, wearing his ordinary clothes, stands gossiping with her. LAURA comes in through the door in the background.

BERYL: *Stan, you are awful!*

STANLEY: *I'll wait for you in the yard.*

BERYL: *Oh, all right.*

STANLEY goes out.

LAURA: *I'd like a glass of brandy, please.*

BERYL: *We're just closing.*

LAURA: *I see you are, but you're not quite closed yet, are you?*

BERYL sullenly: *Three Star?*

LAURA: *Yes, that'll do.*

BERYL getting it: *Tenpence, please.*

LAURA taking money from her bag: *Here — and — have you a piece of paper and an envelope?*

BERYL: *I'm afraid you'll have to get that at the bookstall.*

LAURA: *The bookstall's shut — please — it's very important — I should be so much obliged. . . .*

BERYL: *Oh, all right — wait a minute.*

BERYL goes out.

LAURA sips the brandy at the counter. She is obviously trying to control her nerves. After a moment BERYL can be heard walking back across the refreshment room. She enters the shot and puts down some notepaper and an envelope.

LAURA: *Thank you so much.*

BERYL: *We close in a few minutes, you know.*

LAURA: *Yes, I know.*

BERYL goes out of shot and the camera pans with LAURA as she takes a few paces along the counter in order to be under the light. She stares at the paper for a moment, takes another sip of brandy, and then begins to write.

BERYL looks at LAURA with exasperation.

Close shot of LAURA. BERYL can be heard walking away across

the refreshment room and slamming the door at the other end. LAURA falters in her writing, then breaks down and buries her face in her hands. In the background the door to the platform opens and ALEC comes in. He looks hopelessly round for a moment, then, seeing her, walks forward.

ALEC: *Thank God — Oh, darling. . . .*

LAURA: *Please go away — please don't say anything. . . .*

ALEC: *I've been looking for you everywhere — I've watched every train.*

LAURA: *Please go away. . . .*

ALEC: *You're being dreadfully cruel. It was just a beastly accident that he came back early — he doesn't know who you are — he never even saw you.*

LAURA: *I suppose he laughed, didn't he?* Bitterly. *I suppose you spoke of me together as men of the world?*

ALEC: *We didn't speak of you — we spoke of a nameless creature who had no reality at all.*

LAURA: *Why didn't you tell him who I was? Why didn't you tell him we were cheap and low and without courage — why didn't you. . . .*

ALEC: *Stop it, Laura — pull yourself together.*

LAURA: *It's true! Don't you see? It's true. . . .*

ALEC: *We know we really love each other — that's true — that's all that really matters.*

LAURA: *It isn't all that matters — other things matter too, self-respect matters, and decency — I can't go on any longer.*

ALEC: *Could you really say good-bye — not see me any more?*

LAURA: *Yes — if you'd help me.*

ALEC after a pause: *I love you, Laura — I shall love you always until the end of my life — all the shame that the world might force on us couldn't touch the real truth of it. I can't look at you now because I know something — I know that this is the beginning of the end — not the end of my loving you — but the end of our being together. But not quite yet, darling — please not quite yet.*

LAURA in a dead voice: *Very well — not quite yet.*

ALEC: *I know what you feel about this evening — I mean about the beastliness of it. I know about the strain of our different lives; our lives apart from each other. The feeling of guilt, of doing wrong is a little too strong, isn't it? Too persistent? Perhaps too great a price to pay for the few hours of happiness we get out of it. I know all this because it's the same for me too.*

LAURA: *You can look at me now — I'm all right.*

ALEC *looking at her: Let's be careful — let's prepare ourselves — a sudden break now, however brave and admirable, would be too cruel. We can't do such violence to our hearts and minds.*

LAURA: *Very well.*

ALEC: *I'm going away.*

LAURA: *I see.*

ALEC: *But not quite yet.*

LAURA: *Please — not quite yet.*

A train bell goes.

The door leading to the staff-room opens and BERYL comes in.

BERYL: *That's the ten-ten. It's after closing time.*

ALEC: *Oh, it is?*

BERYL: *I shall have to lock up.*

BERYL escorts LAURA and ALEC to the door of Number 3 platform. They go out and the camera remains on BERYL as she slams the door and bolts up.

Outside, LAURA and ALEC walk up and down the platform.

ALEC: *I want you to promise me something.*

LAURA: *What is it?*

ALEC: *Promise me that however unhappy you are, and however much you think things over, that you'll meet me next Thursday.*

LAURA: *Where?*

ALEC: *Outside the hospital — twelve-thirty?*

LAURA: *All right — I promise.*

ALEC: *I've got to talk to you — I've got to explain.*

LAURA: *About going away?*

ALEC: *Yes.*

LAURA: *Where are you going? Where can you go? You can't give up your practice.*

ALEC: *I've had a job offered me. I wasn't going to tell you — I wasn't going to take it — but I know now, that it's the only way out.*

LAURA: *Where?*

ALEC: *A long way away — Johannesburg.*

LAURA *stopping still: Oh, Alec. . . .*

ALEC: *My brother's out there. They're opening a new hospital —*

they want me in it — it's a fine opportunity really. I'll take Made-leine and the boys. It's been torturing me — the necessity of making a decision one way or the other. I haven't told anybody — not even Madeleine. I couldn't bear the idea of leaving you — but now I see, it's got to happen soon anyway — it's almost happening already.

LAURA: *When will you go?*

ALEC: *Almost immediately — in about two weeks' time.*

LAURA: *It's quite near, isn't it?*

ALEC: *Do you want me to stay? Do you want me to turn down the offer?*

LAURA: *Don't be foolish, Alec.*

ALEC: *I'll do whatever you say.*

LAURA her eyes filling with tears: *That's unkind of you, my darling.*

Close-up of the station loudspeaker.

LOUDSPEAKER: *The train for Ketchworth, Longdean and Perford is now entering Number Three platform.*

A train can be heard entering the station.

Dissolve to LAURA and ALEC. He opens the door of an empty third-class compartment and LAURA gets in. ALEC shuts the door after her and LAURA leans out of the open window. (*Still*)

ALEC: *You're not angry with me, are you?*

LAURA: *No, I'm not angry — I don't think I'm anything really — I feel just tired.*

ALEC: *Forgive me.*

LAURA: *Forgive you for what?*

Close-up of ALEC over LAURA's shoulder.

ALEC: *For everything — for having met you in the first place — for taking the piece of grit out of your eye — for loving you — for bringing you so much misery.*

Close-up of LAURA over ALEC's shoulder.

LAURA trying to smile: *I'll forgive you — if you'll forgive me.*

Close-up of ALEC over LAURA's shoulder. There is the sound of the guard's whistle and the train starts to move. The camera and LAURA track away from ALEC as he stands staring after the train which pulls out of the station. Fade out.

LAURA'S VOICE: *All that was a week ago — it is hardly credible that it should be so short a time.*

Fade in on hospital. It is day time. LAURA is standing by a lamp post in the foreground of the shot. After a moment ALEC comes down the hospital steps and joins her.

LAURA'S VOICE: *To-day was our last day together. Our very last together in all our lives. I met him outside the hospital as I had promised at 12.30 — this morning — at 12.30 this morning — that was only this morning.*

Dissolve to ALEC and LAURA sitting in a car.

LAURA'S VOICE: *We drove into the country again, but this time he hired a car. I lit cigarettes for him every now and then as we went along. We didn't talk much — I felt numbed and hardly alive at all. We had lunch in the village pub.*

Dissolve to ALEC and LAURA leaning over the bridge. The car is parked nearby.

LAURA'S VOICE: *Afterwards we went to the same bridge over the stream — the bridge that we had been to before.*

Cut to Milford Junction Station and yard. It is night time. LAURA and ALEC are crossing the station yard towards the booking hall. (*Still*)

LAURA'S VOICE: *Those last few hours together went by so quickly. We walked across the station yard in silence and went into the refreshment room.*

ALEC and LAURA are sitting at the refreshment room table. The voices of ALBERT and MYRTLE fade away to a murmur in the background.

ALEC: *Are you all right, darling?*

LAURA: *Yes, I'm all right.*

ALEC: *I wish I could think of something to say.*

LAURA: *It doesn't matter — not saying anything, I mean.*

ALEC: *I'll miss my train and wait to see you into yours.*

LAURA: *No — no — please don't. I'll come over to your platform with you — I'd rather.*

ALEC: *Very well.*

LAURA: *Do you think we shall ever see each other again?*

ALEC: *I don't know.* His voice breaks. *Not for years anyway.*

LAURA: *The children will all be grown up — I wonder if they'll ever meet and know each other.*

ALEC: *Couldn't I write to you — just once in a while?*

LAURA: *No — please not — we promised we wouldn't.*

ALEC: *Laura, dear, I do love you so very much. I love you with all my heart and soul.*

LAURA *without emotion: I want to die — if only I could die.*

ALEC: *If you died you'd forget me — I want to be remembered.*

LAURA: *Yes, I know — I do too.*

ALEC *glancing at the clock: We've still got a few minutes.*

DOLLY *off: Laura! What a lovely surprise!*

LAURA *dazed: Oh, Dolly!*

> DOLLY *joins* LAURA *and* ALEC.

DOLLY: *My dear, I've been shopping till I'm dropping. My feet are nearly falling off, and my throat's parched, I thought of having tea in Spindle's, but I was terrified of losing the train.*

LAURA'S VOICE: *It was cruel of Fate to be against us right up to the last minute. Dolly Messiter — poor, well-meaning, irritating Dolly Messiter. . . .*

> The camera is slowly tracking in to a close-up of LAURA.

DOLLY: *I'm always missing trains and being late for meals, and Bob gets disagreeable for days at a time.* Her voice is fading away. *He's been getting those dreadful headaches, you know. I've tried to make him see a doctor but he won't.*

> Her voice fades out.

LAURA'S VOICE: *. . . crashing into those last few precious minutes we had together. She chattered and fussed, but I didn't hear what she said. I was dazed and bewildered. Alec behaved so beautifully — with such perfect politeness. Nobody could have guessed what he was really feeling — then the bell went for his train.*

> The platform bell rings.

LAURA: *There's your train.*

ALEC: *Yes, I know.*

DOLLY: *Aren't you coming with us?*

ALEC: *No, I go in the opposite direction. My practice is in Churley.*

DOLLY: *Oh, I see.*

ALEC: *I am a general practitioner at the moment.*

LAURA *dully: Doctor Harvey is going out to Africa next week.*

DOLLY: *Oh, how thrilling.*

> There is the sound of ALEC's train approaching.

ALEC: *I must go.*

LAURA: *Yes, you must.*

ALEC: *Good-bye.*

DOLLY: *Good-bye.*

He shakes hands with DOLLY, and looks swiftly once only at LAURA.

Close-up of LAURA. ALEC's hand comes into the shot and gives her shoulder a little squeeze.

LAURA's VOICE: *I felt the touch of his hand for a moment and then he walked away*. . . .

ALEC is seen from LAURA's view-point. He crosses the refreshment room and goes out of the door on to the platform.

LAURA's VOICE: *. . . away — out of my life for ever.*

Close shot of LAURA and DOLLY. LAURA is gazing out of the door through which ALEC has just passed. She seems almost unaware of DOLLY at her side, who proceeds to fumble in her handbag for lipstick and a mirror. DOLLY is chattering, but we do not hear her voice.

LAURA's VOICE: *Dolly still went on talking, but I wasn't listening to her — I was listening for the sound of his train starting — then it did*. . . .

The sound of ALEC's train is heard as it starts to move out of the station.

Close-up of LAURA.

LAURA's VOICE: *I said to myself — 'He didn't go — at the last minute his courage failed him — he couldn't have gone — at any moment now he'll come into the refreshment room again pretending that he'd forgotten something.' I prayed for him to do that — just so I could see him once more — for an instant — but the minutes went by*. . . .

There is the sound of the station bell.

Close shot of LAURA and DOLLY.

DOLLY: *Is that the train?*

She addresses MYRTLE.

DOLLY: *Can you tell me, is that the Ketchworth train?*

MYRTLE off: *No, that's the express.*

LAURA: *The boat-train.*

DOLLY: *Oh, yes — that doesn't stop, does it?*

DOLLY gets up and moves out of shot towards the counter.

LAURA jumps to her feet and rushes blindly out of the door leading to Number 2 platform. As the camera pans to the door it goes off level, giving the effect of LAURA running uphill.

She runs out of the refreshment room towards the camera and

the railway lines.

The railway lines are seen from above. An express train hurtles through the scene. The camera is tilted.

Close-up of LAURA from a low angle. She is swaying on the edge of the platform. The lights from the express streak past her face. The noise is deafening. She stands quite still. The lights stop flashing across her face and the sound of the train dies away rapidly. Slowly the camera returns to a normal angle.

LAURA'S VOICE: *I meant to do it, Fred, I really meant to do it — I stood there trembling — right on the edge — but then, just in time I stepped back — I couldn't — I wasn't brave enough — I should like to be able to say that it was the thought of you and the children that prevented me — but it wasn't — I had no thoughts at all — only an overwhelming desire not to be unhappy any more — not to feel anything ever again. I turned and went back into the refreshment room — that's when I nearly fainted. . . .*

Dissolve to the library at LAURA's house. It is night time. Close-up of LAURA, who is sitting with her sewing in her lap. She is staring straight in front of her.

Close-up of FRED, who is looking at her. He continues to look at her in silence for a moment or two.

FRED gently: *Laura!*

She doesn't answer. He gets up.

Close shot of LAURA. FRED kneels beside her and softly touches her hand.

FRED: *Laura. . . .*

LAURA turning her head slowly and looking at him — her voice sounds dead: *Yes, dear?*

FRED: *Whatever your dream was — it wasn't a very happy one, was it?*

LAURA in a whisper: *No.*

FRED: *Is there anything I can do to help?*

LAURA: *Yes, my dear — you always help. . . .*

FRED: *You've been a long way away?*

LAURA nodding, her eyes fill with tears: *Yes, Fred.*

FRED moves a little closer to her and quietly rests his face against her hand.

FRED with a catch in his voice: *Thank you for coming back to me.* Fade out.

CREDITS:

Production	Alexander Korda/David O. Selznick/London Films
Produced and directed by	Carol Reed
Original story and screenplay by	Graham Greene
Music by	Anton Karas
Associate Producer	Hugh Perceval
Production Manager	T. S. Lyndon-Haynes
Art Director	Vincent Korda
Assistant Art Directors	John Hawkesworth
	Joseph Bato
Director of Photography	Robert Krasker
Edited by	Oswald Hafenrichter
Camera Operators	Edward Scaife
	Denys Coop
Additional photography by	John Wilcox and Stan Pavey
Sound	John Cox
Make-up	George Frost
Chief Hairdresser	Joe Shear
Wardrobe	Ivy Baker
Set Dresser	Dario Simoni
Continuity	Peggy McClafferty
Zither music arranged and played by	Anton Karas
Length	9,428 ft.
Time	1 hour 44 minutes
Shot	At the London Film Studios, Shepperton, England, and on location in Austria

The Third Man won the Grand Prix for the best feature film in the 1949 International Film Festival at Cannes.

CAST: *

Holly Martins	Joseph Cotten
Anna	Alida Valli
Harry Lime	Orson Welles
Major Calloway	Trevor Howard
Sergeant Paine	Bernard Lee
Porter	Paul Hoerbiger
Porter's Wife	Annie Rosar
' Baron ' Kurtz	Ernst Deutsch
Popescu	Siegfried Breuer
Dr Winkel	Erich Ponto
Crabbit	Wilfrid Hyde-White
Anna's Landlady	Hedwig Bleibtreu
Hansl	Herbert Halbik
Brodsky	Alexis Chesnakov
Hall Porter at Sacher's	Paul Hardtmuth

---

* See appendix for Graham Greene's own description of his characters.

THE THIRD MAN

Because of Graham Greene's reputation as a writer, the screenplay of *The Third Man* has been printed in full. Notes in an appendix and brackets show the additions and omissions made by Carol Reed, and even Orson Welles, in the final version of the film. Minor transliterations of Greene's phrases by other actors are omitted. The script serves as a model lesson in how even the most brilliant and detailed of screenplays has to be changed in the process of making the film. Most of the changes are for the purpose of clarifying the action of the well-made film. Other changes have to do with problems of casting; the parts of Tomb and Carter were originally written for the comedy pair of Basil Radford and Naunton Wayne, but their dialogue had to be scrambled together when Wilfred Hyde White was cast to play both of the parts as one man, Crabbit. Other changes have to do with the suggestions of the stars; Orson Welles' famous speech on the Swiss cuckoo clock, as he leaves the Great Wheel, is very much his own inspiration. Some written action is simply not translatable in terms of the cinema, or is better done another way on the spot. Some small changes creep in for the sake of improvement or plausibility: Rollo Martins becomes Holly Martins, Anna comes from Czechoslovakia, Tyler is a sauve Rumanian called Popescu. The world-famous shots of the hands of the zither-player, Anton Karas, playing the ' Harry Lime ' theme, come from Carol Reed's chance use of a local café, where Karas played for tips. Above all, the opening of the film had to be shot three months after the main shooting was officially completed, because the producer found that the location and situation in Vienna was insufficiently explained for a mass audience. Carol Reed himself narrated the opening.

Such are the changes and compromises that lie between a screenplay and a film. Yet all in all, the film of *The Third Man* shows incredible devotion by the director to the script. Carold Reed was kind enough to lend his personal copy of the script for printing, and Graham Greene personally vetted it before publication, for he has wisely retained all literary rights in the property (a rare and right and usually impossible thing to do). Thus the decision to print the screenplay in full, after the most important addition to it — the opening sequence which sets the scene in Occupied Vienna, 1945.

[1. INSERT CANADIAN PASSPORT (Before main title).*

The passport is on a desk. A pair of hands opens it showing the identification photograph with the name below — ROLLO MARTINS. Over scene we hear the faint clicking of a typewriter.
VICE CONSUL voice only: *Remember, Vienna is an occupied city. You must be extremely careful to observe all official regulations.*
MARTINS voice only: *I know.*
VICE CONSUL voice only: *Just one more thing . . . whom are you staying with in Vienna?*
MARTINS voice only: *With a friend of mine named Lime . . . Harry Lime.*
VICE CONSUL voice only: *Address?*
MARTINS voice only: *15 Stiftgasse.*
One hand holds the passport while the other goes out of frame a moment, brings in a stamp and presses it to the opposite page of the passport picture. As it is lifted we see the printed impression — it is a visa to the military zone of Vienna.

ALLIED MILITARY PERMIT
VIENNA

The strains of a Strauss waltz swell up. The hand closes the passport and holds it up. Another hand takes it, camera pulls back to interior Canadian Passport office. ROLLO MARTINS is taking passport, says something in thanks to the official who has stamped it and turns to go out of the office.

2. EXTERIOR. AERODROME (DAY):

A Constellation is warming up, MARTINS goes aboard, waving back off scene to someone very cheerfully.

3. CREDIT TITLES:

(After each title card the following background scenes remain in the clear for a few feet, establishing the progress of

---

* See appendix for opening sequence of film version.

Martins' journey.)

1. Martins in his seat looks round at his fellow passengers, then out of the window — settles down and opens a book.
2. Aerial shot of Constellation over the ocean.
3. Martins in his seat, eating from a tray. The plane dips suddenly, spilling a glass of tea into his lap.
4. Night, over the ocean. (The titles are now in white.)
5. Martins, dozing uneasily in his seat, wakes up, tries to find a comfortable position for his legs as he turns from one side to the other.
6. Dawn, and the plane coming in over Paris, with the Eiffel Tower in the background. (The titles are in black again.)
7. French Customs and Immigration Officials examining Martins' passport and papers, as he explains at length some story which we cannot hear.
8. Martins getting aboard another plane — a different plane this time.
9. Aerial shots crossing countryside which changes from fertile valleys to Swiss Alps.
10. Martins asleep in the plane weary and unshaven, getting progressively untidier and unhappier.
11. Martins feeling ill.
12. Another set of Customs and Immigration officials examining his passport and another explanation by Martins; this time he is very weary of the whole business.
13. Martins looking eagerly out of his plane window, bleary-eyed with a very unsightly stubble covering his face.
14. As the credits dissolve out, we see Vienna in the clear. Then the word:

VIENNA

As this dissolves out again:

4. ANIMATION (over the aerial shot)

Heavy black lines that show the various zones of the occupying powers. The names of the area are established simultaneously: Russian — French — British — American. Hold on this long enough to establish the crazy patchwork that is Vienna today.

MARTINS' plane swoops past camera and down towards the city.

5. AIRPORT (DAY):

The passengers disembark from the plane and line up at the barrier where soldiers of the four powers, all in full uniform and armed, are examining their papers. All types are in the line — an American business man, a British officer, a young woman and her child, etc. MARTINS is about fourth in line, carrying his passport in his hand and looks eagerly towards the barrier, as though searching for someone in the waiting throng at the other side. The passengers in front and behind him are waving to relatives and friends who have come to meet them, talking in all languages of the occupying forces, as well as German. MARTINS seems a little anxious as he reaches the soldiers of the four powers, not having spotted the person he is looking for. One of the soldiers takes his passport, glances at it and passes it to the other three in routine fashion.]

BRITISH OFFICER [to others: Canadian — Martins.] To MARTINS, as they glance over his papers: *What is the purpose of your visit, Mr Martins?*

MARTINS: *I've been offered a job by a friend of mine. . . .*

BRITISH OFFICER: *Where are you staying?*

MARTINS: *With him . . . Stiftgasse 15.*

BRITISH OFFICER: *His name?*

MARTINS has had to repeat this too many times.

MARTINS: *Lime — Harry Lime.*

As the OFFICER makes a note of this, MARTINS looks towards barrier anxiously.

MARTINS: *I thought he'd be here to meet me.*

[During this the men look at the papers, pass them around, glance somewhat strangely at MARTINS, then hand them back to the BRITISH OFFICER, who returns them to MARTINS.

BRITISH OFFICER nods him on: *Right, Mr Martins. . . .*][1]

MARTINS stows his papers away and moves on, through the barrier. He looks around hopefully for a sign of his friend, watches as a man greets the woman with the baby, hugging and kissing her lovingly, then moves on towards a desk marked

' Information '.

MARTINS to girl at desk: *Has anyone left a message for me? Martins — Rollo Martins . . .?*

GIRL glancing at her papers: *No, sir. . . .*

MARTINS: *You sure? I'm expecting a friend — his name's Lime — he said he'd be here. . . .*

GIRL: *I'm sorry. . . .*

MARTINS nods and crosses thoughtfully to the baggage section where the other passengers are busy claiming their bags.

6. AIRPORT. LOCATION (DAY):

As MARTINS stands outside a crowded bus, his valise in hand, still looking around for his friend, the last passengers are aboard and the DRIVER starts up his motor, looking out at MARTINS warningly.

DRIVER in German: *We're leaving, sir. . . .* In English. *We go now. . . .*

MARTINS turns and gets into the bus, taking a seat up front near the DRIVER. The bus pulls out of scene.

7. TRAVELLING SHOTS. LOCATION (DAY):

As the bus makes its way through the ruined and devastated parts of Vienna, we see MARTINS' reactions to the scenes, obviously new to him, for he looks with great interest and with a sense of revulsion.

8. STREET. LOCATION (DAY):

As MARTINS gets out of the bus with his bag, the DRIVER pointing down the street and saying something we cannot hear. MARTINS nods and starts off in the direction he has been shown. A ratty little MAN has been watching him surreptitiously. Now he falls in beside him, and in a whining manner, asks him something. MARTINS glances at him, then turns away, shaking his head in dismissal as he walks.

The MAN continues to follow him, pleading. MARTINS gives him a cigarette. The man slouches away, satisfied.

MARTINS arrives at a flat and looks up at the entrance, comparing the address to the one on a paper in his hand. The address on the door reads 15 Stiftgasse. He hurries in.

9.   15 STIFTGASSE STAIRCASE. PART LOCATION (DAY):

MARTINS is making his way as rapidly as he can with his bag up the stairs. He rings the bell of HARRY LIME's flat which he can recognise on the third floor by the name plate, and opening the letter box, he whistles. While he waits, he examines such things as the hooks for brushing the clothes outside the doors and the spy holes to observe people. There is no reply to his ring and no answer comes. He rings a second and then a third time. Suddenly a voice speaks to him in German. The PORTER is standing two floors above.

PORTER: *Es hat keinen Zweck so zu lauten, es ist niemand hier.*
MARTINS: *Huh? Speak English?*
PORTER in bad English, shouting to make himself understood: *You have just missed them.*
MARTINS: *Missed who?*
PORTER: *His friends and the coffin.*

MARTINS looks up with surprise and apprehension.

MARTINS: *Coffin?*
PORTER: *Mr Lime's.*

MARTINS stares at the PORTER who realises his mistake.

PORTER: *[Didn't you know?] . . . An accident . . . run over by a car . . . saw it myself . . . on his own doorstep . . . bang, bowled down like a rabbit. Killed at once.*[2] *They'll have a difficult time burying him in this frost.*

On the PORTER's voice and the look of distress on MARTINS' face, slowly dissolve.

10.   CENTRAL CEMETERY. LOCATION (DAY):

MARTINS is looking about him — he speaks to an official who points down the huge snow-bound park. Avenues of graves, each avenue numbered and lettered, stretching out like spokes of an enormous wheel. [On some gravestones are the photographs of the occupants. Respectable faces with waxed moustaches and morning coats. A huge figure in armour on the

96

family vault of a steel manufacturer; the bust of a dandified gentleman with hair parted in the middle — the master of a dancing school. The statue of a woman in an attitude of despair, raising her arms towards the portrait in relief of her husband.] A long way away a small group seems to be gathered together on some very private business. MARTINS is walking down the avenue towards them, still carrying his bag. Still further away stands a man in a mackintosh. He stands there more like an observer than a participant in the scene. He is CALLOWAY. MARTINS comes up to him.

MARTINS quietly: *Could you tell me . . . is this . . .?*

CALLOWAY not at all moved: *A fellow called Lime.*

As MARTINS approaches the group, we can see a coffin is on the point of being lowered into a grave and we hear a passage of prayer the PRIEST is saying.

PRIEST mumbling rapidly: *Anima ejus, et animae omnium fidelium defunctorum, per misericordiam Dei requiescant in pace.*

Two men in heavy overcoats stand close to the grave. One carries a wreath that he has obviously forgotten to lay on the coffin; his companion touches his elbow, and he comes to with a start. A girl stands a little distance away from them and she puts her hands over her face as the coffin is lowered. We shall know her later as ANNA SCHMIDT. (*Still*)

MARTINS stands watching the scene with tears gathering in his eyes. The PRIEST puts a spoon of earth on the coffin, and then the two men do the same. One of the men approaches the girl and offers her the spoon. The girl shakes her head and turns away with tears in her eyes. The man is left holding the spoon uncertainly. MARTINS approaches him, takes the spoon from him, and adds his earth to the others. All the time CALLOWAY watches the scene from a distance. The two men, whom we know later on as KURTZ and WINKEL, stand side by side watching MARTINS, whom they have never seen before; they are uneasy and puzzled. As he turns away from the grave, they say something to each other in low voices. The PRIEST goes up to them, speaks a few words and shakes their hands; he turns to MARTINS, but MARTINS is walking rapidly away. He stumbles on a loose stone as he walks.

CALLOWAY follows him, catching him up.

Calloway loudly: *I've got a car here. Like a lift to town?*
Martins stares at this man who offers him a lift as if they were leaving a party.
Martins: [*No*] *thanks.*
He starts to walk ahead, then changes his mind and returns to the taxi. There is a jeep in the background, driven by a Sergeant Paine, whom we meet later. Paine watches, starts up and follows:

11. INTERIOR. TAXI. BACK PROJECTION (DAY):

Calloway looks back towards the group by the grave, but Martins stares straight ahead.
Calloway: *My name's Calloway.*
Martins does not at first answer; his thoughts are elsewhere.
Martins: *Martins.*
Calloway: *You a friend of Lime's?* Martins will not answer. *Been here long?* [*I haven't seen you around.*]
[No reaction from Martins.][3] Calloway sees someone out of the window of the taxi and leans forward to get a better view.

12. MAIN ROAD. LOCATION (DAY):

The girl who was at the graveside is walking towards the city, by the wall of the cemetery. Trams run beside it. Behind are rows of monumental masons and flower shops, grave-stones waiting for the owners and wreaths for mourners.

13. TAXI. BACK PROJECTION (DAY):

Calloway is now looking out of the back window at the receding figure. He turns to Martins, who is staring straight ahead, and speaks with a voice out of mood with the situation.
Calloway: *You've had a bit of a shock, haven't you?* No notice taken. *You need a drink.*
For the first time, at the word ' drink ' he gets a reaction.
Martins: *Could you buy me one? I haven't got any Austrian money.*
Calloway: *Of course.*
As he leans forward to give the driver instructions, dissolve.

14. KARNTNERSTRASSE BAR (DAY):

A small bar consisting of two rooms. A self-absorbed courting couple sits in the first room. CALLOWAY and MARTINS, with his back to the entrance. A bottle of cognac is on the table and at intervals CALLOWAY fills MARTINS' glass, always giving him a little more than he does himself. MARTINS is already half-drunk. He twirls the bottom of his glass through the spilt drink on the table.

MARTINS: *I guess there's nobody knew Harry like he did . . .*
Corrects himself . . . *like I did.*

CALLOWAY's lighter stays a moment half-way to his cigarette.

CALLOWAY: *How long ago?*

MARTINS: *First term at school. Never felt so damned lonely in my life — and then Harry showed up . . . [showed me the ropes.*

He takes a swallow of brandy and spills some from his glass. Dipping his fingers in the spilled brandy he anoints himself on the top of the head and behind each ear.

MARTINS: *He even taught me that.]*

CALLOWAY: *When did you see him last?*

MARTINS: *September '39. When the business started.*[4]

CALLOWAY: *See much of him before that?*

MARTINS: *Once in a while. [Once a month we might get pie-eyed — for the good of our health.]*

[CALLOWAY: *What were you going to do here?*

MARTINS: *You know this medical thing . . . this unit he ran?*

CALLOWAY: *Not exactly — no. . . .*

MARTINS: *Some sort of charity organisation which helped to get medical supplies. That was him, you know. Anyway he asked me to write some propaganda for him. I guess he knew I was broke.* His thoughts return to LIME. *It seems like yesterday — that school corridor and the cracked bell and all those British children kidding me about my accent.*

CALLOWAY: *And Lime?*

MARTINS: *He and I got up to a lot of things.* He laughs ruefully. *I was always the one who got caught.*

CALLOWAY: *That was convenient for Lime.*

MARTINS reaching the point of alcoholic irritation: *What are you getting at?*

99

CALLOWAY: *Well, wasn't it?*

He is watching MARTINS' reactions closely. He is dead sober, and we begin to notice the little barbed shafts he is sticking in MARTINS' sides. He wants to make his bull angry.

MARTINS: *That was my fault. He was the* . . . circling the stem of the glass again.] . . . *best friend I ever had.*

CALLOWAY: *That sounds like a cheap novelette.*

MARTINS: *I* write *cheap novelettes.*

CALLOWAY: *I've never heard of you. What's your name again?*

MARTINS: *Rollo Martins.*[5]

CALLOWAY: *No. Sorry.*

MARTINS: [used to not being known: *You know, I don't write masterpieces, I don't like masterpieces.*] As English as possible: *Ever heard of ' The Lone Rider of Santa Fe '?*

CALLOWAY: *No.*

MARTINS very American: *' Death at Double X Ranch '?*

CALLOWAY: *No.*

MARTINS: [*Nobody reads Westerns nowadays. Harry liked them though.*][6] *It's a damned shame.*

CALLOWAY: *What?*

MARTINS: *Him dying like that.*

CALLOWAY: *The best thing that ever happened to him.*

[MARTINS hazy with drink: *You mean — being killed quick.*

CALLOWAY: *He was lucky in that way too.* He is now speaking in a deliberately insulting way.]

MARTINS at last sees that there is a hidden meaning in CALLOWAY's words. He becomes quieter and more dangerous. His right hand lets go of the brandy glass and lies on the table ready for action.

MARTINS: *What are you trying to say?*

CALLOWAY knows what is coming. He moves his chair very slowly back, calculating MARTINS' reach. (*Still*)

[CALLOWAY: *You see, he'd have served a long spell — if it hadn't been for the accident.*

MARTINS: *What for?*]

CALLOWAY: *He was about the worst racketeer who ever made a dirty living in this city. Have another drink.*

MARTINS: *You some sort of a policeman?*

CALLOWAY sitting back: *Mmm.*[7]

100

MARTINS: *I don't like policemen.*

MARTINS edges his chair round to block CALLOWAY's way out; CALLOWAY catches the waiter's eye. The waiter obviously knows what is expected of him and goes out.

MARTINS gently with a surface smile: *I have to call them sheriffs.*

CALLOWAY: *Ever seen one?*

MARTINS: *You're the first. I guess there was some petty racket going on with gasoline and you couldn't pin it on anyone, so you picked a dead man. Just like a cop. You're a real cop, I suppose?*

CALLOWAY: *Yes, but it wasn't petrol.*

MARTINS: *Tyres?*[8] . . . *Saccharine?* . . . *Why don't you catch a few murderers for a change?*

CALLOWAY: *Well, you could say that murder was part of his racket.*

MARTINS pushes the table over with one hand and makes a dive at CALLOWAY with the other; the drink confuses his calculations. Before he can try, his arms are caught behind him. Neither we nor MARTINS have seen the entrance of SERGEANT PAINE, who has been summoned by the waiter and who now pinions MARTINS.

CALLOWAY: *[Don't treat him roughly.]*[9] *He's only a scribbler with too much drink in him.* With contempt. *Take Mr Rollo Martins home.*

PAINE impressed: *Rollo Martins, sir?* MARTINS struggles. *[Be quiet, can't you, sir.]* To CALLOWAY. *The writer? ' The Lone Rider of Santa Fe '?*

CALLOWAY nods and moves away to collect his mackintosh.

MARTINS: *Listen, Callaghan, or whatever your name is. . . .*

CALLOWAY: *Calloway, I'm English, not Irish.*

[MARTINS: There's one dead man you aren't going to pin your unsolved crimes on.]

CALLOWAY: *Going to find me the real criminal? It sounds like one of your stories.*

[MARTINS: You can let me go, Callaghan. If I gave you a black eye, you'd only go to bed for a few days. When I've finished with you — you'll leave Vienna, you'll look so silly.]

CALLOWAY takes out a couple of pounds' worth of Bafs and sticks them in MARTINS' breast pocket.

CALLOWAY: *This is Army money. Should see you through tonight at Sacher's Hotel if you don't spend too much in the bar. We'll keep a seat for you on tomorrow's plane.*

[MARTINS: *You can't throw me out. My papers are in order.*
CALLOWAY: *This is like other cities: you need money here. Let him go.*

PAINE lets go of his arms and dusts MARTINS down.

MARTINS: *I'd thank you for the drinks — but I guess they were on expenses.*
CALLOWAY: *Yes.*]

MARTINS [steps to one side as though to make way for the waiter and] slashes out at CALLOWAY. [CALLOWAY just avoids him, but stumbles against the table.] Before MARTINS can try again, PAINE, who has been greatly impressed by meeting MARTINS, has to land him one on the mouth. He [goes bang over in the alleyway, between the tables and] comes up bleeding from a cut lip.

[CALLOWAY: *You promised not to fight.*]

PAINE lifts him up and dusts him down again.

PAINE: *Please be careful, sir.*[10] *Written anything lately?*

MARTINS wipes some of the blood away with his sleeve.

CALLOWAY has had a long day and is tired of MARTINS.

CALLOWAY: *Take him to Sacher's. Don't hit him again if he behaves. You go carefully there — it's a Military Hotel.*

CALLOWAY turns away from both of them and leaves the bar.
PAINE still dusting MARTINS down: *I'm so glad to have met you, sir.* [*I know all your books.*] He leads MARTINS towards the door — he holds his arm — he carries his bag and smiles at him. *I like a good Western.*[11] Dissolve.

15. SACHER'S HOTEL LOUNGE (DAY):

Sacher's Hotel, which may roughly be compared to Brown's Hotel in London, has been taken over by the British Army, but this has not altered its atmosphere of red plush and Edwardian pictures, nor the old world courtesy of the PORTER who treats every subaltern like a grand duke. [Two men with a distinctly ex-officer look are having tea. Their lounge suits have rather a mothball air, and their faces are anxious. Their names are CARTER and TOMBS. TOMBS is the more pessimistic and saturnine. CARTER gives an appearance of ill-directed energy. A

102

young OFFICER passes by them.

OFFICER: *Hello, you chaps, how's the culture going?*

TOMBS: *It's an uphill climb, old man.*

OFFICER: *Heard you were going to be back in uniform next week.*

He picks up a biscuit off their tea tray.

CARTER: *That joke's in the worst possible taste.*

OFFICER: *Hear the Brigadier didn't like last week's striptease.*

TOMBS: *It wasn't striptease. It was Hindu dancing.*

The OFFICER moves on, munching their biscuit.

TOMBS: *Sometimes, old man, one gets discouraged.*

CARTER: *Tombs, do you think there's anything in what he said?*

TOMBS: *Frankly, yes.*

CARTER: *After all we've done for re-education.*

TOMBS: *It would seem strange to be in uniform again.*

He shivers slightly and his cup shakes.

CARTER: *Don't . . . . If only we could put on one really good show.*

TOMBS: *I saw nothing wrong with last week's. Perhaps they should have had a larger loin cloth.*

A SENIOR OFFICER enters with a WOMAN.

TOMBS in a whisper: *Don't look round. Slip quietly out, old man. It's the Brigadier.*

They leave with the utmost caution.][12]

16. SACHER'S RECEPTION HALL (DAY):

PAINE leads MARTINS to the HALL PORTER's desk. he is carrying MARTINS's bag for him, and MARTINS has a handkerchief pressed to his mouth. [CARTER and TOMBS approach from the lounge.]

PAINE to the PORTER: *Colonel Calloway says this gentleman is to have a bed for the night.*

[PORTER: *Your passport, please.*]

As MARTINS is producing it, PAINE moves over to CARTER and TOMBS who are staring at this strange-looking tourist.

PAINE: *Rollo Martins, sir, the writer. Thought you'd be interested.*

[TOMBS turning away: *Never heard of him.*]

CARTER: *Did you say* writer, *Paine?*

TOMBS turns back.

PAINE: *Of books, sir. Yes, Westerns, sir.*[13] [Very seriously. *I enjoyed*

103

the striptease last week, sir.]

[As PAINE moves back to the desk, CARTER and TOMBS both stare at MARTINS.

PAINE to MARTINS: *Good night, sir, I hope you'll be comfortable.*
MARTINS nods good night, as the PORTER gives MARTINS the usual papers to sign.

CARTER doubtfully: *A writer, Tombs.*

TOMBS: *Not very high class, old man.*

CARTER: *Well, they're books, aren't they? We've got to take a chance.*

TOMBS: *I've got a foreboding.*

CARTER: *You chose the Hindu dancing, Tombs. Leave this to me.*
He approaches MARTINS who is receiving his key at the desk. TOMBS lags a little way behind.]

CARTER: *Mr Martins, isn't it?*

MARTINS: *Yes.*

[CARTER: *My name's Carter — Captain Carter, and this is Tombs — Captain Tombs.*

MARTINS: *Yes?*

CARTER: *We run the C.R.S. of G.H.Q., you know.*

MARTINS: *You do?*

CARTER: *Cultural Re-education Section. Directly I heard you were here, I thought — there's the man for us. We are having a little discussion at our Institute the day after tomorrow on the — well, you know, the usual literary subjects. Sort of lecture, you know — we thought you might like to speak.*

MARTINS: *They wouldn't know me.*

CARTER: *Nonsense, your books are very popular here — aren't they, Tombs?*

TOMBS: *Staying here long, Mr Martins?*][14]

MARTINS showing Bafs: *How long can you stay on a couple of pounds of this [funny money?]*

CARTER: *We'd like you to be our guest, sir. Glad to have you here.*

MARTINS: *Did you say . . . guest?*

CARTER: *As long as you care to stay.*

[TOMBS in an undertone: *Careful.*

CARTER: *But, of course, do say yes — it is really great fun — isn't it, Tombs?*

TOMBS: *Great.*

104

MARTINS speaking into his handkerchief: *Okay.*][15]
TOMBS: *Got toothache, sir? I know a very good dentist.*
MARTINS: *I don't need a dentist. Somebody hit me, that's all.*
CARTER: *Trying to rob you?*
MARTINS: *Just a soldier.*
   MARTINS removes the handkerchief and gives them a view.
[CARTER: *American?*
MARTINS: *British. I punched his colonel in the eye.*
TOMBS smiling: *Really. a colonel?*
MARTINS: *I came here to stay with a friend of mine.*][16] *And he died last Thursday — then. . . .*
CARTER: *Goodness, that's awkward.*
MARTINS: *Is that what you say to people after a death? Goodness, that's awkward!*
PORTER holding up telephone: *Mr Martins, excuse me, Baron von Kurtz.*
MARTINS: *It's a mistake.*
   But he takes the telephone. CARTER and PAINE move a little away and converse together in undertones.
MARTINS: *Yes.*
VOICE: *I was a friend of Harry Lime's.*
MARTINS his attitude changing: *I would much like to meet you, Baron. Come around.*
VOICE: *Austrians aren't allowed in Sacher's. May we meet at the Mozart Café? Just around the corner.*
MARTINS: *How will I know you?*
VOICE: *I'll carry a copy of one of your books.* He sniggers. *Harry gave it to me.*
MARTINS: *Be there in a moment.*
   He hangs up and goes over to CARTER.
MARTINS: *If I do this, I can be your guest for a week? Can I?*
CARTER: *Certainly, You're just the man we need.*
MARTINS: *Fine.* He starts for the door, excited, then turns. *Ever read a book of mine called ' The Lone Rider of Santa Fe '?*
CARTER: *No. . . . Trying to remember. . . . Not that one.* [. . . Turns to TOMBS. . . . *Did you?* TOMBS cannot help.
TOMBS: *I don't think so.*]
MARTINS: *This lone rider has his best friend shot unlawfully by a sheriff. The story is how this lone rider hunted that sheriff down.*

TOMBS: *Sounds exciting.*
MARTINS: *It is. I'm gunning just the same way for your Colonel
Callaghan.*[17]

As MARTINS turns to the door, TOMBS speaks uneasily to
CARTER.
TOMBS: *Sounds anti-British,* [*old boy.*
CARTER: *So were your Hindu dancers.*]

17. MOZART CAFE. PART LOCATION (DAY):

MARTINS enters the café and examines the occupants. Several
are reading newspapers — they do not interest him. He passes
by a group playing cards, but there remain two or three, reading books, and the audience is given time to decide for themselves which of these is KURTZ: the young man with the arrogant
Hitler Jugend look about him? MARTINS passes by to catch his
eye — looking as if ready to smile — he gets no reaction. He
turns away and at that moment KURTZ enters the café. MARTINS
recognizes him at once because he holds well to the fore the
gaudy paper-covered Western, with a picture of a cowboy
leaping from a horse onto the horns of a galloping steer. He
wears a toupée: flat and yellow, with the hair straight at the
back and not fitting close. He carries a stick with an ivory top.
MARTINS meets him.
MARTINS: *Baron Kurtz?*
KURTZ: *Martins? Delighted to meet you.*
His English accent is really too good. A man ought not to speak
a foreign language so well.
KURTZ: *Let us sit here.* [*This is my usual seat. I come here, you
know, out of the cold. . . .*]
His clothes are shabby, but not too shabby. His overcoat looks
quite adequate compared with the poor clothes of the other
men. When they are seated, he calls a waiter and orders coffee.
That done, he leans back with a sigh.
KURTZ: *It's wonderful how you keep the tension.*
MARTINS: *Tension?*
KURTZ: *Suspense. At the end of every chapter, you are left guess-
ing . . . what he'll be up to next.*
[MARTINS: *You really liked it?*

106

KURTZ: *The best I've read of yours.*

The waiter brings the coffee, and KURTZ takes out of his waist-coat pocket an elegant little 18th century snuff box.

KURTZ: *A saccharine tablet?*

MARTINS: *Thank you. There's only one left!*

KURTZ: *Oh, dear, I knew I was short, but I don't take sweetening myself. I carry them for my friends.*

He takes a small leather-bound notebook out of his pocket and makes a note.

KURTZ: *My memory is so bad.*]

MARTINS: *So you were a friend of Harry's?*

KURTZ: *I think his best.* A small pause in which his brain must have registered the error. *Except you, of course.*

MARTINS: *The police have a crazy notion that he was mixed up in some racket. (Still)*

KURTZ: *Everyone in Vienna is — we all sell cigarettes and that kind of thing. Why, I have done things that would have seemed unthinkable before the war. Once when I was hard up, I sold some tyres on the black market. I wonder what my father would have said.*

MARTINS: *The police meant something worse.*

[KURTZ: *Sometimes they get things mixed. Who was that man at the cemetery who spoke to you?*

MARTINS: *He's the one — the policeman who made Harry out to be every kind of crook.*]

KURTZ: *They get rather absurd ideas sometimes.*

[MARTINS: *They can't monkey around with Harry even if he's dead.*]

KURTZ: *He's somewhere now he won't mind about that.*

MARTINS: *Well, anyway, I'm not going to leave it at this — will you help me?*

KURTZ has a cup of coffee halfway to his lips; he takes a slow sip.

KURTZ: [*One begins to forget what real Vienna coffee tasted like.*][18] *You know I am an Austrian — I have to be careful with the police; no, I can't help you — except with advice, of course, advice.*

[MARTINS: *I'm bad at taking that.*

Pause. MARTINS glances at KURTZ, feeling that HARRY's friend should be more helpful.]

[MARTINS: *Well, anyway, show me how it happened.*
Dissolve.

18. OUTSIDE LIME'S FLAT. LOCATION (DAY):

KURTZ is standing at the door of LIME's flat, and holding
MARTINS' arm.
KURTZ: [*You see, you might be Harry.*] *We came out like this and
were walking this way.* . . .
He points to a doorway on the other side of the road; the
the camera follows imaginary figures while the voice continues.
KURTZ: *An* [*American*] *friend of his, Tyler,*[19] *called to him from
over there. Harry went across, and from up there* . . . Points down
the road . . . *came the truck.* [*It was Harry's fault, really, not the
driver's.*] Looking down on the ground. *It was just about here.*[20]
[The noise of an approaching truck sounds like an illustration
to KURTZ's story, but as he utters the last words, he pulls
MARTINS on one side and a real truck drives quickly by.]
KURTZ: *These military cars aren't safe.*
MARTINS: *It was here?*
He kicks with his foot at a broken stone on the kerb. From
out of the doorway to HARRY's flat comes the PORTER sweeping
the steps. They nod to each other. KURTZ sees this.
KURTZ: *Tyler and I carried him across to the doorway over there.*
He leads MARTINS to the other side of the road. The PORTER con-
tinues sweeping, his eyes on the two of them.

19. [DOORWAY. PART LOCATION (DAY):

It leads to some cheap apartments. There are a couple of dustbins in the porch.][21]
KURTZ: *And this is where he died.* [MARTINS takes in the dreary
doorway and the dustbins.] *Even at the end his thoughts were of
you.*
MARTINS greatly moved: *What did he say?*
KURTZ: *I can't remember the exact words. Rollo — I may call you
Rollo, mayn't I? — he always called you that to us — he was
anxious I should look after you when you arrived — to see that you
got safely home. Tickets, you know, and all that.*
MARTINS indicating PORTER: *He told me he died instantaneously.*

108

KURTZ: *No. But he died before the ambulance could reach us.*
[MARTINS: *There was an inquest?*
KURTZ: *Of course. The driver was exonerated. It really was Harry's fault.*]
MARTINS: *So you were here, and this man Tyler. I'd like to talk to him.*
KURTZ: *He's left Vienna.*
    MARTINS walks across to the PORTER.
MARTINS: *You remember me?*
PORTER: *Yes.*
MARTINS: *I wanted to ask you some questions about Harry Lime.*
    The PORTER'S WIFE has come out and gives an angry look at MARTINS and KURTZ.[22]
PORTER'S WIFE in German: *Don't stand there gossiping.*
    She hustles him in. MARTINS returns thoughtfully to KURTZ.
MARTINS: *Who was at the funeral besides you?*
KURTZ: *Only his doctor, Dr Winkel.*
MARTINS: *The girl?*
KURTZ: *Oh, you know what Harry was. Some girl from the Josefstadt Theatre.* He sees an intention in MARTINS's face and adds quickly. *You oughtn't to speak to her. It would only cause her pain.*
MARTINS: *We don't have to think about her. We've got to think about Harry.*
KURTZ: *What's the good of another post mortem? Suppose you dig up something — well, discreditable to Harry?*
    MARTINS shakes his head. It is not an idea he will entertain.
MARTINS: *Could I have your address?*
KURTZ: *I live in the Russian Sector.* [*One has to work the best way one can, you know. Poor mother — I keep it from her.*][23]
MARTINS: *What was the girl's name?*
KURTZ: *I don't know. I don't think I ever heard it.*
MARTINS: *But the theatre where she works?*
KURTZ: *The Josefstadt. I still think it won't do Harry any good. You'd do better to think of yourself.*
MARTINS: *I'll be all right.*
    They turn to go.
KURTZ: *I'm glad to have met you, Rollo.*
    KURTZ holds up the book, showing the cowboy on the cover.
KURTZ: *A master of suspense. Such a good cover, I think.*

[KURTZ leads the way from the porch. As he steps onto the pavement an Austrian police officer approaches, and KURTZ makes way for him with sudden subservience as they walk down the street.] Dissolve.

20. SACHER'S HOTEL. RECEPTION DESK (DAY):

MARTINS comes in and finds Sergeant PAINE waiting. PAINE advances to meet him and holds out an envelope.

PAINE: *Colonel Calloway sent this, with his compliments. It's the ticket for the plane tomorrow. He said I was to drive you out to the airfield or take you to the bus, whichever you prefer.*

MARTINS: *Tell Colonel Calloway I won't need it.*[24] He hands the ticket back to the sergeant and turns to the PORTER. *Please get me a ticket for the Josefstadt theatre tonight.*

He walks slowly up the staircase one step at a time — feeling he has started to put CALLOWAY in his place. Dissolve.

21. JOSEFSTADT THEATRE (NIGHT):

MARTINS is seated in the stalls. A play is in progress. He cannot understand a word of it, and gazes bewilderedly at his neighbours when they rock with laughter at a situation which visually seems serious enough. On the stage an elderly man and a woman are storming at a girl — the girl from the cemetery [all the easier to recognise because she wears the same mackintosh as she did there][25] — who protests something, he does not know what. At every sentence, the audience howls with laughter. He looks at his programme and we see the name of ANNA SCHMIDT. As he looks up at the stage again, the curtain falls. The audience remain in their seats, but MARTINS scrambles out and goes through the small door at one side of the stage.

22. BACKSTAGE. LOCATION (NIGHT):

A quick change of scene is taking place on the stage. MARTINS watches from the wings as the scene-shifters are at work. ANNA SCHMIDT comes up hurriedly and stands near him, doing up her dress; the clasps will not fasten — she does not notice him.

[MARTINS: *Fraulein Schmidt?*

110

ANNA: *Yes?* She glances up at him and back to her dress.]
MARTINS: *I was a friend of Harry Lime's.*

ANNA stops and stares at him. The curtain is rising and her entrance has to be on the rise of the curtain.

ANNA quickly: *Afterwards.* [*Afterwards.*]

She goes onto the stage and, playing her first lines towards him, watches with a puzzled and distressed expression, the stranger who has broken into her grief. For the first time we really take her in: an honest face, a wide forehead, a large mouth which does not try to charm; the kind of face which one can recognise at once as a friend's. The opening lines of this scene demand that she should approach the wings. Dissolve.

23. ANNA'S DRESSING ROOM (NIGHT):

ANNA opens the door to MARTINS. [Unlike most actresses' rooms, this one is almost bare: no wardrobe packed with clothes, no clutter of cosmetics and greasepaint. On the door hangs a sweater one recognises from the first act.] On the only easy chair lies a tin of half-used paints and grease. A kettle hums softly on a gas ring.[26]

MARTINS: *My name's Rollo Martins. Perhaps Harry told you about me.*

ANNA: *No. He never told me about his friends.*

[MARTINS: *I think I was his oldest.*]

ANNA: *Would you like a cup of tea? Someone threw me a packet last week — sometimes the British do, instead of flowers, you know, on the first night.*

She opens a cupboard under the dressing table to get the tea, and shows a bottle of Canadian Club.

ANNA: *That was a bouquet too, from an American.* Reluctantly. *Would you rather have a whisky?*

MARTINS: *Tea's okay.*

ANNA: *Good.* She closes the cupboard. *I wanted to sell it.*

He watches her while she makes the tea. She does it all wrong: the water not on the boil, the teapot unheated, too few leaves. She pours it out immediately.

[ANNA: *I never understand why the English like tea.*
MARTINS: *Oh, I like it.*] *You'd known him some time?*

Her mouth stiffens to meet the dreaded conversation.

ANNA: *Yes.*

MARTINS: [*I knew him twenty years.*] Gently. *I want to talk to you about him.* . . .

ANNA stares back at him.

ANNA: *There's nothing really to talk about, is there? Nothing.*

He drinks his cup quickly like a medicine and watches her gingerly and delicately sip at hers.

MARTINS: *I saw you at the funeral.*

ANNA: *I'm sorry . . . I didn't notice much.*

MARTINS: *You loved him, didn't you?*

ANNA: *I don't know. You can't know a thing like that — afterwards. I don't know anything any more except.* . . . She hesitates; MARTINS looks at her. . . . *I want to be dead too.* There is silence for a while. *Another cup of tea?*

MARTINS too promptly: *No, no thank you.* . . . *Cigarette?* He offers a Lucky Strike packet.

ANNA: *Thank you . . . I like Americans.*

He lights it, but during the following scene she lets it go out.

MARTINS: *I've been talking to a friend of Harry's, Baron Kurtz. Do you know him?*

ANNA: *No.*

MARTINS: [*He wears a* toupée.] *I can't understand what Harry saw in him.*[27]

ANNA: *Oh, yes.* She does not like him. *That was the man who brought me some money when Harry died. He said Harry had been anxious — at the last moment.*

MARTINS: *He must have been very clear in his head at the end: he remembered about me too. It seems to show there wasn't really any pain.*

ANNA: *Doctor Winkel told me that.* . . .

MARTINS: *Who's he?*

ANNA: *A doctor Harry used to go to. He was passing just after it happened.*

MARTINS: *Harry's own doctor?*

ANNA: *Yes.*

MARTINS: *Did you go to the Inquest?*

ANNA: *Yes. They said it wasn't the driver's fault. Harry had often said what a careful driver he was.*

112

MARTINS astonished: *He was Harry's driver?*
ANNA: *Yes.*
MARTINS: *I don't get this. Kurtz and [the American] — his own driver knocking him down — his own doctor — not a single stranger.*
He is brooding on this new fact.
ANNA: *I've wondered about it a hundred times — if it really was an accident.* MARTINS is astonished. *What difference does it make? He's dead.*
VOICE from outside: *Fraulein Schmidt.*
ANNA: *They don't like us to use the light. It uses up their electricity.*
MARTINS up to this point had never thought of murder.
MARTINS: *The porter saw it happen. It couldn't have been. . . .*[28]
Dissolve.

24. HARRY'S FLAT. SITTING ROOM (NIGHT):

The PORTER throws open the window. MARTINS stands behind him. ANNA is a little distance away, examining the room as though it was a home to which she had returned after many years.
PORTER: *It happened right down there.*
He leans out and we look down with him to the pavement, five storeys below. ANNA turns abruptly away and walks through an open door into the bedroom.
MARTINS: *And you saw it?*
PORTER: *Well, not saw. I heard it though. I heard the brakes [put on and the sound of the skid and I got to the window] and saw them carry the body to the other side of the [road]*[29] . . . He points . . . over there.
While the PORTER is talking, MARTINS turns and watches ANNA in the next room.

25. BEDROOM (NIGHT):

She stands beside the bed with her head down, and every now and then she raises it and takes a quick look here and there.

26. SITTING ROOM (NIGHT):

MARTINS says in a low voice so as not to carry to the next room. . . .

113

MARTINS: *Could he have been conscious?*
PORTER: *Oh no, he was quite dead.*
MARTINS: *I've been told he* didn't *die at once.*
PORTER: *He couldn't have been alive, not with his head in the state it was.*[30]

27. BEDROOM (NIGHT):

ANNA moves from the bed. Twice she puts out her hand and touches the wall. She comes to the dressing table. In the mirror is stuck a snapshot. It is of herself, laughing into the camera. Above it she sees her face in the mirror: tousled hair and hopeless eyes. Automatically she puts her hand down to the right hand drawer. She does not have to look. She opens the drawer and pulls out a comb. Still only half-conscious of what she is doing, she raises it to her head and is just going to use the comb when her eye falls on something in the drawer belonging to HARRY. She drops the comb, slams the drawer to, and puts her hand over her face.

28. SITTING ROOM (NIGHT):

MARTINS: *Why didn't you say all this at the Inquest?*
PORTER: *It's better not to be mixed up in things like that.*
MARTINS: [*It was your duty.*][31]
PORTER: *I was not the only one who did not give evidence.*
MARTINS: *What do you mean?*
PORTER: *Three men helped to carry your friend to the [house.]*[32]
MARTINS: *No — only Kurtz and the American.*
PORTER: *There was a third man. He didn't give evidence.*
MARTINS: *Three men carried the body?*
PORTER: *Yes. The third one held his head.*
MARTINS: *You don't mean the doctor?*
PORTER: *Oh no, he didn't arrive till after they got him to the doorway.*
MARTINS: *Can't you describe this — third man?*
PORTER: *No. He didn't look up. He was just — ordinary. He might have been anybody.*
  MARTINS looks down at the pavement. At the PORTER's last sentence, MARTINS looks down at two or three people passing

114

in the street.

MARTINS almost to himself: *Just anybody. But I think he murdered Harry.*

A telephone starts to ring in the bedroom.

29. BEDROOM (NIGHT):

ANNA picks up the receiver. (*Still*)

ANNA: *Hello, [wer ist da?] Hello.*

There is no reply, but whoever it is remains on the line.

ANNA: [*Warum antworten Sie nicht?*] *Hello.*

She puts the receiver down and turns to MARTINS.

ANNA: [*Nobody.*][33]

MARTINS turns back into the other room.

30. SITTING ROOM (NIGHT):

The PORTER does not want to continue the discussion.[34]

MARTINS: *You've got to tell the police your story.*

Through the open door of the room from the landing outside, trickles a child's ball — nobody sees it.

PORTER: *Nonsense. It is all nonsense. It was an accident I saw it happen.*

A child (little HANSL) comes to the door and looks in — the ball is too far across the floor for him to reach it unobserved — and he skulks there, watching the scene, waiting his opportunity.

MARTINS: *Be accurate. You saw a dead man and three men carrying him.*

The PORTER is working himself up from self-protection into rage.

PORTER: *You have no business forcing your way in here and talking nonsense. I ought to have listened to my wife. She said you were up to no good. Gossip.*

MARTINS: *Don't you see your evidence is important?*

PORTER: *I have no evidence. I saw nothing. I'm not concerned. You must go at once please. Fraulein Anna.*

ANNA SCHMIDT comes in from the bedroom.

ANNA: *What is it?*

PORTER: *I have always liked you, Fraulein Anna, whatever my wife*

115

may say, but you must not bring this gentleman again.
The PORTER shepherds them towards the door. The child backs out of sight onto the landing. As the PORTER reaches the ball and kicks it angrily through the door — it bounces into the corridor and off down the stairs. The child follows it. Dissolve.

31. ANNA'S STREET. LOCATION (NIGHT):

ANNA and MARTINS walk up to the door of an ancient bombed house where ANNA has a room — she looks in her bag for the key.[35]

32. DOORWAY. PART LOCATION (NIGHT):

The door of the house has been broken away and a makeshift door has been made out of planks nailed roughly together. Between the planks can be seen an OLD WOMAN hurrying towards the door. She starts to talk to ANNA excitedly in German, through the cracks in the door. ANNA steps back on the pavement and looks up to a lighted window.
MARTINS: *What is it?*
ANNA: *The Police.*[36]

33. HALLWAY AND STAIRCASE (NIGHT):

A once grand house, badly bombed, and with half the walls out — a large staircase leads upstairs. The OLD WOMAN follows behind ANNA and MARTINS, to whom she behaves like a hostess, muttering all the time and not able to keep up with them. She stops on the first landing, looking up. . . .

34. STAIRCASE AND LANDING (NIGHT):

ANNA's bedroom had once been a reception room; it is large with a high ceiling, but is now a cheaply-furnished room with bare necessities. ANNA and MARTINS can see no one through the half-opened door, but the drawers of a chest are open, and her things are piled in neat heaps on top. Photographs have been removed from frames, etc. Reaction of bewilderment and fear on ANNA's face. MARTINS swings the door open with his foot.

35. ANNA'S BEDROOM (NIGHT):

The opening of the door has taken no one by surprise. CALLO-
WAY stands inside while PAINE and two Austrian POLICEMEN,
paying no attention whatever to the arrival of ANNA and
MARTINS, continue their search.

MARTINS: *What the devil?* . . .

CALLOWAY: *Getting around, Martins?*

MARTINS: *Pinning things on girls now?*

CALLOWAY ignoring him: *I want to see your papers, Miss Schmidt.*

MARTINS: *Don't give him a thing.*

ANNA opens her bag, hands over her papers.

CALLOWAY: *Thank you.*

He begins to turn them over.

[MARTINS: *I'm going to your superiors . . . you'll find out. . . .*]

CALLOWAY: *You were born in Graz, of Austrian parents?* . . .

ANNA in a low voice: *Yes.*

CALLOWAY lifts the document to the light and examines it at
eye-level.

CALLOWAY: [*Take a look,*] *Paine.* PAINE repeats the action. *See
what I mean?*

PAINE: *Yes, sir.*[37]

CALLOWAY: *I'll have to keep these for a while, Miss Schmidt.*

She is too scared to protest. MARTINS does it for her.

MARTINS: [*You can't go that far, Callaghan.*] *She can't live in this
city without papers.*

CALLOWAY: *Write her out a receipt, Paine. That will serve. Give
her a receipt for the other things too.*

PAINE: *This way, miss.*

He leads the way through into the sitting-room.[38]

36. ANNA'S SITTING ROOM (NIGHT):

PAINE seats himself at a table where a number of objects are
already stacked, including a bundle of letters.

ANNA: *You aren't taking those?*

PAINE writing on a leaf of his notebook: *They'll be returned, miss.*

ANNA: *They are private letters.*

PAINE: *Don't worry, miss. We are used to it. Like doctors.*

ANNA leaves him and goes to the doorway.

117

37. ANNA'S BEDROOM (NIGHT):

MARTINS is in the middle of a tirade. ANNA listens.

MARTINS: *And there was a third man there. I suppose that doesn't sound peculiar to you.*

CALLOWAY: *I'm not interested in whether a racketeer like Lime was killed by his friends or in an accident. The only important thing is that he's dead.*

As he speaks the last words, he turns and sees ANNA in the doorway.

CALLOWAY: *I'm sorry.*

MARTINS: [*What an inhuman so-and-so you are, Callaghan.*][39]

CALLOWAY with good humour: *Calloway.*

ANNA: *Must you take those letters?*

CALLOWAY: *Yes, I'm afraid so.*

ANNA: *They are Harry's.*

CALLOWAY: *That's the reason.*

ANNA: *You won't learn anything from them. They are only — love letters. There are not many of them. . . .*

CALLOWAY: *They'll be returned, Miss Schmidt, after they've been examined.*

ANNA: *There's nothing in them. Harry never did anything.* She hesitates. *Only a small thing, once, out of kindness.*

CALLOWAY: *What was that?*

ANNA turning to the other room: *You've got it in your hand.*

CALLOWAY lifts his hand, holding ANNA's papers. PAINE comes through from the other room and gives ANNA the receipt for her letters, etc.

[PAINE: *Shall we clean up for you, miss?*

He makes to put one of the photographs back in its frame.

ANNA quickly, sharply: *No. Don't touch it again.*]

CALLOWAY to Austrian POLICEMAN in German: *Finished?*

POLICEMAN in German: *Nearly.*

CALLOWAY: *You'll have to come with us, Miss Schmidt. Martins, go home like a sensible chap. You don't know what you are mixing in. Get the next plane.*

MARTINS: *You can't order me around, Callaghan. I'm going to get to the bottom of this.*

CALLOWAY: *Death's at the bottom of everything, Martins. Leave death to the professionals.*[40]

CALLOWAY crosses to PAINE, where some of ANNA's belongings are being put back. ANNA goes to the chest and begins to put one of the photographs back in its frame. MARTINS watches her. The photograph is of a man grinning with great gaiety and vitality at the camera.

MARTINS: [*That's him all right. He would have known how to handle that. . . .*] Whispers . . . *Why did they take your papers?*

ANNA: *They are forged.*

MARTINS: *Why?*

ANNA: *The Russians would claim me. I come from Estonia.*[41]

In the open doorway stands the OLD WOMAN. She does not come in.

OLD WOMAN in German: *The way they behave — breaking in like this. I am sorry. . . .*

ANNA takes no notice — the WOMAN goes on talking in German to MARTINS.

MARTINS: *What's she say?*

ANNA: *Only complaining about the way they behave — it's her house.*

MARTINS looking around: *Is it. . . .*

ANNA: *Give her some cigarettes.*

MARTINS gives her four cigarettes, which she will not at first accept, but finally does so with great grace. MARTINS goes back to ANNA.

CALLOWAY: *Ready, Miss Schmidt?*

MARTINS: *Don't be scared. If I can only clear up this mess about Harry — you'll be okay.*

ANNA glancing up at the picture: *Sometimes he said I laughed too much.* To CALLOWAY. *Yes.*

MARTINS: *What was that doctor's name?*

ANNA spelling it: *Winkel.*

CALLOWAY: *What do you want to see a doctor for?*

MARTINS touches his mouth where PAINE hit him.

MARTINS: [*About my mouth.*][42]

The OLD WOMAN watches them going downstairs. Dissolve.

38. DR WINKEL'S FLAT. DINING ROOM (NIGHT):

A chicken is being carefully dissected. The bell rings.

39. DR WINKEL'S FLAT. PASSAGE (NIGHT):

A MAID passes along and opens the door. MARTINS stands outside.

MARTINS: *Is Dr Winkel in?*

MAID: *Die Sprechstund ist von drei bis fünf.* (*His consulting hours are 3 till 5.*)

She prepares to close the door.

MARTINS: *I want Dr Winkel. Don't you speak any English?*

MAID: *Nein.*

MARTINS: *Dr Winkel, I . . .* He points at himself *. . . want to see Dr Winkel. Tell him, a friend of Harry Lime's.*

40 DR WINKEL'S DINING ROOM (NIGHT):

We cut back to the hands carving the chicken. They suddenly stay still. The knife is put down. A voice calls out something in German.

VOICE in German: *Show him into the waiting-room, Hilda.*

41. DR WINKEL'S WAITING-ROOM (NIGHT):

The MAID shows MARTINS into the waiting-room and leaves him there. DR WINKEL's waiting-room reminds one of an antique shop that specializes in religious objets d'art. There are more crucifixes hanging on the walls and perched on the cupboards and occasional tables than one can count; none are of later date than the seventeenth century. There are statues in wood and ivory. There are a number of reliquaries: little bits of bone marked with saints' names and set in oval frames on a background of tinfoil. Even the high-backed, hideous chairs look as if they had been sat in by cardinals. Through the open doorway can be seen the stick with the ivory top that KURTZ was carrying earlier. A sneeze disturbs MARTINS.

DR WINKEL is very small, neat, very clean, in a black tail-coat and a high stiff collar; his little black moustache is like an evening tie. He sneezes again. Perhaps he is cold because he is so clean.

WINKEL: [*Mr Martins?*]

MARTINS: *Dr Winkel?*[48]

120

MARTINS always pronounces this name wrong, as though it were the name of the shellfish, so that the ' W ' is pronounced like an English ' W ' and not as in German as a ' V '. This annoys WINKEL.

WINKEL: *Vinkel.*

When he bows, there is a very slight creak as though his shirt front is celluloid. Or does he wear stays?

MARTINS: *You have an interesting collection here.*

WINKEL: *Yes.*

[MARTINS: *These saints' bones. . . .*

WINKEL: *The bones of chickens.*

MARTINS pauses by yet another crucifix; a figure hanging with arms above the head; a face of elongated El Greco agony.

MARTINS: *That's a strange crucifix.*

WINKEL: *Jansenist.*

MARTINS: *Never heard the word. Why are the arms above the head?*

WINKEL: *Because he died, in their view, only for the elect.*

DR WINKEL takes a large white handkerchief out of his sleeve, rather as though he were a conjuror producing his country's flag. He blows his nose neatly and thoroughly twice, closing each nostril in turn. One expects him to throw away the handkerchief after one use.][44]

WINKEL: *Would you mind, Mr Martins, coming to the point? I have guests waiting.*

MARTINS: *You and I were both friends of Harry Lime's.*

WINKEL unyieldingly: *I was his medical adviser.*

MARTINS: *I want to find out all I can.*

WINKEL: *Find out?*

MARTINS: *Hear the details.*

WINKEL: *I can tell you very little. He was knocked over by a car. He was dead when I arrived.*

MARTINS: *Who was there?*

WINKEL: *Two friends of his.*

MARTINS: *You're sure. . . . Two?*

WINKEL: *Quite sure.*

MARTINS: *Would he have been conscious at all?*

WINKEL: *I understand he was . . . yes . . . for a short time . . . while they carried him into the house.*

MARTINS: *In great pain?*
WINKEL: *Not necessarily.*
MARTINS: *Would he have been capable of . . . well, making plans to look after me and others? In those few moments?*
WINKEL looks at the nails on one hand.
WINKEL: *I cannot give an opinion. I was not there.*
[DR WINKEL takes a silver pencil out of his pocket and cleans one nail with the point.]⁴⁵
WINKEL: *My opinion is limited to the causes of death. Have you any reason to be dissatisfied?*
MARTINS: *Could his death have been . . . not accidental?*
DR WINKEL puts out a hand to straighten a crucifix on the wall, and flicks some imaginary dust off the feet.
MARTINS trying to make himself clear: *Could it have been. . . .*
WINKEL: *Yes?*
MARTINS: *Could he have been pushed, Dr Winkel?*
WINKEL stonily correcting him: *Vinkel, Vinkel.*
DR WINKEL is a very cautious doctor. His statements are so limited that one cannot for a moment doubt their veracity.
WINKEL: *I cannot give an opinion. The injuries to the head and skull would have been the same.*
Dissolve.

42. CALLOWAY'S OFFICE (NIGHT):

[CALLOWAY sits at his desk with ANNA before him. On his desk, a bundle of letters.]⁴⁶
CALLOWAY: *I can let you have these back, Miss Schmidt. Will you look through, see that they are right, and sign the receipt?*
He pushes the receipt across to her, watching her closely.
ANNA: *But my passport?*
CALLOWAY: *We need that for a while longer.*
[ANNA begins to count the letters. The door opens and a Russian Officer, BRODSKY, enters.
BRODSKY: *I've brought the passport back. Very cleverly done.* He drops the passport on the desk. *You know we are interested in this case. Have you arrested the girl?* He takes a long look at ANNA.
CALLOWAY: *Not yet.*
BRODSKY: *You'll remember we have a claim to the body. See you*

tonight, Calloway. He goes out.]
ANNA *with fear: What did he mean?*
CALLOWAY: *You know as much as I do.*
[ANNA: *There is a letter missing.*
CALLOWAY: *Yes.*
ANNA: *Why did you keep it?*
CALLOWAY: *To have a photostat made.*

CALLOWAY, to prevent himself embarrassing ANNA, goes to the window and speaks his next lines with his back turned.]
CALLOWAY: *Miss Schmidt, you were intimate with Lime, weren't you?*
ANNA: *We loved each other. Do you mean that?*

CALLOWAY is looking through the window.

[43. STREET. LOCATION (NIGHT):

MARTINS is waiting on the other side of the road. We see him from CALLOWAY's viewpoint.]

44. CALLOWAY'S OFFICE (NIGHT):

CALLOWAY turning from the window and picking a photograph from the desk: *Know this man?*
ANNA after a quick look at the photograph: *I've never seen him.*
CALLOWAY: *But you've heard of him — Joseph Harbin.* [*A medical orderly.*][47]
ANNA: *No.*
CALLOWAY: *It's stupid to lie to me, Miss Schmidt. I am in a position to help you.*
ANNA: *I am not lying. You are wrong about Harry. You are wrong about everything.*
CALLOWAY: *In the letter we've kept, Lime asked you to telephone a good friend of his called Joseph. He gave you the number. . . .* [*It's the number of the hospital where Harbin worked.*][48]
ANNA: [*Oh, that. Yes. I remember that.*] *It wasn't important.*
CALLOWAY: *What was the message?*
ANNA: [*I can't remember.*][49]
CALLOWAY: *Harbin disappeared the day you telephoned — I want to find him.* He picks up the passport and turns it over in his hands. *You can help us.*

ANNA: *What can I tell you but. . . . * CALLOWAY looks up. *You've got everything upside down.* CALLOWAY gets up.

CALLOWAY: *Right, Miss Schmidt. We'll send for you when we want you. That friend of yours is waiting for you — a rather troublesome fellow.*

Dissolve.

45. THE CASANOVA CLUB (NIGHT):

A dance floor with tables round it; up a short flight of stairs, a bar and cloakroom. KURTZ, playing a violin with two other players, is going from table to table. As he passes one table, we see CARTER and TOMBS. They go up the stairs to the bar and cloakroom. As they reach the cloakroom, the street door opens and MARTINS and ANNA enter. ANNA goes up to the bar. CARTER sees MARTINS as he turns, struggling to get into his overcoat.

CARTER: *Hello, Mr Martins. [Goodness, I'm glad I ran into you.]*

MARTINS: *Good evening.*

CARTER: *I've been looking all over town for you, Mr Martins. [I've arranged a lecture at Innsbruck.*

MARTINS: *You what?*

TOMBS gloomily: *Wait till you hear the subject.]*[50]

CARTER: *They want you to talk on the Crisis of Faith.*

MARTINS: *What does that mean?*

TOMBS: *We thought you'd know. You're a writer, old chap.*

CARTER: *We'll talk again after the discussion. I'll let you know the time.*

[MARTINS: *What discussion?*

CARTER: *The lecture on the modern novel. You remember — what we arranged at the hotel.*

MARTINS: *Oh yes, that's right.*

TOMBS: *So long, old man.]*

ANNA is at the bar. MARTINS comes up.

MARTINS: *Drink?*

He takes out his army money.

ANNA: *And they won't take that stuff here.* To BARMAN. *Two whiskies.* She opens her bag.

MARTINS turning round on his stool sees KURTZ playing at a

table below, where a fat woman is sitting with an elderly man. He is pouring it out with great emotion — eyes slit and swimming, his shoulders move with the slow rhythm and his head nods with appreciation. MARTINS watches him with suspicion. KURTZ has not yet seen him.

ANNA: *Your whisky.*

He half-turns back to the bar. ANNA, who has turned her bag out, is putting her change back. She picks up a snapshot and is about to put it back in her bag.

MARTINS: *Harry?*

She gives it to him — they stare at it together.

ANNA: *He moved his head, but the rest is good.*

KURTZ is playing from table to table, followed by a double bass and second violin. He sees MARTINS and ANNA, leaves the others and moves to the bar. He seems completely unperturbed and comes up the stairs to the bar. He bows to ANNA.

KURTZ: *Miss Schmidt. You've found out my little secret. A man must live.* To MARTINS. *How goes the investigation? Have you proved the policeman wrong?*

MARTINS: [*Yes.*][51]

KURTZ, who is aware he has carried off a tricky situation well, has been a little over-exhilarated, but this plain statement damps him.

KURTZ: *Our friend Winkel said you had called. Perhaps he was helpful?* He cannot avoid a shade of anxiety.

MARTINS: *No.*

KURTZ: *Mr Tyler is here tonight.*

MARTINS: *I thought he left Vienna.*

KURTZ: *He's back now.*

MARTINS: *I want to meet all Harry's friends.*

KURTZ: *I'll bring him to you.*

KURTZ goes back to the dance floor.

ANNA: *Haven't you done enough today?* She is worn out with reminders of HARRY.

MARTINS: *That porter said three men carried the body, and two of them are here.*

MARTINS turns from the bar and sees TYLER: a man with tousled grey hair, a worried, kindly, humanitarian face and long-sighted eyes.

KURTZ: *Mr Tyler, Mr Martins.*

TYLER: *Any friend of Harry's is a friend of mine.*

KURTZ: *I'll leave you together.* He goes.

TYLER: *Good evening, Miss Schmidt. You remember me?*

ANNA: [*Yes.* The memory is obviously not pleasant.]

TYLER: *I helped Harry fix her papers, Mr Martins. Not the sort of thing I should confess to a stranger, but you have to break the rules sometimes. Humanity's a duty. Cigarette, Miss Schmidt? Keep the pack.*

MARTINS is growing impatient with all this talk.

MARTINS: [*I want to hear about Harry's death.*][52]

ANNA SCHMIDT takes her glass and moves away down the bar. She cannot bear any more of this. She sits there, during the ensuing scene, smoking cigarette after cigarette.

TYLER to BARMAN: *Two large whiskies and a small one for the lady.* To MARTINS. *It was a terrible thing. I was just crossing the road to go to Harry. He and the Baron were on the sidewalk.*

MARTINS'S eyes go to KURTZ who has come into sight below, playing at a table as before. He glances towards MARTINS and nods at him with a smile.

TYLER: *Maybe if I hadn't started across the road, it wouldn't have happened. I can't help blaming myself and wishing things had been different. Anyway he saw me and stepped off the sidewalk to meet me, and the truck . . . it was terrible, Mr Martins, terrible.* He swallows his whisky. *I've never seen a man killed before.*

MARTINS: *There was something wrong about Harry's death.*

TYLER: *Of course, there was.* [*Two more whiskies.*]

MARTINS: *You think so too?*

TYLER: *It was so damned stupid for a man like Harry to be killed in a* [*piddling*] *street accident.*

MARTINS: *That's all you meant?*

TYLER: *What else?*

MARTINS: *Who was the third man?*

TYLER takes up his glass.

TYLER: *I oughtn't to drink it. It makes me acid. What man would you be referring to, Mr Martins?*

MARTINS: *I was told a third man helped you and Kurtz with the body.*

TYLER: *I don't know how you got that idea. You'll find all about*

126

it in the Inquest report. There was just the two of us. Me and the Baron. Who could have told you a story like that?

MARTINS: *I was talking to the porter at Harry's place. He was cleaning the window and looked out.*

TYLER with great calm: *And saw the accident?*

MARTINS: *No. Three men carrying the body, that's all.*

TYLER: *Why wasn't he at the Inquest?*

MARTINS: *He didn't want to get involved.*

TYLER: *You'll never teach these Austrians to be good citizens. It was his duty to give the evidence, even though he remembered wrong. What else did he tell you?*

MARTINS: *That Harry was dead [when he was carried into the house.]*[53] *Somebody's lying.*

TYLER: *Not necessarily. [It's an odd thing, Mr Martins, with accidents. You'll never get two reports that coincide. Why, even the Baron and I disagreed about details. The thing happens so suddenly, you aren't prepared to notice things.]*

MARTINS watching the other man's reactions: *The police say Harry was mixed up in some racket.*

TYLER: *That's quite impossible. He had a great sense of duty.*

MARTINS: *Kurtz seemed to think it was possible.*

TYLER: *The Baron doesn't understand how an Anglo-Saxon feels.*[54]

He looks across at ANNA and finishes his drink. [He speaks as he rises.]

TYLER: *That's a nice girl, that. But she ought to be careful in Vienna. Everybody ought to be careful in a city like this.*

Dissolve.

[46. ANNA'S ROOM (NIGHT):

ANNA lies awake in bed, with her arms behind her head, staring at the ceiling. The street lamps outside cast shifting shadows on the ceiling, and something goes tap, tap, tap. ANNA looks in the direction of the sound and sees what it is — the cord of the window shade hitting the back of HARRY's photograph. She puts out her hand and lays the photograph face down.

47. STREET. LOCATION (DAWN):

International Patrol car passes along empty streets. In the

background is one lighted window — the silhouette of a figure is seen telephoning.

48. TYLER'S ROOM. LOCATION (DAWN):

TYLER is putting down the receiver of his telephone. He opens a drawer and takes out two packets of American cigarettes, looks in a mirror, carefully rumples his hair and makes for the door.

49. WINKEL'S FRONT DOOR. LOCATION (DAWN):

DR WINKEL, dressed as always very neatly, comes out of his door, carrying a briefcase. He trots down the stairs, expressionless, giving nothing away.

50. KURTZ'S FLAT. EXTERIOR. LOCATION (DAWN):

Through the open front door we see KURTZ adjusting his toupée. He walks down the street.

51. VIENNA EXTERIOR. LOCATION (DAWN):

Dawn over the canal and the ruined quays; the Russian zone notice; the Prater with the idle wheel; the Danube. KURTZ walks through these scenes.] [55]

52. REICHSBRUCKE. EXTERIOR. LOCATION (DAWN):

A man with his back turned to the camera waits on the bridge. He is joined one after the other by TYLER, KURTZ and WINKEL. They talk together out of hearing.

[53. ANNA'S ROOM (MORNING):

ANNA is at last asleep. Dissolve.]

54. STREET. EXTERIOR. LOCATION (DAY):

In the middle of the dissolve there is the sound of a crash which continues into this scene. A tram is stopping suddenly with a jerk. MARTINS is seen from the rear, getting out; he walks towards the Public Library. Dissolve.

55. PUBLIC LIBRARY. INTERIOR. LOCATION (DAY):

OFFICIAL is finishing his translation of the Inquest report to
MARTINS. He has been making endless notes and has obviously
spent some time here.
OFFICIAL in a broken accent: . . . *exonerated the driver and brought
in a verdict of accidental death.*]
Dissolve.

56. HARRY'S FLAT. EXTERIOR. LOCATION (DAY):

MARTINS is pacing out the distance from the door to the point
where HARRY was killed, and various other distances. Then he
paces back along the pavement where the body was carried,
and looks up to the window of HARRY's flat, from which the
PORTER had seen the third man. Staring down at him is the
PORTER, duster in hand.
PORTER calling softly down: *Mein Herr.*
MARTINS: *Yes?*
PORTER: *I am not a bad man, mein Herr. Not a bad man. Is it
really so important?*
MARTINS: *Very important.*
PORTER: *Come this evening when my wife is out then.*
MARTINS: *I'll come, but tell me now. Was the car. . . .*
PORTER: *Shsh.* He slams the window.

57. HARRY'S FLAT (DAY):

The PORTER slams the window and turns towards the camera.
He stays still, listening. There is a sound of squeaking shoes,
approaching from the next room. As they come close, we see a
look of horror on the PORTER's face.
Dissolve.

58. ANNA'S ROOM (DAY):

The grey early-evening time, before it is quite dark enough to
switch on the lights. ANNA is standing by the table on which
are the roneoed sheets of a play. She has been trying to learn
a new part. She turns and the camera turns with her to pick
up MARTINS in the doorway. He wears a wet mackintosh. For a

129

moment, because her mind is in the past, she almost thinks it is HARRY. She makes a motion towards him and then turns away.

ANNA: *Come in. [I can't give you a drink. Except tea. There's some of that packet left.*

MARTINS: *No, thank you. You know I can't stand tea.* He sits down on the divan. *I'm feeling cross-eyed — been looking at Inquest Reports — Police Reports — but I finally got something.]* *The porter's going to talk to us tonight.*

ANNA: *Need we go through it all again?*

MARTINS: *I can manage alone.* He picks up the play. *Busy?*

ANNA: *Another part I've got to learn.*

MARTINS: *Shall I hear you?*

ANNA sceptically: *In German?*

MARTINS: *I can try. Tragedy or comedy?*

ANNA: *Comedy, I'm not the right shape for tragedy.*

She hands him the part and shows him the cue, which he ludicrously mispronounces. They go on for a few lines, but she is obviously getting them wrong.

ANNA: *It's no good.*

MARTINS: *One of the bad days?*

ANNA: *It's always bad about this time. He used to look in round six. I've been frightened, I've been alone, I've been without friends and money, but I've never known anything like this.*

ANNA plonks herself down on a hard chair opposite him. It is as if she had been fighting for days not to say this, and now surrenders.

ANNA: *Please talk. Tell me about him; tell me about the Harry you knew.*

MARTINS takes a long look at her. All the grace she may have had, seems to have been folded up with her dresses and put away for professional use. This ANNA is for everyday. Suddenly it is he who is less willing to talk of HARRY.

MARTINS: *What kind of things?*

ANNA: *Anything. Just talk. Where did you see him last? When? What did you do?*

MARTINS: *We drank too much. We quarrelled. I thought he was making a pass at my girl.*

ANNA: *Where's she?*

MARTINS: *I don't know. That was nine years ago.*

ANNA: *Tell me more.*

MARTINS: *It's difficult. You knew Harry; we didn't do anything terribly amusing — he just made it all seem such fun.*

ANNA: *I know a little what you mean. Was he clever when he was a boy?*

He gets up restlessly and looks out of the window.

MARTINS: *I suppose so. He could fix anything.*

ANNA: *Tell me.*

MARTINS: *Oh, little things — how to put up your temperature before an exam — the best crib — how to avoid this and that.*

ANNA: *He fixed my papers for me. He heard the Russians were repatriating people like me who came from Estonia. He knew the right man straight away for forging stamps.*

MARTINS: *When he was only fourteen, he taught me the three card trick. That was growing up fast.*

ANNA: *He never grew up. The world grew up round him, that's all — and buried him.*

[She begins to cry quietly, and MARTINS suddenly turns from the window.

MARTINS: *He's dead. You can't go on remembering him for ever.*

ANNA: *Something may happen.*

MARTINS: *What do you mean?*

ANNA: *Perhaps there'll be another war or I'll die or the Russians will take me.*

MARTINS: *Anna, life goes on. It'll get better.*] *You'll fall in love again.*

ANNA turns to the sink with the remains of a dinner.

ANNA: *Don't you see I don't want to. I don't ever want to.*

MARTINS moving away from the window, passes her and sympathetically scratches the top of her head.

MARTINS: *Come out and have a drink.*

ANNA looks quickly up.

ANNA: *Why did you say that?*

MARTINS: *It seemed like a good idea.*

ANNA: *It was just what he used to say.* [*And when I said ' I've got to be at the theatre ', he'd say. . . .*

MARTINS: *' Time for a quick one '.*][56]

They laugh a moment.

131

ANNA: *If we've got to see the porter, we'd better go. . . .*
She picks up her part and starts for the door.
MARTINS: *I thought you didn't want. . . .*
ANNA: *We're both in it, Harry.*
MARTINS: *My name's Rollo.*
ANNA: *I'm sorry.*
MARTINS: *You needn't be.* [*I'm bad at names too. Ask Callaghan.*][57]
In the doorway she turns and speaks with the first real friend-
liness.
[ANNA: *What fun we all might have had, him and you and me.*
MARTINS: *As long as I kept off the extra glass.*]
ANNA: *You know, you ought to find yourself a girl.*
Dissolve.

59. HARRY'S STREET. PART LOCATION (NIGHT):

As ANNA and MARTINS walk along the street, lights go on. At
the end of the road a group of people are gathered inspite
of thin icy rain. The lights are reflected in the puddles. ANNA
is staring down the road with some uneasiness, trying to make
out what is happening.
MARTINS: *Isn't that Harry's?* [*It looks like a wedding.*
ANNA: *At this time of day?*
She walks more slowly. The crowd makes her uneasy.
MARTINS: *A demonstration?*
ANNA: *They don't allow demonstrations.*] She stops altogether. *Let's
go away.*
MARTINS: *Stay here. I'll see what it's about.*
MARTINS walks slowly on alone. It is not a political meeting,
for no one is making a speech. Heads turn to watch him come,
as though he is somebody expected. MARTINS reaches the fringe
of the little crowd and speaks to a MAN there.
MARTINS trying out some bad German: *Was ist?* He waves his hand
at the crowd.
[MAN: *They wait to see him brought out.*
MARTINS: *Who?*
MAN: *The porter.*
MARTINS: *What's he done?*
MAN: *Nobody knows yet. They can't make their minds up in there*

132

— it might be suicide, you see, but why should he have cut his own throat . . .?]

The small child, called HANSL, whom MARTINS saw on his visit to HARRY's flat, comes up to his informant and pulls at his hand.

HANSL: *Papa, papa.*

His face is pinched and blue with cold, and more unpleasant than ever.

HANSL in German: *Papa, I heard the big man say, ' Can you tell me what the foreigner looked like? '*

MAN to MARTINS: *Ha. He had a row with a foreigner, they think he did it. . . .*

HANSL: *Papa, papa.*

MAN: *Ja, Hansl?*

HANSL: *Wie ich durch's Gitter geschaut habe, hab'ich Blut auf'm Koks gesehen. (When I looked through the grating, I could see some blood on the coke.)*

MAN admiringly to MARTINS: *What imagination! He thought when he looked through the grating, he could see blood on the coke.*

The child stares solemnly up at MARTINS.

HANSL: *Papa.*

MAN: *Ja, Hansl?*

HANSL in German: *Das ist der Fremde. (That's the foreigner.)*

The MAN gives a big laugh which causes a dozen heads to turn.

MAN: *Listen to him, sir. He thinks you did it because you are a foreigner. There are more foreigners here these days than Viennese.*

HANSL: *Papa, papa.*

MAN: *Yes, Hansl?*

HANSL points. A knot of police surrounds the covered stretcher which they lower down the steps. The PORTER's wife comes out at the tail of the procession; she has a shawl over her head and an old sackcloth coat. Somebody gives her a hand and she looks round with a lost, hopeless gaze at this crowd of strangers. If there are friends there, she does not recognise them, looking from face to face. To avoid her look, MARTINS bends to do up his shoelace, but kneeling there, he finds himself on a level with HANSL's scrutinizing gaze. Walking back up the street towards ANNA, MARTINS looks behind him once: the child is pulling at his father's hand, and he can see the lips forming

133

round those syllables, ' *Papa, papa* '.

MARTINS: *The porter's been murdered. Let's get away from here. They're asking about the foreigner who called on him.*

They hurry away. Unknown to them, they are followed at a distance by little HANSL, who drags his father after him.

ANNA and MARTINS walk as naturally as they can, but sometimes hurrying too much, and then slowing too much.[58]

ANNA: *Then what he said was true. There* was *a third man.*

MARTINS does not reply. The tram-cars flash like icicles at the end of the street. MARTINS turns round and sees HANSL and his father following with a few of the man who were outside the PORTER's doorway.

MARTINS: *Anna.* He indicates their pursuers.

ANNA: *That child?*

MARTIN nods. They hurry round the corner.

60. CINEMA. LOCATION (NIGHT):

Outside a cinema a small queue is just moving in.

MARTINS: *Come in here.*

ANNA takes money from her bag, and they buy tickets. They go into the dark cinema.

61. CINEMA. INTERIOR. LOCATION (NIGHT):

The film which is being shown is a well-known Hope-Crosby-Lamour film, with voices dubbed in German. Big laughs come from the audience. Crosby begins to sing in German.

ANNA: *Be careful. The porter knew so little and they murdered him. You know as much. . . .*

MARTINS: *You can't be careful of someone you don't know.*

The camera takes in the anonymous, shadowy faces sitting round them.

MARTINS: *Go on to the theatre. I'd better not come near you again till this is fixed.* ANNA gets up.

ANNA: *What are you going to do?*

MARTINS with harassed bewilderment: *I wish I knew.* He looks back at the screen.

ANNA: *Be sensible. Tell Colonel Calloway.* Dissolve.

[62. SACHER'S HOTEL. LOCATION (NIGHT):

MARTINS hurries up — a taxi is waiting outside the Hotel.
MARTINS is about to get in, but there is no driver — he turns
into the hotel.]

63. SACHER'S RECEPTION DESK (NIGHT):

A MAN, with a chauffeur's cap and a shifty expression, is just
leaving the desk as MARTINS comes hurriedly in. The MAN turns
and stares at him as he passes. MARTINS' mind is made up.
MARTINS to PORTER: *Get Colonel Callaghan on the 'phone.*
PORTER: *I don't know him, sir.*
MARTINS: *Calloway then. I don't care what his name is. Get him
quickly. It's urgent.*
PORTER: *Do you know his number, sir?*
MARTINS: *Of course, I don't. Is there a car I can use?*
PORTER: *There's one right here for you, sir.*
MARTINS: *Fine.*
He strides out, followed by a sub-porter.
[The PORTER calls after him.
PORTER: *Captain Carter has been on the 'phone to you, sir. He was
anxious to speak to you. About a lecture. . . .*
MARTINS: *Tell him he can put his damned culture in the dustbin.*]

64. SACHER'S HOTEL. LOCATION (NIGHT):

The sub-porter opens the door of a car driven by the shifty
MAN in the chauffeur's cap.

65. CAR. BACK PROJECTION (NIGHT):

As MARTINS sits down, the car immediately begins to move off.
MARTINS: *International Police Headquarters. Colonel Calloway's
Office.*
The MAN does not reply and the car gathers speed. It plunges
into ill-lit streets. MARTINS peers anxiously out.

66. CAR. STREET. LOCATION (NIGHT):

The taxi speeds around a corner — it almost mounts the kerb.
It is driving to a more deserted part of the city.

67. CAR. BACK PROJECTION (NIGHT):

MARTINS: *Slower. Slower.*[59] The DRIVER pays no attention. *This isn't the way to the International Police. Where are we going?*
   The DRIVER turns his head and speaks in German, with a malevolent ring. MARTINS makes a joke which sounds hollow to his own ears. . . . .
MARTINS: *Have you got orders to kill me?*
DRIVER: [*Ich kann nicht English.*] (*I do not speak English.*)

68. CULTURAL CENTRE. LOCATION (NIGHT):

   The car pulls through the open gates of a courtyard and drives around to the rear of a house, stopping with a jerk alongside a big doorway. The DRIVER opens the door.
DRIVER: *Bitte.* (*Please.*)
MARTINS: *This isn't Police Headquarters.*
DRIVER: *Bitte.*
   The DRIVER puts his hand into the car to help MARTINS out, and MARTINS shakes it off.
DRIVER: *Bitte.*
   The DRIVER turns towards the big doors and starts to push them open. MARTINS edges out of the car and turns to try to escape, but the car blocks his way. The light from the now open doorway falls across him.
VOICE: *Oh, Mr Martins.*
   He looks up startled.

69. CULTURAL CENTRE. HALLWAY (NIGHT):

   Bright lights shine out. MARTINS sees CARTER advancing through a throng of women.
CARTER: *Better late than never.* He draws MARTINS inside.

70. CULTURAL CENTRE. RECEPTION AND ANTEROOM (NIGHT):
   Hemmed in by CARTER and TOMBS and the attendant women, MARTINS is hustled like a Führer through the anteroom which is being used as a cloakroom. His mackintosh is drawn off him as he walks. In the large inner room where the discussion will be held, the uncomfortable chairs are arranged in rows; a buffet

136

has been set up, laden with nothing more exhilarating than cocoa; an urn steams; a woman's face is shiny with exertion; and huddled in the background, like faces in a family album, the earnest and dreary features of constant readers. MARTINS looks behind him, but the door has closed. There is no escape.

[MARTINS desperately to CARTER: *I'm sorry, but.* . . .

CARTER: *For goodness sake, do your stuff, old man. The Brigadier's here.*

Three chairs for CARTER, TOMBS and MARTINS face the others. CARTER in an undertone to TOMBS: *You give them the works?*

TOMBS: *Oh no. This is your funeral, old man.*

CARTER: *Well, you read one of his books, didn't you?*

TOMBS: *Nothing doing.*

CARTER knocks on the table, and as he begins to speak, people drift to their seats. The BRIGADIER listens and hangs on every word.]

CARTER: *Ladies and Gentlemen, we have with us tonight Mr Rollo Martins, one of the great writers from the other side. Here he is. We've all of us read his books. Wonderful stuff. Literature depends on character — I've read that somewhere — and Mr Martins' characters — well, there's nothing quite like them, is there? You know what I mean. We ought to give him a great welcome.*

The faces of the listeners watch with avid expectancy; one figure jumps up to ask a question. Dissolve.[60]

71. RECEPTION ROOM (NIGHT):

It is some time later and MARTINS already looks harried and confused by the questions. CARTER is worried. [and TOMBS sits in despair — with one eye on the BRIGADIER.]

AUSTRIAN WOMAN: *Do you believe in the stream of consciousness?*

MARTINS to CARTER: *Stream of what?*

CARTER gives a gesture of despair.

[72. STAIRCASE (NIGHT):

A bowed figure slowly mounts the stairs towards the double doors. It is dark on the stairs and we cannot make out the face. By now we are prepared to see in all strangers, in all mysterious figures, the possible features of the third man.

145

73. RECEPTION ROOM (NIGHT):

We can see, though MARTINS cannot, right through the ante-room to the door. Somebody opens the door and the figure from the stairs comes in. We still do not see the face.

AUSTRIAN YOUNG MAN with rather an effeminate manner: *Among the great English poets, where would you put Oscar Wilde?*

MARTINS: *What do you mean, put? I don't want to put anybody anywhere.*][61]

TYLER: *Can I ask Mr Martins if he's engaged on a new book?*

MARTINS, CARTER [and TOMBS] look at the doorway. TYLER stands there. MARTINS takes him in for a moment in silence. He recognises the challenge.

MARTINS: *Yes . . . yes. . . . It's called ' The Third Man '.*

WOMAN: *A novel, Mr Martins?*

MARTINS: *It's founded on fact.*

[CARTER: *I'm so glad you were able to come, Mr Tyler. To MARTINS. Mr Tyler is here on a cultural mission.*][62]

[TYLER: *I guess we all have to get together against the common enemy.*

MARTINS: *Who's that, Mr Tyler?*

TYLER: *Ignorance, Mr Martins. You know the saying — to know all is to forgive all.*

MARTINS: *You have to know all first.*

CARTER to his assistant: *Get a chair for Mr Tyler.*

TYLER: *Just let me squat here on the edge of the buffet, Captain Carter.* He does so. *I've got to push off in a few minutes.*

A WOMAN, wearing a meagre bit of rabbit round her throat, asks the question she has been dying to get out all through the last interchange.

AUSTRIAN WOMAN: *Mr Martins, what author has chiefly influenced you?*

MARTINS: *Gray.*

ELDERLY AUSTRIAN: *Grey? What Grey? I do not know the name.*

MARTINS: *Zane Gray — I don't know any other.*

TOMBS: *Don't get above their heads, old chap.*

AUSTRIAN: *He is a greater writer?*

CARTER: *Terrific. Read him myself.*

AUSTRIAN YOUNG MAN: *And James Joyce, Mr Martins?*

146

CARTER to TOMBS: *Joyce?*

TOMBS to CARTER: *Lord Haw Haw. Don't like the way this is going, old man.*

MARTINS: *I've never heard of him.*

TOMBS: *Good line, old chap.*

There is a lot of ill-suppressed discontent in the audience by this time. A YOUNG WOMAN calls out insultingly.

YOUNG WOMAN: *He wrote Ulysses.*

MARTINS: *I don't read Greek.*

TYLER *his voice breaking clearly through the titters: Mr Martins, I'd like a word with you about your new novel.*

MARTINS: *' The Third Man '?*

TYLER: *Yes.*

The meeting slowly quiets to hear them.]

MARTINS: [*It's a murder story.*] *I've just started it.*

TYLER: *Are you a slow writer, Mr Martins?*

MARTINS: *Pretty quick when I get interested.*

TYLER: *I'd say you were doing something pretty dangerous this time.*

MARTINS: *Yes?*

TYLER: *Mixing fact with fiction, like oil and water.*

MARTINS: *Should I write it as straight fact?*

TYLER: *Why no, Mr Martins. I'd say stick to fiction, straight fiction.*

MARTINS: *I've gone too far with the book, Mr Tyler.*

TYLER: *Haven't you ever scrapped a book, Mr Martins?*

MARTINS: *Never.*

TYLER gets lazily up from the edge of the buffet. He touches the urn with his finger.[63]

[TYLER: *Pretty hot. Do you mind if I use your telephone, Captain Carter?*

CARTER: *Please go ahead. In the anteroom.*

TYLER strolls out.

WOMAN: *Do you think there's any future, Mr Martins, for the historic novel?*

74. THE ANTEROOM (NIGHT):

TYLER is at the telephone. While he waits, TYLER speaks to the girl who is looking after the coats. People are fetching their

147

coats and going out all the time. Snatches of dissastified conversations are going on.

TYLER: *You people are doing a wonderful job.*

GIRL: *Bitte?*

TYLER: *Never mind.* Into the telephone. *Oh, hello. Yes, I'm at the Cultural Centre. Our friend's here. Very interesting talk, I thought you might like to meet us. We could have a little party. Bring the car and anyone else who'd like to come. Don't be long.* He puts down the receiver.

75. RECEPTION ROOM (NIGHT):

MARTINS is wiping perspiration off his forehead and TOMBS is leaning gloomily back in his chair. Half the chairs are empty and several others are leaving.

MARTINS: *I've never heard of him.* Desperately. . . . *I don't read many books.*

TOMBS to CARTER: *This is disaster, old man.*

CARTER: *Mr Martins has had a trying time since he came to Vienna. If there are no more questions. . . .*

The meeting breaks up. Those that have not already left stand up to go.

The BRIGADIER approaches TOMBS and CARTER. The shadow of the approaching reprimand clouds the two men's faces. MARTINS is about to leave.

BRIGADIER eyeing CARTER and TOMBS: *Good evening, Mr Martins. Hope you're having a pleasant time in Vienna? Where are you staying?*

MARTINS: *They've put me up at Sacher's.*

A look of uneasiness on the faces of CARTER and TOMBS.

BRIGADIER with a look at CARTER and TOMBS: *You're lucky. It's usually reserved for officers.* As MARTINS moves away. . . . *Good night, Mr Martins.*

CARTER: *We understand, sir, Colonel Calloway. . . .*

BRIGADIER: *You fellows come and see me tomorrow. 9.30 in my office. In uniform.*

76. FRONT DOOR (NIGHT):

TYLER is standing there, looking down the road expectantly as the people are leaving.]

148

77. ANTEROOM (NIGHT):

[MARTINS is coming through in a hurry and stops as he looks down the few stairs and sees a car drive up. TYLER is speaking to the two men who are hurriedly getting out.] TYLER speaks quietly to them, and we do not hear what is said, but the three men now stand in the narrow hallway obviously waiting for MARTINS to come down. They look up the stairs towards him. MARTINS looks above him and sees a narrow staircase that leads along a corridor. He makes a dash for this. TYLER and the two men have seen him vanish and start up the stairs.

78. CORRIDOR (NIGHT):

MARTINS opens a door at random and shuts it behind him. We can hear the three men go by. The room where he stands is in darkness. A curious moaning sound makes him turn to face whatever is in the room. He can see nothing and the sound has stopped. He makes a tiny movement and once more it starts, like an impeded break. He remains still and the sound dies away. Outside somebody calls.

TYLER'S VOICE: *Mr Martins. . . .*

Then a new sound starts. It is like somebody whispering — a long continuous monologue in the darkness.

MARTINS: *Is anybody there?*

The sound stops again. He can stand no more of it. He takes out his lighter. Footsteps go up and down the stairs. He scrapes and scrapes at his lighter in the dark, and something rattles in mid-air like a chain.

MARTINS with the anger of fear: *Is anybody there?*

[Only the click of metal answers him. MARTINS feels for a light switch, to his right and then to his left. He does not dare to go further because he can no longer locate his fellow occupant; the whisper, the moaning, the click have all stopped. Then he is afraid that he has lost the door and feels wildly for the knob. He begins to be far less afraid of the police than he is of the darkness. Somebody outside switches on the landing light, and the glow under the door gives MARTINS his direction.] He turns the light switch, and the eyes of a parrot chained to a perch stare beadily at him. Somebody turns the handle of the

149

door, and MARTINS has only just the time to turn the key. A hand beats on the door.

MARTINS sees an open window behind the parrot. He tries to avoid the parrot; it snaps at him, as he squeezes by, and wounds his hand. MARTINS reaches the window and gets out, just as the door is forced open.

79. EVADING. STREETS. LOCATION (NIGHT):

These shots show MARTINS evading his pursuers. He manages to get to the International Police Headquarters over bomb-sites.

80. CALLOWAY'S OFFICE (NIGHT):

MARTINS sits gloomily in front of CALLOWAY. He has bound up his left hand, where the parrot bit him, with a handkerchief.

CALLOWAY furiously: *I told you to go away, Martins. This isn't Santa Fe, I'm not a sheriff, and you aren't a cowboy. . . . You've been wanted for murder, you've been associating with suspicious characters. . . .*

MARTINS: *Put down drunk and disorderly too.*

CALLOWAY: *I have. What's the matter with your hand?*

MARTINS: *A parrot bit me.*

CALLOWAY looks up sharply and then lets it go. He rings a bell. PAINE enters.

CALLOWAY: *Give me the Harry Lime file, Paine, and better give Mr Martins a double whisky.*

PAINE very efficiently does both.

MARTINS: *I don't need your drinks, Callaghan.*

CALLOWAY: *You will. I don't want another murder in this case, and you were born to be murdered, so you're going to hear the facts.*

MARTINS: *You haven't told me a single one yet.*

CALLOWAY: [*You're going to hear plenty now, I suppose*] *you've heard of penicillin.*

MARTINS: *Well?*

CALLOWAY: *In Vienna there hasn't been enough penicillin to go round. So a nice trade started here. Stealing penicillin from the military hospitals, diluting it to make it go further, selling it to patients. Do you see what that means?*

MARTINS: *So you're too busy chasing a few tubes of penicillin to investigate a murder.*

CALLOWAY: *These* were *murders. Men with gangrened legs, women in childbirth. And there were children too. They used some of this diluted penicillin against meningitis. The lucky children died, the unlucky ones went off their heads. You can see them now in the mental ward. That was the racket Harry Lime organized.*

MARTINS: *Callaghan, you haven't shown me one shred of evidence.*

CALLOWAY: *We're coming to that.* He crosses and pulls a curtain over the window. *A magic lantern show, Paine.*

PAINE fetches a lantern, pulls down a sheet, and turns out the light. While he is doing this, CALLOWAY cheerfully changes the subject.

CALLOWAY: *You know, Paine's one of your devoted readers. He's promised to lend me — what is it? ' The Lone Rider '?*

MARTINS does not reply.

PAINE: *' I'd Like to See Texas Before I Die ', sir.*

MARTINS' nerves give way.

MARTINS: *Show me what you've got to show and let me get out.*

PAINE works the slides. The first slide is of a man caught unawares by the camera — HARBIN. He is talking to some friends.

[CALLOWAY: *We put the screws on one of the racketeers' agents, an orderly in a military hospital. That's him. A chap called Harbin. He led us to Kurtz and Lime. Next, Paine.*

The next slide is the photostat of a note which is signed by HARRY LIME.

CALLOWAY: *Can you identify that?*

MARTINS: *It's Harry's hand.*

CALLOWAY: *You see what I mean?*

A world is beginning to come to an end for MARTINS; a world of easy friendship, hero-worship, confidence that had begun twenty years before . . . but he will not admit it. He sips his whisky. . . .

MARTINS: *It* looks *like Harry's hand. But people are framed sometimes, Callaghan, even by the police. Why should Harry do a thing like that?*

CALLOWAY: *For seventy pounds a tube.*][64]

MARTINS: *I'd like a word with your agent, Harbin.*

CALLOWAY: *So would I.*

151

MARTINS: *Bring him in then.*
CALLOWAY: *I can't. He disappeared a week ago.*
MARTINS: *That's convenient.* [*A missing man, witness against a dead man.*][65]
CALLOWAY: *We have better witnesses.*
Dissolve.

81. MONTAGE (NIGHT):

Microscope — finger prints, threads from coat, files about Lime — still photographs — and MARTINS' reaction to all this. Dissolve. (*Still*)

82. CALLOWAY'S OFFICE (NIGHT):

CALLOWAY is dropping a pile of photographs on his desk. MARTINS is sunk in a chair. He has nothing to say; he is convinced.[66]

CALLOWAY kindly: *You see how it is, Martins.* MARTINS gets up and drinks his whisky. *Go back to bed, and keep out of trouble. You're all right in the hotel,* [*and I'll try to fix things with the Austrian police,*] *but I can't be responsible for you on the streets.*
MARTINS: *I'm not asking you to be.*
CALLOWAY: *I'm sorry, Martins.*
MARTINS: [*Awkward. Sorry. What a vocabulary you English have got.*][67]

He goes. CALLOWAY picks up the receiver.
CALLOWAY: *Get me the Austrian Police H.Q.*

While he waits for the call to come through, BRODSKY enters.
BRODSKY: *Can I have that passport? The Schmidt one?*

It lies on CALLOWAY's desk. He pushes it with a ruler towards BRODSKY.
CALLOWAY: *We're not going to pick her up for that, are we?*
BRODSKY: [*We treat these things more seriously, and your colleagues have agreed.*][68]

BRODSKY exits with passport. Dissolve.[69]

[83. SACHER'S HOTEL, RECEPTION DESK (NIGHT):

MARTINS goes up to the desk.
MARTINS: *256, please.*

PORTER: *I'm afraid your room has been cancelled, sir.*
MARTINS: *Cancelled?*
PORTER: *We received instructions, sir, from Captain Carter. They need the room.*
MARTINS: *What can I do?*
PORTER: *Captain Carter suggested you could sleep in the lounge for tonight.* MARTINS looks in the lounge, full of officers and their wives. *It will be quieter after one, sir. I'll find you a blanket.*
MARTINS: *It's a drink I need.*

84. SACHER'S BAR (NIGHT):

CARTER and TOMBS stand at the bar, glasses in hand.
TOMBS: *Don't look round, old chap. It's that fellow. We don't want a scene.*
MARTINS pushes by to the bar, and pulls out a dollar note.
BARMAN: *We aren't allowed to take those, sir.*
MARTINS: *Be a good fellow and change me one note.*
BARMAN: *I'm sorry, sir. It's against the rules.*
MARTINS: *But what can I do for money?*
The BARMAN whispers in his ear as he leads him to the door.
Dissolve.

85. THE ORIENTAL. LOCATION (NIGHT):

An International Police car drives up and the patrol enters through a door marked: ' Out of Bounds to Allied Personnel '.

86. THE ORIENTAL. BAR AND DANCE FLOOR (NIGHT):

The patrol enters. It is a dreary, smoky little night club. The same semi-nude photographs on the stairs, the same half-drunk Americans at the bar, the same bad wine and extra-ordinary gins — one might be in any third-rate night haunt in any other shabby capital of a shabby Europe. A waiter is hand-ing out a large pile of notes to MARTINS. The cabaret is on, and the International Patrol waits and takes a look at the scene. The Americans at the bar never stir, and nobody interferes with them. The cabaret comes to an end. MARTIN rises. One of the dance girls, who has been watching the waiter give him the notes, comes up and speaks to him.

153

DANCE GIRL: *It's early, dear.*
MARTINS: *What? What did you say?*
DANCE GIRL puzzled: *It's early.*

He looks at her as if he does not understand a word, and goes to the stairs. Then he comes back to the GIRL who is watching him.

MARTINS: *Did you ever know a fellow called Lime?*
DANCE GIRL: *No. Did you?*

MARTINS shakes his head, less as if he were saying no than getting something out of his hair. Dissolve.

87. EMPTY CLUB (NIGHT):

The seats are being piled up and a waiter and a girl are quietly pushing MARTINS out.

88. ANNA'S STREET (NIGHT):

MARTINS is walking unsteadily in the street. The rain is dripping from gutters, but he has not bothered to put on a coat.

89. ANNA'S LANDING (NIGHT):

MARTINS knocks on the door and ANNA opens it. She is in a dressing-gown.

ANNA: *What is it? What's happened to you?*
MARTINS: *I've found out everything.*
ANNA: *Come in. You don't want to wake the house.*][70]

90. ANNA'S ROOM (NIGHT):

ANNA: *Now, what is it? I thought you were going to keep away. Are the police after you?*
MARTINS: *I don't know.*
ANNA: *You're drunk, aren't you?*
MARTINS sulkily: *A bit.* Angrily. *I'm sorry.*[71]
[ANNA: *Why? Wish I had a drink.*
MARTINS: *I've been with Calloway. Learnt everything. We were both wrong.*
ANNA: *You'd better tell me.*

She sits down on the bed and he begins to tell her, swaying

154

slightly with his back to the window.

MARTINS: *You know what penicillin does.*

ANNA: *Not really.*

MARTINS: *It's supposed to cure people of things. They've been steal-ing penicillin here, mixing it with water, I don't know what. People have been dying from it — wounded people, children. I suppose they were all in it — Kurtz, Tyler — even that doctor.*]

He goes to the window, and turns again to her. Over his shoulder we look down into the dark street.

91. ANNA'S STREET. LOCATION (NIGHT):

Somebody looks up at the lighted window. The shadow of a bombed building falls across his face so that we cannot see it. He walks towards a door and stands in the shadow — we can-not see him — a cat walks across from the other side of the road in his direction — it is mewing.

92. DOORWAY. LOCATION (NIGHT):

The cat comes to the man's legs — purring, it rubs itself around the bottom of his trouser-leg — it is hungry.

93. ANNA'S ROOM (NIGHT):

[MARTINS: *I'm not a doctor: I don't understand it all, except Harry made seventy pounds a tube — he ran the business.*

ANNA looks away from the laughing, cheery photograph of HARRY.

ANNA: *You were sober when they told you? They really proved it?*

MARTINS: *Yes. So you see, that was Harry.*

ANNA puts her hand over her eyes.]

ANNA: *He's better dead. I thought perhaps he was mixed up . . . but not with that.*

MARTINS getting up and walking about: *For twenty years — I knew him — the drinks he liked, the girls he liked. We laughed at the same things. He couldn't bear the colour green. But it wasn't true. He never existed, we dreamed him. Was he laughing at fools like us all the time?*

ANNA sadly: *He liked to laugh.*

MARTINS bitterly: *Seventy pounds a tube. And he asked me to write about his great medical charity. [I suppose he wanted a Press Agent.] Maybe I could have raised the price to eighty pounds.*

[ANNA: *There are so many things you don't know about a person you love, good things, bad things.*

MARTINS: *But to cash in like that. . . .*]

ANNA angrily: *For heaven's sake, stop making him in your image. Harry was real. He wasn't just your friend and my lover. He was Harry.*

MARTINS: *Don't talk wisdom at me. You make it sound as if his manners were occasionally bad. . . . I don't know. . . . I'm just a bad writer who drinks too much and falls in love with girls . . .* [*lots of girls*] *. . . you.*

ANNA: *Me?*

MARTINS: *Don't be such a fool — you know I love you?*

ANNA: *If you'd rung me up and asked me, were you dark or fair or had a moustache, I wouldn't have known.*

MARTINS: *Can't you get him out of your head?*

ANNA: *No.*

MARTINS: *I'm leaving Vienna. I don't care if Kurtz killed Harry or Tyler — or the third man. Whoever killed him, it was justice. Maybe I'd have killed him myself.*

ANNA: *A man doesn't alter because you find out more about him.*

MARTINS: *I hate the way you talk. I've got a splitting headache, and you talk and talk. . . .* [*You make me cross.*]

Suddenly ANNA laughs.

[ANNA: *You come here at three in the morning — a stranger — and say you love me. Then you get angry and pick a quarrel. What do you expect me to do?*]

MARTINS: *I haven't seen you laugh before. Do it again.* [*I like it.*]

ANNA staring through him: *There isn't enough for two laughs.*

MARTINS takes her by the shoulder and shakes her gently.

MARTINS: *I'd make comic faces all day long. I'd stand on my head and grin at you between my legs. I'd learn a lot of jokes* [*from the books on After Dinner Speaking. . . . I'd. . . .*]

ANNA stares at him without speaking.

MARTINS hopelessly: [*You still love Harry, don't you?*][72]

[ANNA picking up the copy of her play: *I've got to learn my lines.*

156

ANNA looks through the pages of her script and back to MAR-TINS. MARTINS drops his hands. As he goes towards the door, he turns and makes half an apology, half an accusation.]
MARTINS: *You told me to find a girl.*
Dissolve.

94. ANNA'S STREET. LOCATION (NIGHT):

MARTINS walks rapidly away. Passing along the street, he becomes aware of a figure in a doorway on the opposite side. The whole figure is in darkness except for the points of the shoes. MARTINS stops and stares while the silent, motionless figure in the dark street stares back at him. MARTINS' nerves are on edge. Is this one of CALLOWAY's men, or TYLER's, or the Austrian police?
[MARTINS sharply: *Do you want anything?*
No reply. MARTINS takes a few steps on and then turns again.]
MARTINS: *Have you been following me? Who's your boss?* Still no reply. MARTINS is irascible with drink. He calls out sharply. *Can't you answer?*[8]
A window curtain opposite is drawn back and a sleepy voice shouts angrily to him.
WOMAN: *Seien Sie ruhig. Gehen Sie weiter.* (*Be quiet. Go away.*)
The light shines across, straight on the other man's face.
MARTINS: *Harry!*
MARTINS, in his amazement, hesitates on the edge of the pavement. The woman has slammed down the window and the figure is again in darkness, except for the shoe-caps. Then it begins to emerge, but before MARTINS has a chance of seeing the face again, an International Police car approaches down the street. The figure steps back, and as the car comes between them, the figure makes off in the dark. By the time the car has passed, there is no sign of the stranger — only the sound of footsteps. MARTINS pursues, but the sound dies out. He passes a kiosk and comes out into a fairly well-lighted square which is completely empty. He stands around in bewilderment, unable to decide whether he was drunk, whether he had seen a ghost, or indeed HARRY.
Dissolve.

95. KIOSK SQUARE. LOCATION (NIGHT):

CALLOWAY stands looking at the square with MARTINS and PAINE.

[MARTINS: *You don't believe me. . . .*

CALLOWAY: *No.*]

MARTINS: *It ran up here and vanished.*

They stare at the empty moonlit square. PAINE and CALLOWAY exchange glances.

CALLOWAY: *Where were you when you saw it first?*

MARTINS: *Down there — fifty yards away.*

CALLOWAY turns his back on the square and looks down the street, past the kiosk.

CALLOWAY: *Which side of the road?*

MARTINS: *This one. And there aren't any side turnings.*

They begin to walk down the street.

CALLOWAY: *Doorways. . . .*

MARTINS: *But I could hear it running ahead of me.*

They reach the kiosk.

CALLOWAY: *And it vanished with a puff of smoke, I suppose, and a clap of. . . .* He breaks off as his eye lights on the kiosk. He walks across to it, pulls open the door. We see the little curling staircase going down. *It wasn't German gin, Paine.*

CALLOWAY leads the way down, shining a torch ahead.

96. THE SEWERS. LOCATION (NIGHT):

A strange world unknown to most of us lies under our feet: a cavernous land of waterfalls and rushing rivers, where tides ebb and flow as in the world above. The main sewer, half as wide as the Thames, rushes by under a huge arch, fed by tributary streams. These streams have fallen in waterfalls from higher levels and have been purified in their falls, so that only in these side channels is the air foul. The main stream smells sweet and fresh with a faint tang of ozone, and everywhere in the darkness is the sound of falling and rushing water.

MARTINS: *What is it?*

CALLOWAY without replying moves ahead, across a bridge which spans a waterfall.

PAINE: *It's only the main sewer, sir. Smells sweet, don't it?* [*They*

158

used it as an air-raid shelter in the war, just like our old tube.]⁷⁴

They come up with CALLOWAY who is leaning over the bridge.

CALLOWAY: [*I've been a fool.*] *We should have dug deeper than a grave.* Dissolve.

97. CENTRAL CEMETERY. LOCATION (DAWN):

[A small group makes its way down an avenue of graves. At the end of the avenue three men are engaged in digging. The group consists of CALLOWAY, a British JUNIOR OFFICER, MARTINS, an Austrian POLICE OFFICER, and an OFFICIAL from the City Council, who carries an umbrella. The group pass the graves of Beethoven, Schubert, and Brahms, and CALLOWAY pauses just long enough for us to take in their inscriptions. As they approach LIME'S grave, thin rain begins to fall, and the Austrian OFFICIAL opens his umbrella and offers to share it with CALLOWAY.] One of the men comes over to CALLOWAY and speaks in German.

MAN: *Wir sind jetzt am Sarg. (We've reached the coffin.)*

CALLOWAY to OFFICIAL: *Tell them to take off the lid.*

CALLOWAY and the OFFICIAL, still under the same umbrella, go up to the graveside and stand looking down. The OFFICIAL moves round the side of the grave to examine the body from another angle. He turns across the grave to CALLOWAY and shrugs his shoulders. CALLOWAY takes one look and moves away, passing MARTINS. He nods to MARTINS to take a look. MARTINS reluctantly does so, then quickly joins CALLOWAY as they walk away.

OFFICIAL: *Did you know him, Colonel?*

CALLOWAY: *Yes. Joseph Harbin, medical orderly at the 43rd General Hospital.* To JUNIOR OFFICER. *Next time we'll have a fool-proof coffin.*⁷⁵ Dissolve.

98. INTERNATIONAL POLICE H.Q. (DAWN):

A doorway marked 'International Police' in three languages. Through the door comes BRODSKY with ANNA's passport. He crosses over the hallway and out into the yard where the International Police car is waiting. He goes up to the car and the Russian member of the patrol gets out and joins him. He speaks to him. Dissolve.

99. ANNA'S STREET. LOCATION (DAWN).

The International Police Patrol drives up and, leaving an Austrian policeman in the car, enters the building.

100. STAIRCASE AND LANDING (DAWN):

The four men run up the stairs, the BRITISH M.P. leading. At ANNA's door, the BRITISH M.P. tries the handle. The RUSSIAN M.P. pushing forward, puts his shoulder to it and breaks in. ANNA has not had time to get out of bed.

101. ANNA'S ROOM (DAWN):

ANNA: [*Was ist es?* (*What is it?*)]

RUSSIAN M.P.: *Sie müssen mit uns kommen.* (*You must come with us.*)[76]

ANNA to the BRITISH and AMERICAN M.P.'s: *Have I got to go?*

BRITISH M.P.: *Sorry, miss, it's orders.*

RUSSIAN M.P. in bad German: *These your papers? Your papers?*
  He shows ANNA's passport. ANNA looks at them and up to the four men, realising there is nothing she can do.[77]

[ANNA: *Please tell him to go while I dress.*

AMERICAN M.P. to RUSSIAN M.P. in very bad German: *Komm in die Vorraum bis sie angezogen.* (*Come in the passage, while she gets her things on.*)

RUSSIAN M.P.: *Nein, nein.*

BRITISH M.P.: *I'm not staying here. Let the girl dress by herself.* He prepares to leave.

AMERICAN M.P.: *You can't leave a little goil alone with Rusky here. I'd better stay.*

BRITISH M.P. to FRENCH M.P.: *You coming, Froggy?* The FRENCH M.P. is amused and speaks in French.

FRENCH M.P.: *Qu'est-ce-ça fait?* (*What does it matter?*) *I will look after both of them.*

  The BRITISH M.P. goes out of the room. The AMERICAN M.P. stays in the room and keeps his back chivalrously turned, but he is restless and takes a bit of chewing-gum. The FRENCH M.P. thinks it fun, lights a cigarette and watches with detached, amused interest the attitude of the other two. The RUSSIAN

160

M.P. is just doing his duty and watches the girl closely all the time without sexual interest.]

102. ANNA'S LANDING (DAWN):

The BRITISH M.P. stands by the wall, yawning. The WOMAN who owns the house comes up and speaks to him in German.
WOMAN in German: *This happens every day. I am getting tired of the police.*
He does not understand a word and, to escape from her, goes back into the room.

103. ANNA'S ROOM (DAWN):

ANNA has finished dressing as the BRITISH M.P. enters.
ANNA: *Where are you taking me?*
AMERICAN M.P.: *International Police Headquarters for a check-up.*
[*The Russkies are claiming the body.*]
ANNA: *Body?*
AMERICAN M.P.: *Just an expression.*
The RUSSIAN M.P. listens suspiciously to their conversation.
BRITISH M.P.: *It's the law, miss. We can't go against the protocol.*
ANNA: *I don't even know what protocol means.*
BRITISH M.P.: *I don't either, miss.*
RUSSIAN M.P.: *Wir müssen gehen. (We must go.)*
ANNA picks up her bag. The RUSSIAN M.P. takes it away from her, looks rapidly through the contents, and then hands it back.
[FRENCH M.P.: *Mademoiselle, your lipstick.*
He picks her lipstick from the dressing-table and hands it to her. The BRITISH and AMERICAN M.P.s go ahead out of the room. The RUSSIAN next, then ANNA, then the FRENCH M.P., tall, undisturbed and uninterested, with his dangling cigarette. In the doorway ANNA suddenly turns and says hopelessly to the divan, the table, the walls. . . .
ANNA: *Good-bye.*
The RUSSIAN swings round with his gun pointing, but there is no one in the room. The FRENCH M.P. laughs. Dissolve.]

104. HALL. INTERNATIONAL POLICE H.Q. (DAWN):

MARTINS is by the stairs when the International Patrol brings

ANNA in.

MARTINS with astonishment: *Anna.*

AMERICAN M.P.: *You can't talk to the prisoner, son.*

MARTINS: *Why are you here?* ANNA shrugs her shoulders. *I've got to talk to you. I've just seen a dead man walking.*

ANNA looks up sharply. They begin to move up the stairs and MARTINS follows.

MARTINS: *I saw him buried, and now I've seen him alive.*

AMERICAN M.P.: *Please, Jock. . . . I don't want no trouble with you. . . .*

ANNA looks at MARTINS with excitement. She cannot bring herself to believe him.

ANNA: *You're drunk?*

MARTINS: *No.*

They come to the head of the stairs. CALLOWAY is about to enter his office — he sees the group who are about to pass by.

CALLOWAY: *One moment. . . . Bring the prisoner in here.*

He motions to the patrol to wait outside. The BRITISH M.P. jerks his hand for ANNA to enter and MARTINS tries to follow.

AMERICAN M.P.: *Not you.*

He pushes him away and the door is slammed on him.

105. CALLOWAY'S OFFICE (DAY):

ANNA is brought in. PAINE is in the office.

CALLOWAY: *Sit down, Miss Schmidt. The Russians have asked for you, but I'm not interested in your forged papers.*

She sits down. She is strung up with excitement at what she has heard from MARTINS. She is waiting to have her hopes confirmed or darkened.

CALLOWAY: *When did you last see Lime?*

ANNA: *Two weeks ago.* She waits hungrily for his next question.

CALLOWAY: *We want the truth, Miss Schmidt. . . . We know he's alive.*

ANNA with excitement and joy: *It is true, then?*

CALLOWAY: *The body of another man, Joseph Harbin, was found in the coffin.*

ANNA cannot attend to anything but this news.

ANNA: *What did you say? I didn't hear you. I'm sorry.*

CALLOWAY: *I said another man was buried in his place.*
ANNA: *Another man? Oh, yes . . . where's Harry?*
CALLOWAY: *That's what we want to find out.*
ANNA: *I'm sorry. I don't seem able to understand anything you say. But nothing matters now. He's [safe.]*[78]
[CALLOWAY: *I wouldn't say safe.*
ANNA: *He's alive. Now, this minute he's doing something. He's breathing.*]
CALLOWAY: *We are pretty sure, Miss Schmidt, that he's somewhere in the Russian sector, across the canal. Sooner or later we'll get him, even if the Russians don't co-operate. You may as well help us.*
ANNA: *Help you? Why?*
CALLOWAY: *The next man you have to deal with is Colonel Brodsky. Tell me where Lime is?*
ANNA: *I don't know. . . .*
CALLOWAY: *If you help us, we are prepared to help you.*
ANNA: *Martins always said you were a fool.*
CALLOWAY: *Miss Schmidt, Vienna is a closed city. [A rat would have more chance in a closed room without a hole and a pack of terriers loose.]*
ANNA: *Poor Harry.* All her joy has gone now. *I wish he was dead. He'd be safe from all of you then.*
CALLOWAY: *Better think about it.* He goes to the door and out.[79]

[106. HALL. INTERNATIONAL POLICE H.Q. (DAY):

MARTINS waits at the bottom of the staircase. CALLOWAY comes slowly down.
MARTINS: *What are you doing with her?*
CALLOWAY: *Her?* He is lost in thought. *Paine!* PAINE comes out from the side room.
PAINE: *Sir?*
MARTINS: *Anna, of course. What's going on?*
CALLOWAY: *The Russians claim the body, Martins.*
MARTINS: *You aren't going to hand her over?*
CALLOWAY: *Her papers are false.*
MARTINS: *Why, you double-timing. . . .*
CALLOWAY: *She's no concern of mine, Martins. It's Lime I want.*
MARTINS: *Damn Lime.*

CALLOWAY continues through the door with PAINE. Dissolve.

163

107. CASANOVA (DAY):

MARTINS enters and goes to the HEAD WAITER after vainly looking for KURTZ upon the floor, where a tea-dance is in progress.

MARTINS: *Is Baron von Kurtz here?*

HEAD WAITER: *I do not know the Baron.*

MARTINS: *Oh, yes, you do. He plays in your orchestra.*

HEAD WAITER: *The Baron von . . . ?*

MARTINS: *Kurtz. Kurtz.*

HEAD WAITER: *We have someone called Freddie Kurtz, but he hasn't turned up today.*

MARTINS: *With a toupée.*

HEAD WAITER: *That is right. His mother works in the cloakroom.*

As MARTINS goes up the stairs to the cloakroom, the door of the club opens and the International Patrol enters, accompanied by Austrian Police. The Austrians stand guard at the door, two M.P.'s go down to the dance floor and do a check of papers there. The others remain above.

108. CLOAKROOM (DAY):

A slatternly woman with a malevolent sour face is looking after the cloakroom.

AMERICAN M.P.: *Papers, please.*

She hands him her papers. MARTINS stands by watching.

AMERICAN M.P.: *Frau Kurtz?*

FRAU KURTZ: *Ja.*

She blows her nose with her fingers. Reaction on MARTINS, who expected to see an aristocratic woman turning her hand nobly to plebeian tasks.

BRITISH M.P. to MARTINS: *Passport, please sir.* He looks through it, and hands it back. *Where are you staying?*

MARTINS: *Nowhere. I've been turned out of the only room I had.*

BRITISH M.P.: *If you'll call at the station, we'll do what we can for you, sir.*

MARTINS: *You'll find me a bed, will you, but you can't find Harry Lime.*

The M.P. gives him a quick look and hands back the passport.

AMERICAN M.P.: *Give us time.*

The other M.P.'s have rejoined them and they go out together.
MARTINS turns to FRAU KURTZ.

MARTINS: *You really are Frau Kurtz?*

FRAU KURTZ: *Ja.*

MARTINS: *Sprechen Sie Englisch?*

FRAU KURTZ: *Little. Very little.*

MARTINS: *I know your son. I thought I'd find him here.*

FRAU KURTZ: *Freddie?*

MARTINS: *The Baron.*

FRAU KURTZ goes off into a peal of laughter, showing one long
dirty tooth like a fossil.

FRAU KURTZ: *Baron? His father was a butcher in Linz. He will be
home today. It is safer so, nein?*

Dissolve.

109. BRIDGE. LOCATION (DAY):

MARTINS walks up from the makeshift bridge over the canal,
past the sign which warns that one is entering the Russian zone,
and into the long, wide, dingy Praterstrasse. In a side-turning
are a number of big houses that have come down in the world
through bombing and abandonment. He consults his notebook
for KURTZ's address. MARTINS stops outside one house. The
bottom floor is gutted, and the doorway smashed in, but the first
floor is habitable. A balcony, half-broken away, is in front of
the windows. MARTINS bangs on the smashed door with his
fist, then finds a makeshift wire bell and pulls it. It jangles
somewhere above, and MARTINS steps back into the roadway
and waits. One of the windows opens and KURTZ looks out.
When he sees MARTINS, he comes forward cautiously onto the
smashed balcony.][80]

KURTZ: [*Why, Rollo, you?*] *Winkel, look who's here.*

WINKEL comes out and joins him on the balcony.

MARTINS: *I want to speak to you, Kurtz.*

KURTZ: *Of course.* [*Come in.*]

MARTINS: [*I'd rather stay where I am. You might be following your
father's profession.*][81]

KURTZ: *I don't understand. . . .*

MARTINS: [*I've been talking to your mother. Now*] *I want to talk to Harry, Kurtz.*

KURTZ: *Are you mad?*

MARTINS: [*Never mind that. Say I'm mad, say*] *I've seen a ghost. But you tell Harry I want to see him.*

[He looks around and sees, between the gap in the shelled houses, the Great Wheel in the fairground.]

KURTZ: *Be reasonable. Come up and talk.*

MARTINS: *I like the open.* [*I like crowds.*] *Tell him I'll wait by the Wheel for an hour. Or do ghosts only rise by night? Have you an opinion on that, Dr Winkel?*

DR WINKEL takes out his handkerchief and blows his nose. MARTINS walks away towards the Great Wheel. Dissolve.

110. THE GREAT WHEEL. PART LOCATION (DAY):

The Wheel on this cold autumn day is not popular, and the Prater itself has not recovered sufficiently from the shelling and bombing to attract crowds. A wrecked pleasure place, weeds growing up round the foundations of merry-go-rounds. In the enclosure one stall is selling big, thin, flat cakes like cart-wheels, and the children queue with coupons. A few courting couples wait and wait on the platform of the wheel, and then are packed into a single car and revolve slowly above the city with empty cars above and below them. As the loaded car reaches the highest point of the Wheel, the machinery stops for a couple of minutes and leaves them suspended. Looking up, MARTINS can see the tiny faces pressed like flies against a glass. He walks up and down to keep warm. He looks at his watch. (*Still*) The time is nearly up. Somewhere behind the cake stall, someone is whistling. MARTINS turns quickly. He watches for him to come into sight with fear and excitement. Life to MARTINS has always quickened when HARRY came; as he comes now, as though nothing much has really happened; with an amused geniality, a recognition that his happiness will make the world's day. Only sometimes the cheerfulness will be suddenly clouded; a melancholy will beat through his guard; a memory that this life does not go on. Now he does not make the mistake of offering a hand that might be rejected. Instead he just pats MARTINS on his bandaged hand.

HARRY: *How are things? They seem to have been messing you about a bit.*[82]

MARTINS: *We've got to talk, Harry.*

HARRY: *Of course, old man. This way.*

He walks straight on towards the platform, in the absolute confidence that MARTINS will follow.

MARTINS: *Alone.*

The Wheel has come round again, and one lot of passengers is getting out on the opposite platform as another enters the same car from their platform. HARRY has always known the ropes everywhere, so now he speaks apart to the PORTERESS, and money passes. The car with the passengers moves slowly up, an empty car passes, and then the Wheel stops long enough for them to get into the third car, which they have to themselves.

111. GREAT WHEEL. BACK PROJECTION (DAY):

HARRY: *We couldn't be more alone. Lovers used to do this in the old days, but they haven't the money to spare, poor devils, now.*

112. TOP SHOT FROM GREAT WHEEL (DAY):

He looks out of the window of the swaying, rising car at the figures diminishing below them, with what looks like genuine commiseration. Very slowly, on one side of them, the city sinks; very slowly on the other, the great cross girders of the Wheel rise into sight. As the horizon slides away, the Danube becomes visible, and the piers of the Reichsbrucke lift above the houses.

113. GREAT WHEEL. BACK PROJECTION (DAY):

HARRY turns from the window.

HARRY: *It's good to see you, Rollo.*

MARTINS: *I was at your funeral.*

HARRY: *That was pretty smart, wasn't it?*[83]

MARTINS: *You know what's happened to Anna? They've arrested her.*

HARRY: *Tough, very tough, but don't worry, old man. They won't hurt her.*

MARTINS: *They are handing her to the Russians. Can't you help her?*

167

HARRY unconvincingly: *What can I do, old man? I'm dead — aren't I? Who have you told about me?*

MARTINS: *The police — and Anna.*

HARRY: *Unwise, Rollo, unwise. Did they believe you?*

MARTINS: *You don't care a damn about her, do you?*

HARRY: *I've got a lot on my mind. (Still)*

MARTINS: *You won't do a thing to help her?*

HARRY: *What can I do, Rollo? Be reasonable. Give myself up? This is a far, far better thing. The old limelight and the fall of the curtain. We aren't heroes, Rollo, you and I. The world doesn't make heroes outside your books.*

MARTINS: *You have your contacts.*

HARRY: *I've got to be so careful. These Russians, Rollo — well, I'm safe so long as I have my uses.*

MARTINS with sudden realisation: *You informed on her.*

HARRY with a smile: *Don't become a policeman, old man.*

MARTINS: *I didn't believe the police when they told me about you. Were you going to cut me in on the spoils?*

HARRY: *I've never kept you out of anything, old man, yet.*

> HARRY stands with his back to the door, as the car swings upward, and smiles back at MARTINS.

MARTINS: *I remember that time at that Club, ' The 43 ', when the police raided it. You'd learnt a safe way out. Absolutely safe for you. It wasn't safe for me.*

HARRY: [*You always were a clumsy devil, Rollo.*][84]

MARTINS: *You've never grown up, Harry.*

HARRY: *Well, we shall be old for a very long time.*

MARTINS: *Have you ever seen any of your victims?*

> HARRY takes a look at the toy landscape below and comes away from the door.

HARRY: *I never feel quite safe in these things.* He feels the door with his hands. *Victims? Don't be melodramatic. Look down there.*

114. TOP SHOT FROM GREAT WHEEL. LOCATION (NIGHT):

He points through the window at the people moving like black flies at the base of the Wheel.

115. GREAT WHEEL. BACK PROJECTION (DAY):

HARRY: *Would you really feel any pity if one of those dots stopped moving for ever? If I said you can have twenty thousand pounds for every dot that stops, would you really, old man, tell me to keep my money — or would you calculate how many dots you could afford to spare? Free of income tax, old man. Free of income tax.* He gives his boyish, conspiratorial smile. *It's the only way to save nowadays.*

MARTINS: [*You're finished now. The police know everything.*]⁸⁵

HARRY: *But they can't catch me, Rollo. They can't come in the Russian Zone.*

[The car swings to a standstill at the highest point of the curve, and HARRY turns his back and gazes out of the window. MARTINS draws his arms back; he thinks one good shove would be strong enough to break the glass. His arms drop again.

MARTINS: *The police have dug up your coffin.*

HARRY: *I couldn't trust Harbin. Look at the sunset, Rollo.*

MARTINS looking at the sunset: *You know I love Anna.*

HARRY: *That's fine, old man. If she gets out of this hole, be kind to her. She's worth it.*

He gives the impression of having arranged everything to everybody's satisfaction.

MARTINS: *I'd like to knock you through the window.*

HARRY: *But you won't, old man. Our quarrels never lasted long. You remember that time in The Monaco? Kurtz tried to persuade me to, well, arrange an accident.*

MARTINS: *It wouldn't be easy.*

HARRY: *I carry a gun. You don't think they'd look for a bullet wound after you hit that ground.*]⁸⁶

Again the car begins to move, sailing slowly down, until the flies become midgets, and recognisable human beings.

HARRY: *What fools we are, Rollo, talking like this, as if I'd do that to you — or you to me.* Deliberately he turns his back and leans his face against the glass. *In these days, old man, nobody thinks in terms of human beings. Governments don't, so why should we? They talk of the people and the proletariat, and I talk of the mugs. It's the same thing. They have their five year plans and so have I.*

MARTINS: *You used to believe in a God.*

That shade of melancholy crosses HARRY's face.

HARRY: *Oh, I still* believe, *old man. In God and Mercy and all that. The dead are happier dead. They don't miss much here, poor devils.*
As he speaks the last words with an odd touch of genuine pity, the car reaches the platform and the faces of the doomed-to-be-victims peer in at them.[87]
HARRY: *I'd like to cut you in, you know. We always did things together, Rollo. I've no one left in Vienna I can really trust.*
[MARTINS: *Tyler? Winkel, Kurtz?*
HARRY: *The police are on to all of them now.*

116. GREAT WHEEL. LOCATION (DAY):

They pass out of the car and HARRY puts his hand again on MARTINS' elbow.
HARRY: *Have you heard anything of old Bracer recently?*
MARTINS: *I had a card at Christmas.*
HARRY: *Those were the days, old man. Those were the days.*
MARTINS: *You'd really cut me in, would you?*
HARRY: *There's plenty for two — with the others gone. Think it over, old man. Send me a message through Kurtz. I'll meet you anywhere, any time.*
He has written the number on the back of an envelope. MARTINS holds it in his hand.
HARRY: *So long, Rollo.*
He turns to go, and MARTINS calls after him.
MARTINS: *And Anna — you won't do a thing to help?*
HARRY: *If I could, old man, of course. But my hands are tied.* When he is a little further away, he suddenly comes back. *If we meet again, Rollo, it's you I want to see, and not the police. Remember, won't you?*
MARTINS stands there watching the figure disappear. Dissolve.][88]

117. CALLOWAY'S OFFICE (DAY):

CALLOWAY is standing with his back to MARTINS, studying a map of Vienna.
CALLOWAY: [*We'd choose the right spot.*][89]
MARTINS: *It wouldn't work.*
CALLOWAY: *We'll never get him in the Russian Zone.*

MARTINS: *You expect too much, Callaghan. Oh, I know he deserves to hang. You've proved your stuff. But twenty [five] years is a long time. Don't ask me to tie the rope.*[90]

MARTINS moves up and down as he speaks. The door opens and Colonel BRODSKY enters.

CALLOWAY: *Evening, Brodsky. Anything I can do?*

BRODSKY: *We've identified the girl.*

CALLOWAY: *I've questioned her. We've got nothing against her.*

BRODSKY: *We shall apply for her at the Four Power meeting tomorrow.*[91]

During their talk we watch MARTINS' reactions.

CALLOWAY: *I've asked your people to help with Lime.*

BRODSKY: *This is a different case. It is being looked into.*

As he goes, he drops ANNA's passport on CALLOWAY's desk and smiles.

[BRODSKY: *It is very clever, but I thought I could rely on my information. Good-night, colonel.*

CALLOWAY: *Good-night.*

CALLOWAY looks down at on open file which has a photograph of LIME in it.]

CALLOWAY: *In the last war a general would hang his opponent's picture on the wall. He got to know him that way. I'm beginning to know Lime, and I think this would have worked. With your help.*

MARTINS: *What price would you pay?*

CALLOWAY: *Name it.*

Dissolve.

118. VIENNA RAILWAY STATION BUFFET. BACK PROJECTION (NIGHT):

A clock shows 8.15 p.m. Atmosphere and description must be left for location. [MARTINS is standing, glass in hand, in the crowded buffet. The windows are frosted up, but whenever the door opens, the clang and clatter of the station and the steam of the engines blows in. ANNA and PAINE enter. MARTINS sees them, puts down his glass and begins to worm his way out. He does not want to be seen.

PAINE: *Well, miss, you'll be having breakfast in the British Zone. You needn't fear the Russkies with those papers.*

ANNA: *I don't understand a thing.*

PAINE: *If I picked up a pound note, miss, I'd put it quick in my pocket, no questions asked. I'll be saying good-night.*

ANNA: *Good-night. Thank you. How kind you've been.*

> PAINE goes out. ANNA looks at the ticket and papers he has given her, and then across the buffet. She sees MARTINS making for another door. Suspicions of what she does not yet know, come to her. MARTINS looks back and meets her gaze — uneasily. He stops. Slowly she thrusts her way through the crowd at the buffet to his side.

ANNA: *What are you doing here?*][92]

MARTINS: *I wanted to see you safely off.* Defiantly. *There's no harm in that, is there?*

ANNA: *How did you know I'd be here?*

> MARTINS sees he has made a mistake and becomes evasive.

MARTINS: *Oh, I heard something about it at Police H.Q.*

ANNA: *Have you been seeing Colonel Calloway?*

MARTINS: *No. I don't live in his pocket.*

ANNA: *Harry, what is it?*

MARTINS: *For heaven's sake, don't call me Harry again.*

ANNA: *I'm sorry.*

LOUDSPEAKER: *Passengers for Klagenfurt take their seats, please.*

> The loudspeaker repeats it in French, German and Russian, while the dialogue goes on.

MARTINS: *It's time to be off, Anna.*

ANNA: *What's on your mind, Rollo? Why did you avoid me just now?*

MARTINS: *I didn't see you. Anna, you* must *come along.*

> He urges her through the buffet door.

119. RAILWAY PLATFORM. BACK PROJECTION (NIGHT):

> Reluctantly, scenting a mystery, ANNA follows MARTINS towards the train.

MARTINS: *Only six hours. It's going to be cold. Take my coat.*

ANNA: *I shall be all right.*

> MARTINS begins to take off his coat.

MARTINS: *Send me a wire from Klagenfurt when you are safe.*

ANNA: *Are you staying in Vienna?*

172

MARTINS evasively: *A day or two.* He puts his coat round ANNA [and opens a compartment door.] *Jump in, my dear.*

ANNA: *What's going to happen? Where is he?*

MARTINS: *Safe in the Russian Zone. I saw him today.*

ANNA: *You saw him?*

MARTINS: *Oh yes, we talked and he laughed a lot. Like the old days.*

ANNA: *How is he?*

MARTINS: *He can look after himself. Don't worry.*

ANNA: *Did he say anything about me?*

MARTINS: *Oh, the usual things.*

ANNA: *What?*

[MARTINS: *He's untouchable, Anna. Why, he even wanted to cut me in.*

Doors of compartments are being slammed. A PORTER approaches.

PORTER: *Please get in.*]

MARTINS: *Good-bye, Anna.*

ANNA: *I don't want to go.*

MARTINS: *You must.*

ANNA: *There's something wrong. Did you tell Calloway about your meeting?*

MARTINS: *No. Of course, not.*

ANNA: *Why should Calloway be helping me like this? The Russians will make trouble.*

MARTINS: *That's his headache.*

[A SOLDIER comes up to him.

SOLDIER: *Colonel Calloway's compliments, sir, and the car's waiting. We've got to get started.*

ANNA: *Why did you lie? . . . What are you two doing?*]

MARTINS: *We're getting you out of here.*

ANNA: *I'm not going.*

MARTINS: *You must.* He puts his hand on her arm as though to force her into the carriage. [*You are more important than a crook like that. Get in.*

She shakes herself free.

ANNA: *What are you doing?*

MARTINS angrily, his nerves breaking: *They want my help and I'm giving it them.*

ANNA: *The police?*

173

MARTINS: *For pete's sake get in.*

ANNA: *And you have the nerve to talk about love. Love for me, love for Harry. How do you spell the word?*

MARTINS: *I asked him to help you, and he wouldn't lift a finger. He called you a good little thing, and said the Russians wouldn't hurt you.*

ANNA: *Poor Harry.*

MARTINS: *Why in heaven's name, poor Harry?*]⁹³

ANNA: *Oh, you've got your precious honesty, and don't want anything else.*

MARTINS fiercely: *I suppose you still want him.*

ANNA: *I don't want him any more. I don't want to see him, hear him. But he's in me — that's a fact. I wouldn't do a thing to harm him.*⁹⁴

[She takes the ticket and her papers and tears them into scraps. MARTINS watches her with gloomy acquiescence.]

ANNA: *I loved him. You loved him, and what good have we done him? Oh love! Look at yourself in the window — they have a name for faces like that . . .*⁹⁵ [*informers.*

MARTINS stares into the window of the compartment.

MARTINS: *You talk too much.*

A long silence follows. When he turns his head again she has gone. His coat lies at his feet. As he stoops to pick it up, the train begins to pull out. Dissolve.]

120. CALLOWAY'S OFFICE (NIGHT):

CALLOWAY and MARTINS are together. CALLOWAY stands with his back to MARTINS, his eyes on the map of Vienna.

MARTINS: *I want to catch the first plane out of here.*

CALLOWAY: *So she talked you round?*

MARTINS holding out the scraps of paper: *She gave me these.*

CALLOWAY sourly: *A girl of spirit.*

MARTINS: *She's right. It's none of my business.*

CALLOWAY: *It won't make any difference in the long run. I shall get him.*

MARTINS: *I won't have helped.*

CALLOWAY: *That will be a fine boast to make* [*to your children.*]
He puts his finger on the map as though he is still planning LIME's

174

capture. Then he shrugs and turns to MARTINS. *Oh, well, I always wanted you to catch that plane, didn't I?*
MARTINS: *You all did.*
CALLOWAY going to the telephone: *I'd better see if anyone's at the terminus still. You may need a priority.*
Dissolve.

121. CALLOWAY'S CAR. BACK PROJECTION (NIGHT):

PAINE is driving. CALLOWAY is sitting in silence. MARTINS beside him.
CALLOWAY: *Mind if I drop off somewhere on the way? I've got an appointment. Won't take five minutes.*
MARTINS nods. They draw up outside a large public building.
CALLOWAY: *Why don't you come in too! You're a writer, it should interest you.*
Dissolve.

122. CHILDREN'S HOSPITAL (NIGHT):

As they come through the doors, a NURSE passes and MARTINS realises he has been shanghaied, but it is too late to do anything.
[CALLOWAY: *I want to take a look in No. 3 Ward.*
NURSE: *That's all right, Colonel Calloway.*
CALLOWAY to MARTINS: *You've been in on this story so much, you ought to see the end of it.*]

123. CHILDREN'S WARD (NIGHT):

He pushes open a door and, with a friendly hand, propels MARTINS down the ward, talking as he goes in a cheerful, professional, apparently heartless way. We take a rapid view of the six small beds, but we do not see the occupants, only the effect of horror on MARTINS' face.
CALLOWAY: *This is the biggest children's hospital in Vienna* [*— very efficient place. In this ward we have six examples — you can't really call them children now, can you? — of the use of the Lime penicillin in meningitis. . . . Here in this bed is a particularly fascinating — example, if you are interested in the medical history of morons . . . now here. . . .*

175

MARTINS: *For pete's sake, stop talking. Will you do me a favour and turn it off?*]⁹⁶

As they continue their walk past the small beds, dissolve.

124. CALLOWAY'S CAR. BACK PROJECTION (NIGHT):

They are driving together again in CALLOWAY's car. MARTINS is not speaking.

CALLOWAY: [*For a good read I like a Western.*] *Paine's lent me several of your books. ' The Lone Rider ' seemed a bit drawn out — you don't mind my talking frankly, do you? But I thought the plot of ' Dead Man's Reach ' was pretty good. You certainly know how to tell an exciting story.*

MARTINS sullenly: *All right, Callaghan, you win.*

CALLOWAY: *I didn't know they had snake charmers in Texas.*

MARTINS: *I said you win.*

CALLOWAY: *Win what?*

MARTINS: *I'll be your dumb decoy duck.*

Dissolve.

125. CAFE (NIGHT):

A thin drizzling rain falls and the windows of the café continually cloud with steam. MARTINS sits gloomily, drinking cup after cup of coffee, and the clock in the café points to a quarter past midnight. There are only two other people in the café. Once, as somebody opens the door of the café, we see MARTINS put a hand to his pocket and we are aware that he has a revolver there.

126. CAFE STREET. LOCATION (NIGHT):

Outside the café, preparations are being made for HARRY's capture; the kiosk and the empty rain-wet street, and then at discreet intervals, well away from the scene, groups of POLICE.

127. SQUARE (WITH MANHOLE IN DISTANCE). LOCATION (NIGHT):

Last, under the trees of a square, sheltering as well as they can from the rain, CALLOWAY, PAINE and a group of SEWER POLICE:

men with peaked caps, rather like lumberjacks, with big thigh-length boots; one man has a small searchlight hung on his chest; all carry revolvers. A manhole in the square is ready open.[97]

[128. TELEPHONE BOX. LOCATION (NIGHT):

A telephone begins to ring in a nearby box, and CALLOWAY answers it. Only half of the conversation is heard, but we can gather MARTINS is on the other end.
CALLOWAY: *I told you to keep away from the telephone unless it was urgent. I don't care if you've drunk twenty cups. They'll help to keep you awake.*

129. CAFE SQUARE. LOCATION (NIGHT):

He goes disgruntedly back to PAINE.
CALLOWAY: *He's getting tired of it already, and he's only had two hours. Listen, Paine, get back to the office, slip on civvies, and go along to him. He'll be doing something foolish. Don't forget your gun.*]

130. ROOF TOP. LOCATION (NIGHT):

We see HARRY beside a chimney stack, silhouetted by bombed ruins against the sky, looking grimly down. From this angle, the square seems deserted. Then he turns and watches the window of the café.
[MARTINS returns to his table from the telephone. HARRY moves forward.]

131. CAFE (NIGHT):

[MARTINS to WAITER: *Coffee, more coffee.*
The clock stands at 12.45. MARTINS rubs the pane free from steam and peers out at the dreary empty street. Then he turns again and sips disconsolately at his coffee. He is divided in mind: between the sight he saw in the hospital of HARRY'S victims, and the consciousness of the role he is himself playing as decoy to his friend. The door of the café creaks, and his hand again goes to his pocket. A girl in a wet mackintosh comes in. It is ANNA.

177

MARTINS: *So it's you.*

ANNA: *It's me. You can take your hand away.*

> She sits down at the table between him and the door, and he sheepishly withdraws his hand with a packet of cigarettes.

MARTINS: *I was only looking for a cigarette.*

ANNA: *How much longer are you going to sit here?*

MARTINS: *Until I'm tired of it.*

ANNA: *Harry won't come. He's not a fool.*

MARTINS: *I wonder.*

ANNA: *What's your price this time?*

MARTINS: *No price, Anna.*

ANNA: *Honest, sensible, sober, harmless Rollo Martins. You are sober, aren't you?*

MARTINS: *They only serve coffee.*

> The door creaks again and he puts his hand to his pocket. He tries to see, but ANNA is between him and the door.

MARTINS: *Get away.*

ANNA: *No.*

> But it is only an OLD WOMAN selling bootlaces.

MARTINS: *I'll have you thrown out.*

> MARTINS gets up and goes to the telephone behind the bar. ANNA follows him. MARTINS dials and waits with his eyes on ANNA. Unseen by both of them, HARRY suddenly appears — not through the main door, but by the back way. He grins when he sees MARTINS by the telephone.

MARTINS: *Is that Calloway? Listen. Anna's here. I can't get her to move.*

> They turn and see HARRY.

ANNA: *Harry! Run, the police.*

MARTINS into the receiver: *He's here, Calloway.*

> HARRY brings out his gun.

ANNA: *No, Harry. . . . Run. . . .*

> She is between HARRY and MARTINS, and HARRY cannot shoot. HARRY wavers. PAINE is passing the window. HARRY lowers his gun and makes for the door. MARTINS drops the receiver and lets it dangle. He makes for the door, pushing ANNA on one side, but HARRY is already reaching the kiosk. PAINE at that moment reaches the café door.][98]

178

[132. KIOSK STREET. LOCATION (NIGHT):

PAINE draws his gun, but it is too late. The kiosk is between them.
PAINE: *Why didn't you shoot, sir?*
They both begin to run down the street.

133. SQUARE WITH MANHOLE. LOCATION (NIGHT):

CALLOWAY drops the receiver back with impatience. Outside the telephone box he calls to the SEWER POLICE in German.
CALLOWAY: *Wir gehen hinunter.* He turns to a young British OFFICER who is with the party. *Carter, get all the manholes closed — he's gone down.*][99]
(*Still. In the film Harry runs across the square and climbs into the manhole*)
The party begin to file down the manhole.

134. WINDING IRON STAIRCASE FROM THE KIOSK. LOCATION (NIGHT):

[The police are clamping them down.][100]

135. THE SEWERS. LOCATION (NIGHT):

(*Stills. In the film Harry hides as the Police pass. The search goes on, and the Police wade through the sewers*)
It is just past high tide when MARTINS and PAINE reach the river: first the curving iron staircase, then a short passage so low they have to stoop, and then the shallow edge of the water laps at their feet. PAINE shines his torch along the edge of the current.
[PAINE: *He's down here, sir.*
Just as a deep stream when it shallows at the rim leaves an accumulation of debris, so the sewer leaves in the quiet water against the wall a scum of orange peel, old cigarette cartons and the like — in this scum HARRY LIME has left his trail as unmistakably as if he had walked in mud. PAINE, shining his torch ahead with his left hand, carries his gun in his right.
PAINE: *Keep behind me, sir, he may shoot.*
MARTINS: *Why the devil should you be in front?*

179

PAINE: *It's my job, sir. You're only a civilian.*

The water comes halfway up their legs. PAINE keeps his torch pointing down and ahead at the disturbed trail of the sewer's edge. He takes a whistle out of his pocket and blows; very far away there come the notes of the reply.

PAINE: *They are all down here now. The sewer police, I mean. They know this place as I know the Tottenham Court Road. I wish my old woman could see me now.*

He lifts his torch to shine it ahead, and at that moment a shot comes. The torch flies out of his hand and falls in the stream.

PAINE: *Nasty!*

MARTINS: *Are you hurt?*

PAINE: *Scraped my hand, sir, that's all. A week off work. Here, take this other torch, sir, while I tie my hand up. Don't shine it. He's in one of the side passages.*

For a long time the sound of the shot goes on reverberating; when the last echo dies, a whistle blows ahead of them. PAINE blows in answer. He gives a low laugh in the darkness.

PAINE: *This isn't my usual beat. Do you know the ' Horseshoe ', sir?*

MARTINS: *Yes.*

PAINE: *And the ' Duke of Grafton '?*

MARTINS: *Yes.*

PAINE: *Well, it's a small world. The things you must have seen in Texas and those parts, sir. Me — I've led a very sheltered life. Careful, sir. It's slippery here. Fancy me being here with Rollo Martins.*

MARTINS: *Let me go first. I want to talk to him.*

PAINE: *I've orders to look after you, sir.*

MARTINS: *That's all right. I don't think he'll shoot at me.*

MARTINS edges round PAINE, plunging a foot deeper in the stream as he goes. When he is in front, he calls out.]

MARTINS: *Harry.*

The name sets up an echo, ' *Harry, Harry, Harry* ', that travels down the stream and wakes a whole chorus of whistles in the darkness.

MARTINS: *Harry. Come out. It's no use.*

A voice startlingly close makes them hug the wall.

HARRY'S VOICE off: *Is that you, old man? What do you want me to do?*

MARTINS: *Come out. And put your hands above your head.*[101]

180

[HARRY'S VOICE: *I haven't a torch, old man. I can't see a thing.*
MARTINS: *Get flat against the wall, Harry. I'm going to shine the torch. . . . Come out. . . . You haven't got a chance.*

He flashes the torch on, and twenty feet away at the edge of the light and the water, HARRY steps into view.

MARTINS: *Hands above the head, Harry.*

HARRY raises his hands and then, snatching his revolver from his breast pocket, fires with his left hand. The shot ricochets against the wall, a foot from MARTINS' head and he hears PAINE cry out. At the same moment a searchlight from fifty yards away lights the whole channel, catching HARRY in its beams. Next to MARTINS, we see the dead eyes of PAINE, who is slumped at the water's edge with the sewage washing to his waist. An empty cigarette carton wedges into his armpit and stays there. CALLOWAY's party has reached the scene. MARTINS stands dithering above PAINE's body, with HARRY LIME halfway between him and CALLOWAY. CALLOWAY's party cannot shoot for fear of hitting MARTINS, and the light of the searchlight dazzles LIME.

CALLOWAY: *Get back against the wall, Martins.*

CALLOWAY's lot move slowly on, their revolvers trained for a chance, and LIME turns this way and that, like a rabbit dazzled by headlights.

MARTINS suddenly: *This way, Harry.*

HARRY turns and runs past MARTINS, and the others cannot shoot. At the edge of the searchlight beam, he takes a flying leap into the deep central rushing stream, and the current carries him rapidly on into the dark.

CALLOWAY: *Shoot, you fool, shoot.*

MARTINS still dithers. CALLOWAY and his party fire blindly into the dark, and a cry comes back to them.

CALLOWAY: *Got him.*

CALLOWAY and his men advance.

CALLOWAY to MARTINS quite gently: *You didn't do him any good.* He halts by PAINE's body. He is dead. His eyes remain blankly opened, the searchlight on him; somebody stoops and dislodges the carton, throwing it in the river which whirls it on.

CALLOWAY: *Poor old Paine.* He looks up to find MARTINS has gone. *Martins! Martins!* His name is lost in a confusion of echoes, in the rush and roar of the underground river.]

MARTINS is wading upstream to find HARRY. He is afraid to lift the torch. He does not want to tempt him to shoot again. HARRY has been struck by the random bullets. He scrambles with difficulty out of the water, falls on his knees and begins to crawl up a side passage. He reaches the foot of the iron stairs. (*Still*) Thirty feet above his head is a manhole, but he would not have the strength to lift it, and even if he succeeded, the police are waiting above. He knows all that, but he is in great pain and cannot think rationally. He begins to pull himself up the stairs, but then the pain increases and he cannot go on. MARTINS wades through the dark.[102]

[MARTINS calling not very loud: *Harry.* He turns back along the edge of the stream and finds his way up the passage which HARRY has taken. *Harry.*

HARRY: *Rollo.*

MARTINS puts his hand on an iron handrail and climbs only three steps up, his foot steps down on a hand, and there is HARRY. MARTINS shines his torch on him; he has not got a gun; he must have dropped it when the bullet hit him. For a moment MARTINS thinks he is dead. But then HARRY whimpers with pain and swivels his eyes with a great effort to MARTINS' face.

CALLOWAY'S VOICE: *Martins, where are you?*

MARTINS: *Here.*

CALLOWAY'S VOICE: *Don't take any chances, Martins. Shoot. . . .*

MARTINS looks down and sees HARRY looking up at him. HARRY winks.] CALLOWAY and his men reach the end of the passage, behind their searchlight. They hear a shot and halt, turning on the light. MARTINS comes out into the beam, with hanging head. Dissolve.

136. THE CENTRAL CEMETERY. LOCATION (DAY):

The coffin of HARRY LIME is being lowered into the grave, just as in the first sequence, except that now only three figures stand around the grave: ANNA, MARTINS, CALLOWAY. But KURTZ and TYLER are missing.

PRIEST: *Anima ejus, et animae omnium fidelium defunctorum, per*

182

misericordiam Dei requiescant in pace.
ANNA: *Amen.*

The PRIEST, again as in the earlier sequence, takes a spoon of earth and drops it onto the coffin. He hands the spoon to MARTINS who does the same. This time ANNA takes it, and she drops the earth too. Then, as before, she walks away without a word. MARTINS and CALLOWAY walk together in silence towards the jeep, down one of the long avenues. [CALLOWAY puts his hand on MARTINS' arm. It is almost the first real gesture of friendship he has shown.

CALLOWAY: *Better dead.*

MARTINS reacts in just the opposite way, as he reacted to ANNA in the café.][103]

MARTINS: *A man's not dead because you put him underground.*

We watch the worried look on CALLOWAY's face. He glances over his shoulder towards the grave, remembering only too well that the first time HARRY LIME was not dead. They reach the car and climb in. There is no PAINE to drive them now. CALLOWAY takes the wheel.

137. CAR. BACK PROJECTION (DAY):

CALLOWAY pushes at the starter. MARTINS is looking ahead down the road, towards the receding figure of ANNA.

MARTINS: *What about Anna, Calloway?*

CALLOWAY: *I'll do what I can — if she'll let me.*

They drive out of the cemetery. This time it is MARTINS who looks out at ANNA.

138. CEMETERY STREET. LOCATION (DAY):

ANNA is on her way to the tram-stop, walking down the long dreary road.

139. CAR. BACK PROJECTION (DAY):

MARTINS: *Put me down a moment, Calloway.*

CALLOWAY: *There's not much time.*

MARTINS: *I can't just leave. . . .*

CALLOWAY slows the car and brings it to a stop.

140. CEMETERY STREET. LOCATION (DAY):

CALLOWAY: *Be sensible, Martins.*

MARTINS as he stands beside the jeep: *I haven't got a sensible name . . . Callaghan.*

He begins to walk down the road. CALLOWAY turns and watches. ANNA is approaching. MARTINS stops and waits for her. (*Still*) [She reaches him and he seeks in vain for a word. He makes a gesture with his hand, and] she pays no attention, walking right past him and on into the distance. MARTINS follows her with his eyes. [Beyond our vision, we can hear a car horn blown again and again.]

THE END

NOTES

1 In the film, the OFFICER lets MARTINS through and says: *Okay.*
2 Here the PORTER adds: *Sorry for the grave-diggers.*
3 In the film, MARTINS replies: *No.*
4 In the film, this line is given to CALLOWAY.
5 In the film, he is called Holly instead of Rollo throughout.
6 Here MARTINS adds: *Must have known I was broke — even sent me an aeroplane ticket.*
7 Here CALLOWAY adds: *Have another drink.*
8 Here MARTINS begins: *So it wasn't petrol. So it was tyres.*
9 In the film, CALLOWAY begins: *That's all right, Paine.*
10 Here PAINE adds: *Up we come.*
11 Here PAINE says: *We read quite a few of your books. I like a good Western. That's what I like about them, sir, pick them up and put them down any time.*
12 In the film, CARTER and TOMBS are amalgamated into one character called CRABBIT.
13 Here PAINE adds: *He's very good, sir. We read quite a few of his books.*
14 In the film, the following sequence is substituted:
   CRABBIT: *The name's Crabbit. I represent the C.R.S. of G.H.Q., you know.*
   MARTINS: *You do?*
   CRABBIT: *Cultural Re-education Section. Propaganda — very important in a place like this. We do a little show each week — last week we had ' Hamlet '. Week before we had — um . . . something. . . .*
   PAINE: *The striptease, sir.*
   CRABBIT: *Oh yes, the Hindu Dancers, thank you, sergeant. This is the first opportunity we've had of making an American author welcome.*
   MARTINS: *Welcome?*
   CRABBIT: *I'll tell you what, on Wednesday night at our Institute, we're having a little lecture on the — er — contemporary novel. Perhaps you'd like to speak?*
   MARTINS: *They wouldn't know me.*
   CRABBIT: *Oh nonsense, your novels are very popular here, aren't they, sergeant?*
   PAINE: *Very popular.*

CRABBIT: *Very popular. Are you staying long?*

15 In the film, PAINE adds: *But he's due to leave tomorrow, sir.*

16 In the film, the sequence is adapted:
MARTINS: *I was trying to punch his major in the eye.*
CRABBIT smiling: *Really, a major?*
MARTINS: *Heard of Harry Lime? I came here to stay with him.*

17 In the film, all MARTINS' preceding four speeches are adapted:
MARTINS says:
(1) *If I do this (lecture business). . . .*
(2) *Fine. (It's a deal.)*
(3) *Story about a rider who hunted down a sheriff who was victimizing his best friend.*
(4) *' Colonel Callaghan ' is called ' Major Calloway '.*

18 In the film, KURTZ begins: *I wish I could.*

19 In the film, the American TYLER becomes the Rumanian POPESCU throughout.

20 Here KURTZ adds: *His friends and I carried him across.*

21 This location is changed to a statue of the Emperor Franz Josef in the middle of the square, and KURTZ adds: *We lay him down there.*

22 In the film, the following sequence is added:
MARTINS: *Who used to visit Mr Lime?*
The PORTER speaks to KURTZ in German.
MARTINS: *What's he say?*
KURTZ: *He says he doesn't know everybody.*

23 In the film, KURTZ adds: *But you'll find me at the Casanova Club every night.*

24 In the film, MARTINS adds: *Didn't you hear Mister Crabbit offer me the hospitality of the H.Q.B.M.C.?*

25 In the film, the actors all wear eighteenth-century costume, and there are three girls and a man in the scene.

26 In the film, the following sequence is added:
MARTINS at the door: *Miss Schmidt?*
ANNA: *Come in.*
MARTINS: *I enjoyed the play very much. You were awfully good.*
ANNA: *You understand German?*
MARTINS: *No — no — I . . . excuse me, I could follow it fine.*

27 In the film, MARTINS says: *He's got a little dog. I can't understand what Harry saw in a fellow like that.*

28 In the film, MARTINS adds: *Do you know that porter?* And ANNA replies: *Yes.*

29 In the film, the PORTER adds: *Emperor Josef statue. . . .* And MARTINS adds: *Why didn't they bring him into the house?*

186

30 In the film, the following sequence is added:
PORTER trying to explain: *Wait a moment, Fraulein Schmidt.*
He asks her a question in German.
ANNA: *He was quite dead.*
PORTER: *He was quite dead.*
MARTINS: *But this sounds crazy. If he was killed at once, how could he have talked about me and this lady after he was dead?*

31 In the film, MARTINS says: *Things like what?*

32 In the film, it is ' *statue* '.

33 In the film, MARTINS asks: *Who was that?* And ANNA replies: *I don't know. He didn't answer.*

34 In the film, MARTINS begins: *But I was told there were only two men there.* And when the PORTER complains: *It's not my business,* MARTINS says: *Make it your business.*

35 In the film, the following sequence is added:
ANNA: *You shouldn't get mixed up in this.*
MARTINS: *Well, if I do find out something, can I look you up again?*
ANNA: *Why don't you leave this town — go home?*

36 In the film, ANNA adds: *They are searching my room.*

37 In the film, PAINE adds: *It's very good, sir, isn't it?* And CALLOWAY asks ANNA: *How much did you pay for this?*

38 In the film, MARTINS says: *I suppose it doesn't interest you to hear Harry Lime was murdered? You've been too busy to get complete evidence.*

39 In the film, MARTINS says: *Tactful too, aren't we, Callaghan?*

40 In the film, the following sequence is added:
MARTINS to CALLOWAY: *Mind if I use that line in my next Western? You can't chuck me out, my papers are in order.*
PAINE to ANNA: *Your receipt for the letters, miss.*
ANNA: *I don't want it.*
PAINE: *Well, I've got it when you want it, miss.*

41 In the film, ANNA comes from Czechoslovakia.

42 In the film, MARTINS says: *A bruised lip.* This scene is followed by a scene at the International Police Headquarters: ANNA's letters are being gone through in detail and photographed, while ANNA herself is told to wait for the result.

43 In the film, WINKEL says good evening in German.

44 In the film, a small and disgusting little dog barks and WINKEL marshals it out of the room with a great rigmarole in German.
MARTIN: *That your dog?*
WINKEL: *Yes.*

45 In the film, WINKEL studies a statuette.

46 In the film, the scene begins with the following sequence: ANNA paces up and down CALLOWAY's office. CALLOWAY enters, but is called back by a Russian Officer, BRODSKY.

BRODSKY: *Major, may I see you for a moment, please?*

CALLOWAY: *Certainly, Brodsky. What is it?*

BRODSKY: *These forgeries, very clever . . . we too are interested in this case. Have you arrested the girl?*

CALLOWAY: *No, not yet.*

BRODSKY: *Please, keep this passport to yourself until I make some enquiries, will you, major?*

CALLOWAY: *Yes, of course.*

BRODSKY: *Thank you.*

CALLOWAY re-enters his office and indicates ANNA's letters on his desk.

47 In the film, CALLOWAY says: *He works in a military hospital.*

48 In the film, CALLOWAY adds: *. . . of the Casanova Club, that's where a lot of friends of Lime's used to go.*

49 In the film, ANNA adds: *Something about meeting Harry at his home.*

50 In the film, the following sequence is played:

CRABBIT: *I've arranged that lecture for tomorrow.*

MARTINS: *What about?*

CRABBIT: *On the modern novel, you remember what we arranged.*

51 In the film, MARTINS says: *Not yet.*

52 In the film, MARTINS says: *I understand you were with Harry. . . .*

53 In the film, this reads: *That Harry was dead before you got him to the statue.*

54 In the film, the following dialogue is added:

MARTINS: *He seems to have been around a bit. Do you know a man called Harbin . . . Joseph Harbin?*

POPESCU: *No.*

55 In the film, four shots replace Scenes 46 to 51.

    (1) POPESCU's room: POPESCU is finishing a telephone call.

        POPESCU: *He will meet us at the bridge, good.* Dissolve.

    (2) KURTZ's house: KURTZ leaves his house surreptitiously. Dissolve.

    (3) WINKEL's house: WINKEL wheels out an old bicycle and rides away. Dissolve.

    (4) POPESCU's front door: POPESCU, dressed in an overcoat, steps out. Dissolve.

56 In the film, MARTINS says: *Well, I didn't learn that from him.*

57 In the film, MARTINS says: *You might get my name right.*

58 In the film, this scene is shot in a very much shortened version,

and far more visually. There is a full extract from the shooting script printed in *The Cinema 1952*, edited by Roger Manvell and R K Neilson Baxter, Penguin Books, 1952.

59 In the film, MARTINS adds: *You don't know where to take me yet.*

60 In the film, the dissolve was to POPESCU on the telephone.
POPESCU: . . . *Bring the car and anyone else who would like to Don't be long.* Dissolve.

61 In the film, the following adaptation of the later part of the screenplay appears here: Two ladies leave the audience.
MAN IN AUDIENCE: *What author has chiefly influenced you?*
MARTINS: *Gray.*
LADY IN AUDIENCE: *Grey? Which Grey?*
MARTINS: *Zane Gray.*
CRABBIT: *That's Mr Martin's little joke, of course. As we all know perfectly well, Zane Gray wrote what we call ' Westerns ' — cowboys and baddies.*
ANOTHER MAN: *This — er — James Joyce now, where would you put him?*
POPESCU has come in and caught MARTINS' attention.
MARTINS: *Would you mind repeating that question?*
MAN viciously: *Where would you put James Joyce — in what category?*

62 In the film, MARTINS adds: *It's a murder story.* CRABBIT quickly interjects: *I'm so glad you were able to come, Mr Popescu.* To MARTINS. *Mr Popescu is a very great supporter of one of our medical charities.*

63 In the film, POPESCU says: *Pity,* as he goes out. Then CRABBIT adds, after everybody has shuffled out in dissatisfaction: *Well, if there are no more questions for Mr Martins, I think I can call the meeting officially closed.*

64 In the film, the following speech now appears:
CALLOWAY: *See this man here? A fellow called Harbin, a medical orderly at the General Hospital. He worked for Lime and helped to steal the stuff from the laboratories. We forced him to give information, which led us as far as Kurtz and Lime, but we didn't arrest them as our evidence wasn't complete and it might have spoilt our chances of getting the others. Next, Paine.*

65 In the film, MARTINS adds: *This is more like a mortuary than a Police H.Q.*

66 In the film, MARTINS then says: *How could he have done it? Seventy pounds a tube.*

67 In the film, the dialogue is:

MARTINS: *I'm sorry, too.* TO PAINE. *Still got that aeroplane ticket on you?*

CALLOWAY: *We'll send it across to the hotel in the morning.*

68 In the film, BRODSKY says: *What can we do? We have our instructions.*

69 In the film, the following scene is substituted:
A cabaret bar: MARTINS sits in a sleazy cabaret bar, drinking and watching the floor show. Hostesses watch him, and a waiter brings him another drink. An old flower-seller persuades him to buy two huge bunches of chrysanthemums. Dissolve.

70 In the film, the scene begins in ANNA's room as follows: There is a knock at the door and ANNA stirs.

ANNA: *Who's that?*

MARTINS: *It's me.*

She opens the door. MARTINS removes his hat, still holding the bunches of flowers.

ANNA: *What is it? What happened to you?*

MARTINS: *Just came to see you.*

71 In the film, the scene continues:

MARTINS: *I did want to say goodbye before I pushed off back home.*

ANNA: *Why?*

MARTINS: *It's what you've always wanted, all of you.* Dangles a string to the cat on the bed. *Kitty, Kitty, don't you want to play?* The cat jumps off the bed. *Not very sociable, is he?*

ANNA: *No, he only likes cats. What made you decide so suddenly?*

MARTINS: *I brought you these. . . .* Offers flowers. *They got a little wet, but. . . .*

ANNA: *What happened to your hand?*

MARTINS: *A parrot. . . .*

ANNA: *Have you seen Calloway?*

MARTINS: *Imagine a parrot nipping a man.*

ANNA: *Have you?*

MARTINS: *Oh. . . . I've been saying goodbye all over.*

ANNA: *He told you, didn't he?*

MARTINS: *Told me?*

ANNA: *About Harry.*

MARTINS: *You know?*

ANNA: *I've seen Major Calloway today.*

Camera tracks to the window and shows the square outside.

72 In the film, MARTINS says: *I wouldn't stand a chance, would I? You did tell me I ought to find myself a girl.*

190

73 In the film, MARTINS begins his speech with the line: *What kind of a spy do you think you are, satchel-foot?* And ends it with the line, chanting childishly: *Come out, come out, whoever you are.*

74 In the film, PAINE adds: *Runs right into the blue Danube.*

75 In the film, CALLOWAY adds: *He's the man I told you was missing. He used to work for Harry Lime.*

76 In the film, the Russian M.P. begins: *International Polizei.*

77 In the film, ANNA merely leaves the room to dress.

78 In the film, ANNA says: *. . . alive.*

79 In the film, there is a dissolve straight to the adapted beginning of the sequence in front of KURTZ's house. (See note 80.)

80 In the film, the scene begins as follows:
The street outside KURTZ's house: MARTINS comes across the courtyard to the house and rings the doorbell. KURTZ comes onto the balcony in his dressing-gown.
KURTZ: *Why, that's you! Come up!*

81 In the film, the dialogue runs:
KURTZ: *Come up.*
MARTINS: *I'll wait here.*

82 In the film, HARRY LIME begins: *Hello, old man, how are you? They seem to have been giving you a busy time.*

83 In the film, HARRY adds: *The same old indigestion.*

84 In the film, HARRY says: *Old man, you should never have gone to the police, you know. You should have left this thing alone.*

85 In the film, MARTINS says: *A lot of good you'll do in jail.*

86 In the film, the dialogue of this sequence is:
MARTINS looking out of the window: *I should be pretty easy to get rid of.*
HARRY: *Pretty easy.*
MARTINS: *Don't be too sure.*
HARRY: *I carry a gun. You don't think they'd look for a bullet wound after you hit that ground.*
MARTINS: *They dug up your coffin.*
HARRY: *Found Harbin? Pity.*

87 In the film, there is more dialogue here:
MARTINS: *What do you believe in?*
HARRY: *If you ever get Anna out of this mess, be kind to her. You'll find she's worth it. I wish I'd asked you to bring some of those tablets. They get off the Wheel.*

88 In the film, HARRY adds a famous parting speech: *When you make up your mind, send me a message — I'll meet you any place, any time, and when we do meet, old man, it's you I want to see, not*

191

the police . . . and don't be so gloomy. . . . After all, it's not that awful — you know what the fellow said. . . . In Italy for thirty years under the Borgias they had warfare, terror, murder, bloodshed — but they produced Michelangelo, Leonardo da Vinci and the Renaissance. In Switzerland they had brotherly love, five hundred years of democracy and peace, and what did that produce . . .? The cuckoo clock. So long, Holly.

89 In the film, CALLOWAY says: *Look here, Martins, you can always arrange to meet him at some little café. . . . Say here, . . .* Pointing at the map . . . *in the International Zone.*

90 In the film, CALLOWAY answers: *Okay, forget it.*

91 In the film, BRODSKY comes in asking: *Busy, Major?* Then adds a remark to each of his two speeches. The first is: *This is her report,* and he hands it to CALLOWAY. The second is: *She has no right to be here.*

92 In the film, the following sequence is substituted:

MARTINS begins by standing at the station barrier. He moves to the buffet to avoid ANNA and PAINE, who sees her onto the train and finds a compartment for her.

PAINE: *Here we are, you'll be all right, miss.*

ANNA: *I don't understand Major Calloway.*

PAINE: *I expect he's got a soft spot for you, miss.*

ANNA: *Why has he done all this?*

PAINE: *Don't worry, miss, you're well out of things. There we are, miss.*

ANNA: *Thank you, you've been so kind.*

PAINE: *Well, I'll be saying good night.*

PAINE leaves, while ANNA inspects her ticket and papers. She looks out of the train window, sees MARTINS in the buffet, and gets off the train to accost him there. Then she asks: *Are you going too?* All her scene with MARTINS takes place in the buffet.

93 In the film, the dialogue runs:

MARTINS: *Anna, don't you recognise a good turn when you see one?*

ANNA: *You have seen Calloway. What are you two doing?*

MARTINS angrily, his nerves breaking: *Well, they asked me to help take him, and I'm helping.*

ANNA: *Poor Harry.*

MARTINS: *Poor Harry? Poor Harry wouldn't even lift a finger to help you.*

94 In the film, MARTINS adds here: *Oh, Anna, why do we always have to quarrel?* The train pulls out past the buffet window. ANNA

replies: *If you want to sell your services, I'm not willing to be the price.*

95 In the film, the scene ends with ANNA leaving the buffet, and MARTINS staring at the swinging door, while his coat lies discarded on the floor.

96 In the film, the scene runs:
CALLOWAY: *. . . All the kids in here are the results of Lime's penicillin racket. . . .* He and MARTINS inspect the beds. MARTINS' face is full of anxiety and compassion, as CALLOWAY indicates a particular child's bed.
CALLOWAY, off-handedly: *Had meningitis. . . . They gave it some of Lime's penicillin. Terrible pity, isn't it?*

97 In the film, the scene continues: A huge shadow looms against a house front near the café. PAINE, CALLOWAY and the soldiers stiffen and signal to each other. An aged BALLOON-SELLER shuffles into shot. While they are distracted, ANNA slips into the café.
PAINE: *Look sir!*
In the café, ANNA sits down and asks MARTINS:
ANNA: *How much longer are you going to sit here?*
Café square: Return to the waiting men:
PAINE: *Shall I go over there, sir?*
CALLOWAY: *No, leave them for a while.*
The BALLOON-SELLER shuffles and sways towards CALLOWAY and PAINE, who try to sink into the shadows. But the old man pesters them until PAINE rapidly makes a purchase to get him out of the way. (The sequence in form and lighting is reminiscent of *M*).

98 In the film, the scene in the café runs:
MARTINS: *You should have gone. How did you know I was here, anyway?*
ANNA: *From Kurtz. They've just been arrested. . . . But Harry won't come. He's not a fool.*
MARTINS: *I wonder.*
Café square: The POLICEMEN wait.
CALLOWAY: *Yes, Paine, slip across and see what's she's up to.*
PAINE leaves.
Café: ANNA is speaking bitterly to MARTINS.
ANNA: *What's your price this time?* The back door of the café opens.
MARTINS: *No price, Anna.*
ANNA: *Honest, sensible, sober Holly Martins. Holly, what a silly name. You must feel very proud to be a police informer.*
HARRY has entered quietly, overhears the word 'informer', and frowns. ANNA turns away from MARTINS and catches sight of

193

HARRY.

ANNA: *Harry, get away, the police are outside!*

HARRY, drawing his gun, signals ANNA out of the line of fire between himself and MARTINS, but PAINE is already making for the main door, so HARRY dashes out of the back door.

99 In the film, the following shots are seen:

The ruins of Vienna: HARRY runs across bomb-sites, as the chase is raised with shrill whistles and shouts. Dogs bark and sirens hoot.

A square: HARRY clatters across a square to an open manhole and leaps in. PAINE, CALLOWAY, MARTINS and the POLICEMEN quickly catch up.

100 In the film, there are the following scenes: The POLICE search, watch and shout in the echoing tunnels. They spot the fleeing HARRY several times. Various shots of HARRY hiding in a gallery. Other shots of him hiding as the POLICE pass. Everywhere, he is stopped by shouts and voices.

101 In the film, the following sequence appears: PAINE dashes out to warn MARTINS.

PAINE: *Get back, get back, sir!*

PAINE is standing right in the middle of the tunnel and does not realise where HARRY is hiding. HARRY shoots him down. The shot echoes round and round as PAINE subsides onto the cobbles.

CALLOWAY strides out of the shadows and shoots HARRY, as the latter makes another break. HARRY falls, and scrambles away.

102 In the film, this sequence continues:

A grille at street level: The wounded HARRY reaches a grille at street level. His fingers clutch and claw at the heavy grating, unable to move it.

The sewers: MARTINS follows HARRY up to the foot of the iron stairway and sees him struggling with the grille. HARRY is in great pain and fear.

103 In the film, the dialogue originally written for the following scene, appears here:

CALLOWAY: *What time is it?*

MARTINS: *Three-thirty.*

CALLOWAY: *We'll have to step on it, if you're going to catch that plane.*

CREDITS:

Produced by	Michael Balcon
Directed by	Robert Hamer
Screenplay by	Robert Hamer
	John Dighton
Associate Producer	Michael Relph
Director of Photography	Douglas Slocombe
Editor	Peter Tanner
Production Supervisor	Hal Mason
Art Director	William Kellner
Sound Supervisor	Stephen Dalby
Camera Operator	Jeff Seaholme
Recordist	John Mitchell
Unit Production Manager	Leigh Aman
Costume Designer	Anthony Mendleson
Hair Styles	Barbara Barnard
	Pearl Gardner
Assistant Director	Norman Priggen
Make-up	Ernest Taylor
	Harry Frampton
Continuity	Phyllis Crocker
Special Effects	Sydney Pearson
	Geoffrey Dickinson
Music played by	The Philharmonic Orchestra
Conductor	Ernest Irving

CAST:

Louis	Dennis Price
Edith	Valerie Hobson
Sibella	Joan Greenwood
The Duke	
The Banker	
The Parson	
The General	
The Admiral	Alec Guinness
Young Ascoyne	
Young Henry	
Lady Agatha	
Mama	Audrey Fildes
The Hangman	Miles Malleson
The Prison Governor	Clive Morton
Lionel	John Penrose
Crown Counsel	Cecil Ramage
Lord High Steward	Hugh Griffiths
Mr Perkins	John Salew
Burgoyne	Eric Messiter
The Farmer	Lyn Evans
The Schoolmistress	Barbara Leake
Maud	Peggy Ann Clifford
The Girl in the Punt	Anne Valery
The Reporter	Arthur Lowe

KIND HEARTS AND CORONETS

The titles and credits appear against a background of net with a frame of fine lace. We see miniature portraits of the principal characters, dressed in Edwardian clothes. The music played is the aria *Il Mio Tesore Intanto* from *Don Giovanni* by Mozart.
There follows a shot of a grim London prison at the turn of the century. It is night.
ELLIOTT, a small middle-aged man, approaches the prison gate. He is wearing a dark overcoat and bowler hat, and looks like an artisan in his Sunday best. He carries a small suitcase.
We see a notice pinned to the prison door:

CAPITAL PUNISHMENT AMENDMENT ACT, 1868
The sentence of the law passed upon Louis D'Ascoyne Mazzini, Duke of Chalfont, found guilty of murder, will be carried into execution at 8 a.m. tomorrow.

> A. LISTER, Sherriff of City of London
> S. E. BROWNLEE, Governor
> Pentonville Prison, 7th Aug. 1902

A WARDER opens the gate to ELLIOTT.
WARDER: *Good evening, Mr Elliott.*
ELLIOTT: *Good evening.*
The WARDER leads the way towards a little office adjoining the gate.
WARDER: *Just sign the book if you will.*
ELLIOTT: *Yes.*
WARDER: *Been keeping you busy, Mr Elliott?*
ELLIOTT: *Oh, just nicely. Went up to Manchester on Monday — a poisoner. A baby-farmer at Holloway this morning. Very ordinary crimes, both of them.*
WARDER: *This one we've got for you tomorrow is something special.*
ELLIOTT: *Yes, very much so. Even after all my years in the profession, I'm quite looking forward to him. He signs in. Ha! Well, I must be getting along.*
WARDER: *Good-night, Mr Elliott.*

ELLIOTT: *Good-night.*

WARDER: *Usual cup of tea at seven?*

ELLIOTT: *Oh, please.*

We are now in a long, gloomy corridor inside the prison.

ELLIOTT and the GOVERNOR are approaching. The GOVERNOR looks like a retired army officer and appears to be grave and abstracted. ELLIOTT can barely mask his excitement in the solemnity of his tone.

ELLIOTT: *Even my lamented master, the great Mr Berry himself, never had the privilege of hanging a Duke!*

GOVERNOR: *Ha!*

ELLIOTT: *What a finale to a lifetime in the public service.*

GOVERNOR: *Finale?*

ELLIOTT: *Yes, I intend to retire. After using the silken rope, never again be content with hemp.*

GOVERNOR: *Quite. Well, here we are.*

ELLIOTT: *Oh, thank you.*

They stop at a door. The GOVERNOR slides back the cover of a peephole, stands aside. ELLIOTT peers through.

We see through the peephole the interior of the condemned cell. LOUIS is sitting writing at a table, with his back to the door.

ELLIOTT closes the peephole and turns to the GOVERNOR.

ELLIOTT: *How will he approach it?*

GOVERNOR: *I should think as the calmest you've ever known.*

ELLIOTT: *Noblesse oblige, doubtless. A difficult client can make things most distressing. Some of them tend to be very hysterical. So inconsiderate. Well, Colonel, considering the importance of the occasion, I shall retire early. The last execution of a Duke in this country was very badly bungled. That was in the old days of the axe, of course.*

GOVERNOR: *Yes.*

ELLIOTT: *Oh, I — I almost forgot. Er — um — You must forgive my ignorance, but when we meet in the morning, what is the correct form of address? Your Lordship?*

GOVERNOR: *Your Grace.*

ELLIOTT: *Your Grace? Oh! Thank you.*

He looks at his watch, hesitates, and moves off muttering to himself.

ELLIOTT to himself: *Good morning, Your Grace. Good morning,*

198

Your Grace.

The GOVERNOR takes a bunch of keys from his pocket and unlocks the door of the condemned cell. LOUIS D'ASCOYNE MAZZINI, tenth Duke of Chalfont, is tall, slim, dark and handsome in a sardonic way. On the desk at which he sits is a silver tray with a carafe of wine and a glass. In the background a WARDER jumps to his feet. LOUIS looks up from his writing as the GOVERNOR enters.

GOVERNOR to WARDER: *All right — sit down.*

LOUIS: *Ah, good evening, Colonel. Glass of wine? (Still)*

GOVERNOR: *Good evening, Your Grace. Er — thank you, no. I — er — I called to enquire whether you had any special wishes for breakfast.*

LOUIS: *Ha — Just coffee and a slice of toast, thank you. Oh, and perhaps a few grapes. I hate to disappoint the newspaper-reading public, but it'll be too early for the conventional hearty breakfast. The appointment is at eight, is it not?*

GOVERNOR: *At eight — er — yes. If I may venture to say so, I am amazed at your calmness.*

LOUIS sips some wine from the glass.

LOUIS: *Dr Johnson was, as always, right when he observed: 'Depend upon it, sir, when a man knows that he is going to be hanged in a few hours, it concentrates his mind wonderfully.'*

GOVERNOR: *Yes . . . well, if there is nothing further I can do for you. . . .*

LOUIS: *Nothing, thank you, Colonel. We shall have the opportunity of making our adieux in the morning, I presume?*

GOVERNOR: *I regret to say, yes. Good-night, Your Grace.*

LOUIS: *Good-night, Colonel.*

The GOVERNOR leaves the cell. LOUIS turns back to the beginning of the sheet of paper, which he has covered with writing. We see the title, while LOUIS' VOICE is heard reading it.

LOUIS' VOICE: *A brief history of the events leading thereto, written on the eve of his execution by Louis D'Ascoyne Mazzini, tenth Duke of Chalfont, who ventures to hope that it may prove not uninteresting to those who remain to read it.*

TWO WARDERS are sitting by the fire in the cell. One of them has dropped off to sleep and is snoring. His companion nudges him, and he wakes with a start. Louis looks up with an expression of annoyance.

Louis to Warder: *My good man, it is not by choice that you keep me company. If you wish to sleep, pray do me the courtesy of sleeping quietly!*

He resumes his reading.

Louis' Voice: *With so little time remaining to complete my story, it is difficult to choose where to begin it. Perhaps I should begin at the beginning.*

We now see Mrs Mazzini lying in bed. In a cot by her side, lies a newly-born Baby Louis. A Nurse bends over him, picks him up and carries him to his mother.

Louis' Voice continuing: *I was a healthy baby, born of an English mother . . .*

Louis' Father is sitting in the parlour. In the doorway stands the Nurse with the small white bundle in her arms.

Louis' Voice continuing: *. . . and Italian father,*

Louis' Father leaps to his feet towards the baby, with arms outstretched.

Louis' Father: *Ahh!*

Just as the Nurse hands him the child, he clutches at his heart and falls to the floor.

Louis' Voice continuing: *. . . who succumbed to a heart attack at the moment of first setting eyes on me.*

We resume on Louis inside the cell. He turns over a page of his memoirs.

Louis' Voice continuing: *In the circumstances, it will be understood that I have but slight memory of him. The little I know comes from what Mama told me.*

In the parlour of the Mazzini house, Louis, now five years old, is standing beside Mrs Mazzini, as she sits at the piano. She is playing an operatic aria and gazing at two photographs on top of the piano. They share a large frame in the shape of a heart. One is of Mrs Mazzini dressed in feathers and a beautiful dress, the other of her husband in full song.

Mrs Mazzini to Louis: *Your father was a very handsome man.*

Mr Mazzini, standing on a dais, is singing the aria from *Don Giovanni*. We are in the main hall of Chalfont Castle. Among

a group of seated people are the DUKE and DUCHESS of CHAL-
FONT and MRS MAZZINI, who is gazing raptly at the singer.
We now see Chalfont Castle in the moonlight.

LOUIS' VOICE: *Mama was the daughter of the seventh Duke of
Chalfont, of Chalfont Castle.*

In the castle grounds MRS MAZZINI is in passionate converse
with MR MAZZINI, who kneels at her feet.

LOUIS' VOICE continuing: *She eloped with her handsome singer* . . .

The magnificent, feudal Chalfont Castle comes into view.

LOUIS' VOICE continuing: . . . *and exchanged the medieval splendours of Chalfont Castle.* . . .

We see a drab little villa in a row of identical villas, on a dull
street in Clapham. An old carriage draws up.

LOUIS' VOICE continuing: . . . *for the modern conveniences of number seventy-three, Balaclava Avenue, S.W.*

It is day time. In the kitchen of the villa MRS MAZZINI is washing the dishes while MR MAZZINI is singing and drying up.

LOUIS' VOICE continuing: *They were poor, but they had five happy
and harmonious years, before my arrival sent Papa to join the
heavenly choir.*

MRS MAZZINI is now seen in deep mourning. She is pushing a
pram outside the Clapham villa. She stops to put a letter in a
pillarbox.

LOUIS' VOICE continuing: *Reduced to even deeper poverty by my
father's death, Mama swallowed her pride and made an effort at
reconciliation with her family. They did not even reply to her letter.*

MRS MAZZINI is showing a room to MR PERKINS, a sancti-
monious looking little man.

LOUIS' VOICE continuing: *In order to keep us both alive, she was
reduced to the horrible expedient of taking in a lodger.*

In the kitchen MRS MAZZINI is distastefully polishing a pair
of MR PERKINS' shoes.

LOUIS' VOICE continuing: *For him she had to perform the most
menial tasks. She felt that her family had conspired to cheat me of
my birthright.*

She crosses the kitchen, shoes in hand, and gazes sadly down
at LOUIS lying in his pram.

We are in the parlour where MRS MAZZINI kneels on the floor,
demonstrating to the five year old LOUIS the intricacies of the

201

family tree. A long parchment scroll, beautifully lettered, is spread out before them.

LOUIS' VOICE continuing: *And I passed from infancy to childhood in an atmosphere of family history and genealogies.*

MRS MAZZINI is dusting a picture hanging on the wall, just above the piano. It is of a breast-plated gentleman with a militant expression.

LOUIS' VOICE continuing: *The Dukedom had been bestowed by Charles the Second on Colonel Henry D'Ascoyne for services rendered to His Majesty during his exile. Later, for services rendered to His Majesty after his Restoration by the Duchess, . . .*

MRS MAZZINI dusts a second picture, portraying a lady.

LOUIS' VOICE continuing: *. . . the title was granted the unique privilege of descending by the female as well as the male line.*

MRS MAZZINI beckons to LOUIS who is playing at the table. She points out the picture to him, while he stares wide-eyed.

MRS MAZZINI: *Louis.*

LOUIS' VOICE continuing: *It was, therefore, theoretically possible that via Mama I might inherit the Dukedom.*

We now see LOUIS, aged ten, wearing a school cap and carrying a satchel. MRS MAZZINI kisses him good-bye at the doorway of the villa.

LOUIS' VOICE continuing: *Mama scraped and saved and sent me to the best school she could afford. One little incident of my schooldays occurs to me as amusing in relation to my present situation.*

We are now in a schoolroom, full of nine and ten-year-olds of both sexes. A prim looking SCHOOL MISTRESS is addressing a rather porcine small boy, LIONEL, who is standing up at his desk.

SCHOOL MISTRESS to LIONEL: *Lionel Holland. . . . What is the Sixth Commandment?*

LIONEL looks uncomfortable and does not reply.

SCHOOL MISTRESS: *Come, come now! Someone else then.*

LOUIS off: *I know . . . please, Miss Waterman.*

LOUIS raises his hand.

SCHOOL MISTRESS: *Louis Mazzini. Tell him.*

LOUIS smugly: *Thou shall not kill.*

SCHOOL MISTRESS: *Quite right, Louis. The Sixth Commandment is*

' *Thou shall not kill.*'

> We resume on LOUIS in the condemned cell, smiling and return-
> ing to his reading.

LOUIS' VOICE: *No, in those days, I never had any trouble with the
Sixth Commandment. As to the Seventh, I was hardly of an age to
concern myself with it.*

> Back in the schoolroom we see young LOUIS smiling at SIBELLA,
> who is a pretty little girl sitting beside him.

LOUIS' VOICE continuing: *Although I was old enough to be in love.
So Sibella enters my story.*

> The scene is now the nursery at the HALLWARD house. LOUIS,
> SIBELLA and GRAHAM, her brother, are roasting chestnuts by
> the fire.

LOUIS' VOICE continuing: *Sibella and her brother, Graham, were
my only close friends, and we grew up together. In their case, Mama
relaxed her objection to my associating with the local children.*

> The door opens and DR and MRS HALLWARD come in.
> LOUIS shakes hands politely.

LOUIS' VOICE continuing: *At least their father, Dr Hallward, was a
professional man!*

> LOUIS, now aged seventeen, is doing his homework in the
> MAZZINI parlour. MRS MAZZINI is sitting at a table, darning
> socks.

MRS MAZZINI: *Louis, we must think very carefully about your
future.*

LOUIS: *Well, it should be quite easy to get a job.*

MRS MAZZINI putting down her sewing: *Not a job, dear. A career.
I had hoped for Cambridge for you. The D'Ascoynes always go to
Trinity, and then, perhaps, the Diplomatic. But I'm afraid it's no
use looking as high as that.* She resumes her sewing. *However, when
you've passed your examination, that should equip you for a start in
one of the professions. People of quite good family go into the professions nowadays, I understand. Now, who do we know who could
help us?*

LOUIS looking up: *We don't really know anyone — except the
family. And they don't know us.*

MRS MAZZINI: *The least we can do is try once more. I shall write
to Lord Ascoyne D'Ascoyne. He can surely do something in that*

bank of his.

LOUIS: *Bank, Mama? Is that a — profession?*

MRS MAZZINI: *This is a private bank, Louis dear. They don't pass money over the counter.*

LOUIS' VOICE: *The letter was duly dispatched . . . and this time we did get an answer.*

In the kitchen, MRS MAZZINI is making pastry.

LOUIS opens a letter, excitedly.

LOUIS reading: *Madam, I am instructed by Lord Ascoyne D'Ascoyne to inform you that he is not aware of your son's existence as a member of the D'Ascoyne family. Signed by his secretary.*

MRS MAZZINI: *It's very stupid of him, of them all, not to admit your existence, when one day you might be Duke of Chalfont.*

LOUIS: *It's a very big might, Mama. There must be at least twelve people before me. To say nothing of the ones who haven't been born yet.*

MRS MAZZINI: *Stranger things have happened. I don't wish to be unchristian, but — in view of their attitude, I could almost wish those twelve people should all die tomorrow.*

LOUIS walks over, puts his arms around her shoulders and kisses her.

LOUIS: *Ha! All except one, Mama! Because you must be Duchess of Chalfont before I'm Duke. It'll have to be a job, not a career after all, Mama.*

MRS MAZZINI: *I'm afraid so, Louis. A D'Ascoyne in trade!*

MRS MAZZINI weeps and wipes her eyes delicately on the edge of her apron. (*Still*) She returns to rolling out the pastry, while LOUIS stokes the fire philosophically.

LOUIS' VOICE: *Did poor Mama's silly dreaming plant in my brain some seed, which was afterwards to grow into the most sensational criminal endeavour of the century? If so, I was not conscious of it at the time, for there were things of more immediate concern. Even potential Dukes have to eat.*

LOUIS is now at the counter of MR PERKINS' drapery shop. He is showing some goods to two lady customers.

LOUIS' VOICE continuing: *Mr Perkins, our lodger for nearly fifteen years, did his best to be helpful. He was employed as shopwalker in a local drapery store and found employment for me there. The possible future Duke of Chalfont became what was known as . . .*

204

Louis now stands in the display window of the drapery store. He places a card labelled 'Spring Model' on a mannequin. Mr Perkins appears in the background and beckons to him urgently.

Louis' Voice continuing: . . . *a general assistant at the drapery. This humiliation continued for two dispiriting years. And then one day, Mama, who had broken her glasses and could not afford to have them mended, was knocked down by a tram near Clapham Junction and fatally injured.*

The scene is now Mrs Mazzini's bedroom. She is lying in bed, clutching the heart-shaped photograph in one hand. Louis kneels by her bedside, looking very anxious.

Mrs Mazzini: *Louis.*

Louis: *Yes, Mama?*

Mrs Mazzini: *I should like to be buried at Chalfont in the family vault.*

Louis: *Yes, Mama.*

Mrs Mazzini closes her eyes, the photograph falls from her hand and crashes to the floor. Louis weeps uncontrollably.

Louis' Voice: *I wrote to the Duke informing him of Mama's dying wish. His reply was the curtest possible refusal.*

We are now in the cemetery. A little bouquet of flowers lies on a newly-filled grave. Dr Hallward and Louis stand sadly beside it. The Doctor moves off, leaving Louis standing there alone for a minute.

Louis' Voice continuing: *Standing by Mama's poor little grave, in that hideous suburban cemetery, I made an oath that I would revenge the wrongs her family had done her.*

Louis returns to his darkened house. He opens a blind, letting in the sunshine, and unrolls the document of the family tree.

Louis' Voice continuing: *It was no more than a piece of youthful bravado, but it was one of those acorns from which great oaks are destined to grow. Even then, I went so far as to examine the family tree, and prune it to just the living members.*

He picks up a pair of scissors and cuts off a portion of the document. He looks thoughtfully at the severed section.

Louis' Voice continuing: *But what could I do to hurt them? What could I take from them? Except, perhaps — their lives? I indulged for a moment in a fantasy of all twelve of them being wiped out simultaneously at a family reunion — by unseen hand . . .*

He walks over to the mantelpiece and studies a watercolour of Chalfont Castle, hanging on the wall.

LOUIS' VOICE continuing: *. . . of the penniless boy from Clapham being miraculously transplanted to his birthright. I even speculated as to how I might contrive it.*

He turns and walks over to MRS MAZZINI's empty bed.

LOUIS' VOICE continuing: *But there were other more urgent problems. Mama's tiny income came from an annuity, and had died with her. The problem of how to live on twenty-five shillings a week was solved for me . . .*

LOUIS now enters a cab drawn by two horses. We follow the cab, as it turns into the drive of the HALLWARD house.

LOUIS' VOICE continuing: *. . . by an invitation from Dr Hallward to lodge with them. It was galling to accept the status of a poor relation,*

SIBELLA is sitting in the nursery by the fire. She is reading, and a large open box of chocolates lies beside her.

LOUIS' VOICE continuing: *. . . but the certainty of seeing Sibella every day was too tempting to be refused.*

She jumps up as LOUIS comes in and walks towards her.

SIBELLA: *Louis! I'm so glad you accepted. It was my idea, you know.*

LOUIS handing her a box: *I've brought you something.*

SIBELLA: *Oh, Louis, you shouldn't have. You can't possibly afford it.*

She starts to open the box when a motor horn honks outside. She pauses.

SIBELLA continuing: *Oh, what a bother, there's Lionel. See you at supper.*

She drops the box on a table, picks up a hat, and is gone in a moment. On the table we see the large opened box of chocolates and LOUIS' small, unopened one. There is the sound of a car engine outside. LOUIS crosses to the window and looks out.

LIONEL HOLLAND is driving away, with SIBELLA seated at his side.

LOUIS' VOICE: *The next few years brought many such heart-breaks. . . . But they also brought promotion.*

Louis is now standing behind the counter in the drapery shop. He is showing some material to two female customers.

Louis' Voice continuing: *Laces and ribbons — at thirty shillings a week. Fabrics at thirty-two and six. Finally* . . . He holds up a pair of bloomers . . . *ladies' underwear at thirty-five.*

Sibella walks into the shop on Lionel's arm. She smiles imperceptibly. Lionel grins unkindly. Louis despatches money and a bill to the cashier, with a savage tug at the mechanism operating the overhead railway.

Louis' Voice continuing: *I decided that if I was to be a draper, at least I would not be a suburban draper.*

Louis is now at a West End shop where he also stands behind a counter, serving two women.

Louis' Voice continuing: *So I migrated to a large modern store which had just been opened in the West End, at the gigantic salary of two pounds a week.*

In the Reading Room of a Public Library, Louis is standing, studying the front page of *The Times.*

Louis' Voice continuing: *Every lunch-time, I went to see how my inheritance was proceeding. Sometimes, the deaths column brought good news.*

We now see him in his bedroom, crossing out a name on the family tree, which is pasted to the back of the watercolour of Chalfont Castle. He turns the picture frontward again.

Resume on Louis in the library.

Louis' Voice continuing: *Sometimes the births column brought bad.*

Resume on Louis in the bedroom, filling in two names.

Louis' Voice continuing: *The advent of twin sons to the Duke was a terrible blow.*

Louis now crosses out the two names and that of the Duchess.

Louis' Voice continuing: *Fortunately, an epidemic of diptheria restored the status quo almost immediately, and even brought me a bonus in the shape of the Duchess.*

It is the drawing-room at the Hallward House. Sibella is in evening-dress and stands in the middle of a crowd of young people. Lionel in a dinner jacket, is beside her. Louis walks up to them and looks admiringly at Sibella.

Louis: *Good evening, Sibella.*

Sibella: *Hello, Louis.*

Louis: *You do look nice.*

Sibella: *So do you. Doesn't he, Lionel?*

Lionel: *Very. Ahem!*

Sibella offers her hand to Louis and they dance away.

Later in the nursery, Louis is standing alone by the window.

Louis' Voice: *Emboldened by her kindness to me. I made a decision I'd been toying with for some time.*

Sibella comes in and flops on a chaiselongue, fanning herself. As they talk she lies back enticingly.

Sibella: *Well that's the last of them, thank heaven. What an evening!*

Louis: *I thought it was a very nice evening.*

Sibella: *It may have been for you. Oh, it's awful being a woman, having to dance with a lot of dull men . . . laugh at their jokes while they're treading on your feet!*

Louis: *I didn't tread on your feet.*

Sibella: *You're not dull. And your jokes are funny!*

Louis: *Thank you, Sibella.*

Sibella: *Hmm?*

Louis goes into a rather theatrical position on one knee.

Louis: *Sibella, will you marry me?*

Sibella: *Ha! Ha! Ha! Hm! Louis, of course not. And do get up. You may be half Italian, but even so, you do look silly playing the stage lover like that.*

Louis: *Oh, I look silly, do I?*

Sibella: *Yes, very.*

He leans forward, pulls her face to his, and kisses her. Sibella's arms go round his neck. After a moment they release each other. (*Still*)

Louis: *Do I still look silly? Now will you marry me?*

Sibella: *No.*

Louis getting to his feet: *Why not?*

Sibella: *Because I just said I'd marry Lionel.*

Louis: *You can't.*

Sibella: *Why not?*

Louis: *Well, he's a clod. He's not a gentleman.*

Sibella: *Listen to who's talking! Who ever heard of a gentleman*

208

blacking the lodger's boots.

LOUIS: *That's a wicked thing to say. Just because Mama was poor.*

SIBELLA: *Lionel will be very rich one day.*

LOUIS: *I might be a Duke one day.*

SIBELLA: *Pigs might fly!*

LOUIS: *No, I might. Really, I might. You see, Mama was the daughter of the Seventh Duke. . . .*

SIBELLA yawning: *Oh, yes, I know. Well, when you are a Duke you just come and show me your crown or whatever it's called, and then I'll feel awfully silly, won't I?*

LOUIS: *Yes, you will.*

SIBELLA: *Anyhow, I'm going to marry Lionel.* She gets up and goes to the door. *And now I'm going to bed.*

LOUIS: *You will.*

SIBELLA: *Hm! Hm! Hm!*

She laughs and goes out without turning her head.

LOUIS leans moodily on the mantelpiece, then crosses the room to light the lamp. He stares thoughtfully at the watercolour of Chalfont.

LOUIS' VOICE: *If there was a precise moment at which my insubstantial dreaming took on solid purpose, that was it. The D'Ascoynes had not only wronged my mother. They were the obstacle between me and all that I wanted. The more I thought of them, these people whom I had studied until I knew their names and histories as well as I knew my own, the more they became monsters of arrogance and cruelty, whose only function in the world was to deprive me of my birthright. I had seen Chalfont only as Mama had painted it.*

The watercolour gives place to the castle in actuality. LOUIS is seen at the main gateway. He is called by a GUIDE, and he joins the rest of the visitors' group.

LOUIS' VOICE: *To pass in through that magnificent gateway . . . on Visitors' Day, at a cost of sixpence, was a humiliating experience, but I forced myself to undergo it. I wanted a closer view of the target at which I had determined to aim.*

The group is now being shown through the hall. LOUIS sees a middle-aged man, dressed in tweeds, pass through the room beyond which is roped off from the public.

LOUIS' VOICE continuing: *I little expected to catch a glimpse of the bull's-eye!*

It is the DUKE. LOUIS attempts to follow him.

GUIDE sharply to LOUIS: *Excuse me, sir.*

LOUIS and the other visitors are now in the grounds. He stops, looking back pensively at the castle.

LOUIS' VOICE: *There were then some eight people between me and the Dukedom, all seemingly equally out of reach. It is so difficult to make a neat job of killing people with whom one is not on friendly terms.*

We now see LOUIS behind the counter of a West End shop, displaying ladies' underwear to a rich-looking YOUNG MAN (D'ASCOYNE) and a GIRL, clinging to his arm.

LOUIS' VOICE: *I was almost resigned to it being an impossibility when one afternoon, at a moment when my thoughts were furthest from the subject, fate took a hand.*

D'ASCOYNE: *If you've nothing better, those will have to do.* To GIRL. *These London shops are so far behind Paris.* To LOUIS. *Parcel them up quickly, and we'll take them with us. Charge them to my account.*

LOUIS: *Yes, sir. What is the name?*

D'ASCOYNE: *Mr Ascoyne D'Ascoyne.*

LOUIS looks up quickly, and then tries to dissemble his interest by busying himself with the packing.

LOUIS' VOICE: *At last, I was face to face with one of them. This was the son of Lord Ascoyne D'Ascoyne, the banker, whose refusal to help me towards a more dignified career had led to my present ignominious occupation. What right had this arrogant puppy to be standing on the other side of the counter, ordering me about? . . . In my excitement and anger, I listened openly to their conversation.*

D'ASCOYNE to GIRL: *I've booked rooms at Cruickshank's at Maidenhead. We'll go down late on Friday afternoon.*

GIRL to ASCOYNE: *Are you sure it's safe?*

D'ASCOYNE: *It's the most discreet place — in fact, anonymous.* To LOUIS. *Hey, you. Get on with that parcel, and never mind what we are talking about.*

D'ASCOYNE prods LOUIS with his cane. (*Still!*)

LOUIS indignantly: *Don't you dare touch me like that!* He knocks the cane away. *I'm not interested in your idiotic conversation.*

D'Ascoyne: *If you want to add impertinence to your eavesdropping, we'll soon see about that!*

He signals to the floorwalker with his cane.

Louis' Voice: *The upshot was that I was dismissed on the spot.*

Louis walks disconsolately from the street up to the front door of the Hallward house.

Louis' Voice continuing: *I decided to repay him in kind by dismissing him with equal suddenness from this world.*

Louis comes into his bedroom and takes a small pill box from his pocket which he hides in a drawer.

Louis' Voice continuing: *His conversation had told me where I could probably find the opportunity to kill him. Dr Hallward's dispensary had provided me with the means.*

We are now in the garden of Cruickshank's Hotel at Maidenhead. It is a summer evening. Louis, in a straw hat, blazer and white flannels, comes out on to the lawn and looks casually around.

Louis' Voice: *With the week's wages I had received in lieu of notice, I invested in suitable apparel for a weekend at Maidenhead.*

The lawn slopes down to the river-bank. There are tables everywhere, with sunshades over them. Louis sees D'Ascoyne and the Girl sitting at a table engrossed in each other. They barely glance up as he passes by and sits at an adjoining table.

Louis' Voice continuing: *It was possible they might remember me, but I thought it unlikely, shop assistants being commonly regarded as an inferior race who never emerge from the other side of the counter. I decided to take the bull by the horns.*

Louis rises and crosses to their table, makes a little bow to the Girl and addresses himself to D'Ascoyne.

Louis: *Forgive me. I wonder if you could oblige me with a match?*

D'Ascoyne: *Certainly.*

He passes Louis a matchbox.

Louis: *Thank you. Haven't we met before somewhere?*

D'Ascoyne turns reluctantly to face Louis.

D'Ascoyne: *I don't think so.*

Louis: *Funny, because I could have sworn I knew your face. Er — were you at Monte last year?*

D'Ascoyne: *The year before.*

Louis: *Ah, that must be it.* The Waiter brings his drink. *Won't you join me?*

D'ASCOYNE: *Thank you, not this evening. We're rather tired.*

D'ASCOYNE glances meaningly at the GIRL and they get up and go. LOUIS watches them go into the hotel.

LOUIS' VOICE: *I deprecated their retiring so early, but it was hard to blame them, for weekends, like life, are short.*

Next day, we see LOUIS come out of the hotel. He goes to a table, sits down and watches the hotel doorway.

LOUIS' VOICE continuing: *The next morning, I waited for them to come down.*

Seated at the same table he is now drinking tea. He yawns.

LOUIS' VOICE continuing: *And the next afternoon. . . .*

Later he is still at the same table, with a glass and a bottle of wine.

LOUIS' VOICE continuing: *They didn't appear the whole day.*

In the garden the following morning, LOUIS is again at the table, trying hard to keep calm.

LOUIS' VOICE continuing: *Nor the morning after. I no longer felt sentimental. The weekend was nearly over, and I could hardly expect Providence to offer me so promising a chance again. I was in a state of desperation.*

Suddenly, with relief, he sees D'ASCOYNE and the GIRL come out of the hotel and walk across the lawn. They approach LOUIS' table, and he stubs out his cigarette, rising expectantly. But they go straight past him, down to the water's edge and into a punt.

LOUIS' VOICE continuing: *And I followed them; hoping for I knew not what.*

D'ASCOYNE is punting along in practised style.

LOUIS follows at a discreet distance in a canoe.

LOUIS' VOICE continuing: *I had the poison with me, but they hadn't even taken a picnic basket. It was possible, however, that they might stop somewhere for refreshment. They did stop, shortly afterwards, but not for that. Judging by past experience, they would be there for hours.*

D'ASCOYNE manoeuvres the punt into the bank, under some overhanging willow trees. He sticks the pole into the mud to keep the punt from moving, and settles down beside the girl, who moves her parasol so as to conceal them both. LOUIS moors on the opposite side of the river. Suddenly he sees a large notice:

WARNING

This reach is DANGEROUS when the weir gates are closed daily at 2 p.m. River users are advised to moor their craft securely. Warning is given by means of a red flag on the bridge.

BY ORDER

LOUIS' VOICE continuing: *The rest followed automatically.*

LOUIS jumps into the river and swims underwater to D'ASCOYNE's punt. He surfaces at the opposite end to the lovers, and frees the mooring rope. (*Still*)

LOUIS' VOICE continuing: *I had fortunately learned to swim at the Clapham Municipal Baths, though I had never had occasion to try it under water. I had no wish to surface under their noses, though I doubt if they would have noticed me even if I had. It was beautifully timed.*

Over the weir the warning flag is hoisted, and the current begins to flow more strongly. The punt glides away and gains speed as it approaches the weir. The couple remain unaware of their predicament, even as the punt disappears over the edge.

LOUIS' VOICE continuing: *I was sorry about the girl, but found some relief in the reflection that she had presumably, during the weekend, already undergone a fate worse than death.*

He rows the canoe back to the mooring.

That night LOUIS is back in his bedroom. He is wearing his pyjamas. He crosses a name off the family tree, turns the picture round again, and gets into bed.

LOUIS' VOICE continuing: *I decided to defer consideration of where and how I should next strike until my nerves were thoroughly restored. It must be remembered that I was very young, and furthermore, I am not naturally callous. I suddenly conceived a brilliant idea. I would write a carefully phrased letter of condolence to old Ascoyne D'Ascoyne. There would be an agreeable feeling of revenge for his cruelty to Mama, and further, it did not fail to occur to me that there was at the moment a vacancy in the Banking House.*

The elderly LORD ASCOYNE D'ASCOYNE is seated, at his desk

213

in the office of a city bank. He rises as LOUIS enters.

LOUIS' VOICE continuing: *Ascoyne D'Ascoyne duly rose to the bait.*

LORD ASCOYNE D'ASCOYNE: *Please be seated, Mr Mazzini. How do you do?*

They shake hands and LOUIS sits, eyeing a photograph on the desk, as he does so.

LORD ASCOYNE D'ASCOYNE: *My late son.*

LOUIS: *A great loss!*

D'ASCOYNE: *He was young and foolish, but I believe that had he been spared until his maturity. . . .*

LOUIS: *It was my consciousness of that which led me to presume to tender you my sympathy.*

D'ASCOYNE: *I am glad that you did so. A loss so tragic serves to put lesser matters in their proper perspective. If I remember rightly, Mr Mazzini, some years ago, I received a communication from your mother.*

Dissolve to the nursery, where SIBELLA is alone waltzing round the room. LOUIS comes in and joins her. They waltz to the mantelpiece and stop.

SIBELLA: *Hullo, Louis. You look very pleased with yourself.*

LOUIS: *So do you.*

SIBELLA: *I have news.*

LOUIS: *And so've I.*

SIBELLA: *What is it?*

LOUIS: *No, yours first.*

SIBELLA: *Lionel and I have fixed a date for our wedding. In two months' time.*

LOUIS: *My congratulations. No, I should congratulate him. I compliment you.*

SIBELLA: *Now yours.*

LOUIS: *Nothing as exciting as yours. I went today to see Lord Ascoyne D'Ascoyne — my cousin, you know. He has a private Banking House in the City. He offered me employment at once at five pounds a week, with excellent prospects of promotion.*

SIBELLA leaning closer to him: *Louis. I'm so glad for you. Louis, do you remember?*

LOUIS: *What?*

SIBELLA: *Once . . . in this room . . . after my party?*

LOUIS: *I kissed you.*
SIBELLA: *Yes.*
LOUIS: *And you were horrible to me.*
SIBELLA: *Yes. I made fun about you being related to the D'Ascoynes. I'm sorry.*
LOUIS: *You take it more seriously now?*
SIBELLA: *Yes. Louis . . . kiss me . . . to show you've forgiven me.*
    LOUIS bends forward to kiss her, then stops himself.
LOUIS: *Er — no, it would be wrong. Your pledge to Lionel. I behaved like a cad that night.*
SIBELLA: *I like you when you behave like a cad.*
    They kiss each other. Suddenly he breaks loose and whirls her into a waltz.
LOUIS: *You're a person who must dance through life, Sibella. I hope Lionel won't tread on your feet too often!*

    LOUIS is now writing at a high clerk's desk, in the Banking House.
LOUIS' VOICE: *My new employment was humble enough, but I had to test the rungs of the ladder before I could climb it.*
    D'ASCOYNE walks past and looks approvingly at LOUIS' work.
D'ASCOYNE: *Very nice.*
    Later in his bedroom, LOUIS studies the family tree. Then he turns back the picture.
LOUIS' VOICE: *The next candidate for removal seemed to be young Henry D'Ascoyne. Twenty-four years old, recently married. As yet without issue.*
    He fetches a scrap-book from the dressing table, and turns the pages until he comes upon a picture of HENRY taking a photo.
LOUIS' VOICE continuing: *I had quite an accumulation by now of D'Ascoyne data, culled from newspapers and periodicals. And I looked through it for a possible approach to Henry.*
    The caption underneath the photograph reads:

MR HENRY D'ASCOYNE, an enthusiastic photographer, has contributed many a beautiful study to our pages.

LOUIS' VOICE continuing: *I found one. I bought the necessary equipment secondhand, and bicycled down the following weekend.*
    We see LOUIS cycling towards a village green.

Louis' Voice: *I had studied a couple of photographic manuals during the week, and found that, in practice, the mysteries of the camera demanded little more than ordinary intelligence, plus the ability to judge a subject upside down.*

Louis sets up his camera outside the village Inn. One or two village children stare curiously at him. He suddenly dives under the velvet cloth in order to make the final adjustments. We see the image as he sees it; upside down and out of focus. The image sharpens and the figure of Henry comes into view, as he surreptitiously emerges from a side door of the Inn.

Louis' Voice continuing: *It was thus indeed, that I first saw Henry D'Ascoyne. My method of approach proved an instantaneous success.*

Henry comes up to Louis and looks at the camera with interest.

Henry: *Excuse me. Isn't that a Thornton Pickard?*

Louis: *Yes. Are you a photographer?*

Henry: *Dabble in it. Got a Sanger Shepherd.*

Louis: *A Sanger Shepherd.*

Henry: *Nice little camera. Focal plane shutter, rapid rectinlinear and all that. Look here, why not come up to my house, and I'll show it to you?*

Louis: *Well, I'd be most interested.*

Henry: *My name's D'Ascoyne, by the way.*

Louis: *Mine is Mazzini.*

Henry picks up the velvet cloth, and together, they pack up the camera.

Louis and Henry are now seen walking through a large gateway, up the drive and towards Henry's house.

Louis' Voice: *He seemed a very pleasant fellow, and I regretted that our acquaintanceship must be so short.*

Henry leads Louis to a small potting shed, and they go inside.

Henry: *Had one of the potting sheds fixed up as a dark room. Couldn't have suited better if it'd been built for it. Had the equip-ment sent down from town.* He lights a gas-lamp. *And I must say the results have been absolutely tophole. I'll show you some quarter-plates I've taken about the village. There we are. Absolutely light-proof, except for this. Er — everything to hand.* He points. *Develop-ing dishes here, toning bath here, whole plate enlarger.*

Louis: *Perfect.*

Henry: *Not too bad, is it? Talking of the village, by the by, I don't know if you're thinking of sending any of your efforts here to some periodical — but there's just one thing. Er* . . . He looks embarassed. *I'm sure you're a good fellow, or I wouldn't like to ask.*

LOUIS: *Ask what?*

HENRY: *I'd be most grateful if you'd keep back that last plate you exposed.*

LOUIS: *The Inn? But it was delightful.*

HENRY: *Yes* . . . *er.* . . .

HENRY: *The — the fact is my wife has views about such places, so I never go in them — you understand.*

LOUIS: *Naturally, I wouldn't dream of embarrassing you.*

HENRY: *I knew you were a good fellow. Suppose we drink on it? Unless you have views yourself, of course?*

LOUIS: *None.*

> HENRY indicates two large bottles on a shelf. They are labelled: ' Developer ' and ' Fixing Solution '.

HENRY: *Splendid. What shall it be? Sherry? Whisky?*

LOUIS: *Oh, I think a small developer.*

> We are now in the drawing-room of HENRY's house.
> EDITH appears in the archway. LOUIS and HENRY are standing by the fireplace.

LOUIS' VOICE: *The mental picture of his wife that I had formed from Henry's words left me unprepared for the charm of the woman I was to meet. She was as tall and slender as a lily, and as beautiful.*

HENRY: *My dear, this is Mr Mazzini. He has a Thornton Pickard. Mr Mazzini, my wife.* (Still)

> EDITH gives LOUIS her hand, and he kisses it.

EDITH: *I'm no photographer myself, Mr Mazzini, but I share my husband's pleasure in welcoming a fellow enthusiast. You'll take some sherry?*

LOUIS: *Well, thank you I.* . . . .

> As EDITH goes to ring for the BUTLER, HENRY nods to LOUIS, indicating that he can accept. He then shakes his head pointing to himself.

EDITH: *My husband and I never touch alcohol, but we see no reason, on that account, to enforce our views on our guests.*

> She turns to the BUTLER, as he appears in the archway.

EDITH to BUTLER: *A glass of sherry, Harwood.*

The prospect of watching LOUIS drinking is too much for HENRY.

HENRY: *I — er — have some printing frames out in the sun. If you don't mind, I'll just run out and see to them.*

He goes out hurriedly.

EDITH: *Have you been in the neighbourhood long, Mr Mazzini?*

EDITH sits and LOUIS follows suit.

LOUIS: *A few hours only. I was — er — cycling through the village and felt compelled to stop and make a study or two of the Inn. It looked so charming.*

EDITH: *It does look charming. But I'm afraid it's by no means an influence for good in the lives of our people here. The landlord is a former coachman of ours. I have spoken to him several times about the amount of drinking that goes on there, but he continues to allow it.*

LOUIS: *It is, after all, I suppose, his livelihood.*

EDITH: *I do not consider he has the right to make a livelihood by exploiting the weaknesses of his fellow men.*

The BUTLER brings in the sherry.

LOUIS: *Put as you put it, it does sound deplorable.*

EDITH: *It is deplorable. Will you excuse me a moment?*

She gets up to speak to the BUTLER, HARWOOD.

LOUIS' VOICE: *I could well understand Henry's visits to the village Inn, and his stock of refreshments in the dark-room. Mrs D'Ascoyne was beautiful. But what a prig she was. I wondered how to ingratiate myself with her, and decided to attack with her own weapons.*

EDITH sitting down again: *I'm afraid we can offer you only a simple luncheon, Mr Mazzini.*

LOUIS: *You are most kind. But I feel I should not intrude.*

EDITH: *It is no intrusion.*

LOUIS: *I'm afraid it is. May I explain?*

EDITH: *Please do.*

LOUIS: *It was only when your husband told me his name that I realised that I'd come by chance into the most embarrassing situation. My mother was a member of the D'Ascoyne family. She married, as they thought, beneath her, and from that day, they refused to recognise her or my existence. I feel, therefore, that although in the circumstances, you might hesitate to say so to my face, you and your husband would prefer not to receive me at your*

218

table. Perhaps you would be good enough to explain matters to your husband for me. I shall naturally leave the neighbourhood at once.

EDITH puts out her hand to stop LOUIS from leaving.

EDITH: *Mr Mazzini, please sit down.*

LOUIS sitting down: *Oh, well. . . .*

EDITH: *You have exhibited the most delicate feelings. I know nothing of the history to which you refer, but I have often felt that the attitude of my husband's family has failed to move with the times, that they think too much of the rights of nobility and too little of its duties. The very honesty of your behaviour would appear to me to prove them wrong. Was Lord Tennyson far from the mark when he wrote — 'Kind hearts are more than coronets, and simple faith than Norman blood.' I hope you will stay to luncheon.*

LOUIS: *Oh, in that case, I should be delighted . . . and honoured.*

Later on the same day, LOUIS is cycling out of the large gateway.

LOUIS' VOICE: *My impersonation of a man of sterling character was such a resounding success that Mrs D'Ascoyne invited me to spend the following Saturday to Monday with them.*

There is a great coming and going at the **Hallward House**. LOUIS walks up the steps and through the front door.

LOUIS' VOICE: *When I returned to the somewhat contrasting atmosphere of Clapham, I found the house in a whirl with preparation for Sibella's wedding to Lionel, which was to take place next day.*

He goes to the nursery where SIBELLA is sitting, gazing into the fire.

LOUIS' VOICE continuing: *Before going to bed that evening, I wandered into the old nursery to fetch a book I'd left there.*

LOUIS: *Penny for them.*

SIBELLA: *Oh, hullo Louis.*

LOUIS: *You're not looking as radiantly happy as young females in your situation are supposed to look.*

SIBELLA: *I was just thinking of all the fun we've had in this room, you and I and Graham.*

LOUIS: *And Lionel.*

SIBELLA: *Yes, and Lionel.*

She turns around and throws herself into LOUIS's arms, sobbing hysterically.

219

SIBELLA continuing: *Oh, Louis, I don't want to marry Lionel.*
LOUIS: *Why not?*
SIBELLA: *He's so dull.*
LOUIS: *I must admit he exhibits the most extraordinary capacity for middle age that I've ever encountered in a young man of twenty-four. However, it's a bit late in the day to think of that, isn't it?*
SIBELLA: *I know. That only makes it worse.*
LOUIS: *I always told you you should marry me.*
SIBELLA: *I know. That makes it worse, too.*

She looks up at him and they embrace.

SIBELLA and LIONEL are now standing, receiving guests after the wedding. LOUIS comes in and kisses SIBELLA's hand.

LOUIS: *You look more lovely today than I've ever seen you.* He turns to LIONEL. *You're a lucky man, Lionel, take my word for it.*

He moves towards a table on which the wedding presents are laid out.

LOUIS' VOICE: *I could not help feeling that even Sibella's capacity for lying was going to be taxed to the utmost. Time had brought me revenge on Lionel, and as the Italian proverb says — ' Revenge is a dish which people of taste prefer to eat cold.'*

LOUIS is now in the grounds of HENRY's house. It is very dark. He creeps towards the shed, carrying a small can.

LOUIS' VOICE: *The following Saturday, I left London in the middle of the night, and reached Henry's house just before dawn.*

He goes into the shed, brings out the dark room lamp, and fills it with the contents of the can.

LOUIS' VOICE continuing: *It took a mere three minutes to substitute petrol for the paraffin in the dark-room lamp.*

He runs towards a haystack and throws himself down in the hay.

LOUIS' VOICE continuing: *And I then repaired to a meadow and took a few hours' sleep, while awaiting the hour at which I could reasonably arrive at the house.*

EDITH is instructing LOUIS in archery, on a lawn in the grounds of the house, HENRY takes their photographs.

LOUIS' VOICE: *The day dragged by in an agony of suspense for me. Henry took photograph after photograph but seemed to have no urge whatever to follow it up . . . with a visit to the dark-room.*

EDITH poses with an arrow and bow. HENRY takes a photograph of her with great enthusiasm. She releases the arrow and it lands dead centre of the target.

HENRY off: *Bravo, Edith.*

LOUIS' VOICE: *I began to fear that he had suddenly taken the pledge....*

HENRY walking towards EDITH: *I think I'll just go and develop these before tea.* Turning to LOUIS. *Care to come?*

LOUIS: *I would indeed, but I have a slight headache. The sun, I think — and I'm afraid the chemicals wouldn't improve it.*

EDITH: *Mr Mazzini and I will have tea under the tulip tree.* Turning to LOUIS. *I've always found that most beneficial for a headache.*

LOUIS and EDITH are seated under a tree.

A table is set out for tea. (*Still*)

LOUIS: *I'm afraid Henry will think me a poor enthusiast.*

EDITH: *I sometimes think that he is too great a one. In a way, I am to blame for it. Before we were married, he had few interests. He used to spend the greater part of each day at his club.*

A loud explosion is heard. EDITH does not seem to hear.

EDITH continuing: *I felt that such a life was unhealthy, and persauded him to come and live here in the country. I hoped that perhaps he would interest himself in the welfare of our tenantry, as I do . . . but he became interested in photography on our honeymoon, and since then it has become the major preoccupation of his life.*

A column of black smoke is beginning to rise in the distance.

LOUIS watches it.

EDITH off: *Mr Mazzini. . . .*

LOUIS: *Yes?*

LOUIS hastily turns his attention to EDITH.

EDITH: *I hope you will forgive my speaking to you on a personal matter. But it worries me that Henry should spend so much time on his hobby that he has little left for any more useful activity. Am I right to let him go on like this?*

LOUIS sips his tea. He appears to ponder EDITH's question.

LOUIS' VOICE: *I could hardly point out that Henry now had no time left for any kind of activity, so I continued to discuss his future.*

LOUIS: *He has never shown any wish for a career in politics?*

EDITH: *None.*

LOUIS: *Nor any other ambitions?*

EDITH: *One only. To win a prize at the Salon of Photography in Brussels.* She breaks off, listening. *What is it?*

LOUIS: *Oh, they're just burning some leaves at the bottom of the garden.*

EDITH: *But they can't be at this time of year.*

She turns and sees the smoke. She springs up with a cry.

EDITH continuing: *Henry!*

LOUIS is also on his feet, and stops her from running towards the shrubbery.

LOUIS: *No, you stay here.*

He runs in the direction of the smoke.

LOUIS' VOICE: *Needless to say, I was too late.*

In the village churchyard the mourners are making their way towards the church.

LOUIS' VOICE: *The funeral service was held in the village church at Chalfont, prior to interment in the family vault.*

A carriage drives up, LOUIS descends and helps out EDITH, who is in widow's weeds.

LOUIS' VOICE continuing: *Mrs D'Ascoyne, who had discerned in me a man of delicate sensibility and high purpose, asked me to accompany her on the cross-country journey.*

REVEREND LORD HENRY D'ASCOYNE is in the pulpit of the church. He is very old and drones on interminably.

LORD HENRY: *To everything there is a season, and a time to every purpose under the Heaven. A time to be born . . . and a time to die.*

LOUIS is sitting in a pew, facing the nave.

LOUIS' VOICE: *The occasion was interesting in that it provided me with my first sight of the D'Ascoynes en masse. (Still) Interesting, and somewhat depressing, for it emphasised how far I had yet to travel. There was the Duke. . . .*

DUKE ETHELRED and EDITH are sitting in the family pew. EDITH is weeping quietly.

LOUIS' VOICE continuing: *There was my employer, Lord Ascoyne D'Ascoyne.*

LORD ASCOYNE D'ASCOYNE removes his monocle.

LOUIS' VOICE continuing: *There was Admiral Lord Horatio D'Ascoyne.*

Admiral Lord Horatio D'Ascoyne looks disdainful.

Louis' Voice continuing: *There was General Lord Rufus D'Ascoyne.*

General Lord Rufus D'Ascoyne is bald and bemedalled.

Louis' Voice continuing: *There was Lady Agatha D'Ascoyne.*

Lady Agatha D'Ascoyne is very stern. She turns to Lord Rufus who is snoring.

Lady Agatha: *Ssh!*

Louis' Voice: *And in the pulpit, talking interminable nonsense, the Reverend Lord Henry D'Ascoyne.*

Lord Henry preaching drearily: *The life cut short . . . was . . . one . . . rich . . . in achievement and promise . . . of service to humanity!*

Louis yawns discreetly behind his hand.

Louis' Voice: *The D'Ascoynes certainly appeared to have accorded with the tradition of the landed gentry, and sent the fool of the family into the Church.*

After the service, Edith, Louis and Duke Ethelred are standing outside the church, awaiting a carriage.

Duke Ethelred to Edith: *Well, goodbye, m'dear!*

Edith weeping: *Goodbye.*

Duke: *No fretting now. After all, one thing to be said, we all have to come to it. Great thing, you know, family vault like ours. Constant reminder of one's heritage. Now, take this new cremation nonsense. . . . Who wants to see his nearest and dearest put in an incinerator?*

Edith is even more upset and Louis intervenes.

Louis to Duke: *I think, sir, Mrs D'Ascoyne should leave. The wind is turning cold.*

Duke: *As Mrs D'Ascoyne thinks best.* Ignoring Louis, he speaks to Edith. *Glad we had Cousin Henry to take the service. Boring old ass, but it keeps the thing in the family.* He opens the carriage door to Edith. *People getting strange ideas these days. Had a fellow write to me not so long age — wanted to bury his mother here. From Tooting or somewhere. Start letting strangers in, the place'll be full up. No room for us, eh?*

Edith gets into the carriage and Louis follows her.

Louis' Voice: *I privately promised him that I would make it my business to see there was room for him.*

Inside the carriage, EDITH is sitting bolt upright.

EDITH: *Uncle Ethelred is not the most tactful of men.*

LOUIS: *I could gladly have struck him.*

EDITH smiling wanly: *Thank you for intervening when you did. The house will be so empty, and yet he will be in it everywhere. I find the thought of life there hard to face.*

LOUIS sympathetically: *Must you stay there? A new environment. . . .*

EDITH: *I must. For one reason, if no other. They would say I was running away, that there was truth in all these rumours.*

LOUIS: *Rumours?*

EDITH: *In the village. There's been gossip. They say that Henry drank, in secret. They even say that that was the cause of the accident.*

She almost breaks down, then recovers herself.

LOUIS: *I am sure that Henry would never have professed one thing, and practised another.*

EDITH: *I too am sure. Otherwise, I think I could not survive.*

LOUIS: *We have a long way to go. Try to sleep a little.*

EDITH: *Sleep does not come easily.*

LOUIS: *Please try. Allow me.*

He settles the rug more comfortably around her knees.

LOUIS' VOICE: *I was conscious that a new obsession was about to join the one that I should wear the coronet of the Duke of Chalfont . . .*

He looks fondly at EDITH. . . . *that Edith D'Ascoyne should wear that of the Duchess beside me.*

The carriage is now arriving at EDITH's house.

LOUIS' VOICE continuing: *Her dignity of bearing in the worst moments of her grief had impressed me with the feeling that here was a woman whose quality matched her beauty.*

LOUIS and EDITH descend from the carriage, and walk towards the house.

LOUIS' VOICE continuing: *I resolved to embark upon her courtship as soon as a decent period of mourning should have elapsed.*

We see a close-up of SIBELLA's photograph. It depicts her on a bicycle and holding an ice-cream cornet.

LOUIS' VOICE continuing: *Sibella? Yes, Sibella was pretty enough in her suburban way. . . .*

LOUIS is back in his bedroom. He is holding SIBELLA's photograph in his hand.

LOUIS' VOICE continuing: *. . . And indeed, there was no reason why* *we shouldn't continue to meet on friendly terms. . . . But her face would have looked rather out of place under a coronet.*

LORD ASCOYNE D'ASCOYNE is sitting in his office.
LOUIS is standing by his side and places some papers on his desk.
LOUIS: *That, sir, is the list of bills due for redemption this week. I've marked in red those asking for renewal.*
LORD D'ASCOYNE: *Aitcheson — yes. Pole and Carter — I suppose so. Knollis, Limited — Oh, no! Redbank and Holland . . . you have a friend there, have you not?*
LOUIS: *An acquaintance. I know Lionel Holland.*
LORD D'ASCOYNE: *Would you say that he's sound?*
LOUIS hesitates momentarily: *I wouldn't say not, sir.*
LORD D'ASCOYNE signs the papers and LOUIS blots his signatures.
LORD D'ASCOYNE: *Hm! Thank you. Mazzini. . . .*
LOUIS: *Yes, sir?*
LORD D'ASCOYNE removing his monocle: *I've watched your progress here with great care, and have been gratified to note that it has fully justified my judgment in inviting you into the firm. In view of that, and in order that you may be able to adopt a style of living befitting a member of the D'Ascoyne family, I have decided to appoint you my private secretary, at a salary of five hundred pounds per annum.*
LOUIS: *Sir, I cannot begin to. . . .*
LORD D'ASCOYNE: *Please do not try. I had intended that my son should occupy that position.*
LOUIS looking moved: *I can only say that I will try to make my occupancy of it worthy of his memory.*

We are in a suite of chambers in St James'. LOUIS is standing by a mantelpiece, over which hangs the painting of Chalfont Castle. He is delicately sipping from a glass of sherry.
LOUIS' VOICE: *I left the Hallward's house and took a bachelor apartment in St James'. Clapham no longer held Sibella's presence to compensate me for the tedious journey between the suburbs and the City. Anyhow, it would be vastly more convenient for her to visit me here.*
A bell rings. He goes to the door and opens it to find SIBELLA, beautifully dressed. She curtsies to him and comes in. He puts out his arms towards her.
LOUIS: *Now, let me have a look at the beautiful Mrs Holland. No,*

I think I prefer Miss Hallward.

SIBELLA turning her back to him: *So do I. Louis, it's very wrong of me to visit you here.*

LOUIS: *Why?*

SIBELLA: *A married woman calling on a bachelor — a dangerous bachelor — in his apartments!*

LOUIS pouring her a glass of sherry: *I . . . dangerous? These things only become wrong when people know about them. This is a very discreet apartment. That's why I chose it.*

SIBELLA: *So that young women could call on you in safety?*

LOUIS: *So that one young woman could.*

SIBELLA: *How did you know she'd want to?*

LOUIS: *I hoped.*

He hands her the glass, and sits down beside her.

LOUIS: *How did you enjoy your honeymoon?*

SIBELLA: *Not at all.*

LOUIS: *Not at all?*

SIBELLA: *Not at all.*

LOUIS: *And how was Italy?*

SIBELLA: *Oh, impossible! Every time I wanted to go shopping, Lionel dragged me off to a church or picture gallery. He said he wanted to improve his mind.*

LOUIS: *He has room to do so.*

SIBELLA: *I should reprove you for saying unkind things about him. But I can't. Louis, I think I've married the most boring man in London!*

LOUIS: *In England!*

SIBELLA: *In Europe!* She sips her sherry. *Oh, the Italian men are so handsome. But I could never get away from Lionel for a moment. But I was forgetting. You're Italian.*

LOUIS: *Half.*

SIBELLA: *Louis, I can speak frankly to you?*

LOUIS: *Well, if not to me, to whom?*

SIBELLA: *I shall go mad. Already when he touches me, I want to scream.*

They fall into a passionate embrace.

SIBELLA pushing him away: *What am I doing?*

LOUIS: *You know very well. Your're playing with fire.*

SIBELLA: *At least it warms me. I must go.*

She gets up and moves towards the door.

SIBELLA: *Lionel is dining at home tonight.*
LOUIS: *And where is Lionel dining tomorrow night?*
SIBELLA: *With some business acquaintances.*
LOUIS: *And where are you dining tomorrow night?*
SIBELLA: *Here?*
LOUIS: *Here.*

> He opens the door to her and bows. She makes her exit and LOUIS returns to the living room.

LOUIS' VOICE: *Poor little imprisoned bird. Well, she was welcome to come and flutter her wings with me. I could think of many more disagreeable ways of killing time, pending the arrival of the moment when the conventional decencies would permit me to make my declaration to Edith.* He takes another drink. *As to the other undertaking, I had not forgotten or forgiven the boredom of the sermon at young Henry's funeral . . .*

> The REVEREND LORD HENRY is walking across Chalfont churchyard, towards the church.

LOUIS' VOICE: *. . . and I decided to promote the Reverend Lord Henry D'Ascoyne to next place on the list.*

> LOUIS, dressed as a bishop and wearing a top hat, is cycling along the road leading to Chalfont Church.

LOUIS' VOICE continuing: *I therefore assumed the garb and character of a Colonial Bishop spending his vacation making a collection of brass rubbings from country churches.*

> LOUIS is now kneeling inside the church. He is taking a brass rubbing on the chancel floor. LORD HENRY approaches him.

LORD HENRY: *Good evening, my Lord.*

LOUIS' VOICE: *It was for a moment a shock to be addressed by my ecclesiastical title, but I recovered quickly.*

LOUIS rising: *Good evening. I was just taking a rubbing of this most interesting brass.*

LORD HENRY: *An ancestress of my dear late wife. Allow me to introduce myself — Henry D'Ascoyne, Rector of this Parish.*

> They shake hands firmly, up and down.

LOUIS: *Septimus Wilkinson, Bishop of Matabeleland. I'm spending my vacation taking a cycling tour round your beautiful country churches.*

LORD HENRY: *Ah! Have you noticed our clerestory?*

Louis puzzled: *Cle.... Ah, exquisite!*

Lord Henry: *The corbals are very fine. Perhaps your Lordship would permit me to show you one or two other things in which we take a pride.*

Louis: *I should be most interested.*

> They begin to take a stroll around the church, Lord Henry leading the way.

Lord Henry with an occasional stutter: *Our most notable features, of course, are the D'Ascoyne memorials. Every member of the family — t-to a cadet branch of which I have the honour to belong — is buried here in the family vault.* They pause a moment in front of two busts. *Here you see the first Duke and his Duchess. . . . The dead watching, as it were, over the living. The Church is exceptionally endowed also with items of architectural interest.* He waves his hand upwards. *You will note that our chantry displays the crocketted and finialed ogee, which marks it as very early perpendicular. Th-the bosses to the pendant are typical.* Louis tries to look impressed. *And I always say that my west window has all the exuberance of Chaucer without happily any of the concomitant crudities of his period.*

Louis to himself: *Hm!*

Lord Henry: *Now we approach the font. . . .*

> They move outside into the churchyard.

Louis' Voice: *At last, he did as I had hoped and invited me to dinner.*

> In the dining room of the rectory, Louis and Lord Henry are sitting over their port.

Louis' Voice: *The Reverend Lord Henry was not one of those new-fangled parsons who carry the principles of their vocation uncomfortably into private life.*

> Lord Henry passes the port decanter to Louis.

Louis' Voice continuing: *However, he exhibited a polite interest in the progress of the Christian faith in Matabeleland which I was at some difficulty to satisfy.*

Louis: *The S.P.C.K. have provided us with a large number of copies of the Good Book, translated into Matabelee, but as none of the natives can read even their own language. . . .* He sighs.

Lord Henry: *You speak Matabelee yourself?*

Louis: *Not as a native.*

Lord Henry: *It — it would be most interesting to hear a sample of the language.*

LOUIS: *I am afraid my Matabelee is a little rusty.*

LORD HENRY: *Oh, come, My Lord. Er — er — Daniel — er — cast into the lion's den, for example.*

LOUIS: *Hm. . . .*

> With an effort LOUIS speaks in gibberish consisting of grunts, groans and clicks. LORD HENRY looks quite horrified.

LOUIS off: *This is a — colloquial rendering, of course.*

LORD HENRY passing more port: *Most interesting! My Lord, the port is with you.*

LOUIS: *Oh!*

LORD HENRY: *How do you find the wine?*

LOUIS: *Admirable.*

LORD HENRY: *Cockburn '69.*

LOUIS: *Hm!*

LORD HENRY: *No finer year, in my view. My doctor, though, is of a different opinion.* He finishes his glass.

LOUIS: *And what does he favour?*

LORD HENRY: *Abstinence!*

LOUIS amused: *Ha! Ha! Ha! Ha!*

LORD HENRY: *Would you care for a cigar?*

LOUIS: *Thank you.*

> LORD HENRY rises to go to the sideboard. While his back is turned, LOUIS tips some poison into the decanter.

LORD HENRY: *Yes . . . he's continually warning me about the state of my arteries. But I say to him — what possible harm can there be in one glass of an evening. . . . Or even two?*

> He returns to the table and hands LOUIS a cigar.

LOUIS: *What harm indeed?*

LORD HENRY: *You do not condemn me, then?*

LOUIS: *Not in the least.*

> LOUIS smiles indulgently, and passes the decanter back to his host who refills his own glass.

LORD HENRY: *If I may say so — without disrespect to my superiors — your visit has brought me something which I could not expect from any churchman in this country.*

> He drinks the poisoned port and, after a pause, looks very ill. He closes his eyes and slumps in his chair. He is dead.
>
> LOUIS looks at LORD HENRY. (*Still*) Picking up the decanter, he goes to the sideboard and disposes of its contents. He then walks

back and places the empty decanter on the table.

LOUIS' VOICE: *I surmised correctly, as it proved, that Lord Henry's doctor would assume that he had succumbed to a surfeit of port, and would politely ascribe death to a heart attack.*

LOUIS is back in his room, crossing off another name on the family tree.

LOUIS' VOICE continuing: *On my return to London, I decided to proceed methodically with the remaining minor obstacles. Lady Agatha D'Ascoyne was a pioneer in the campaign for Women's Suffrage . . .*

We now see LADY AGATHA D'ASCOYNE walking down a street and breaking windows with her umbrella. She is suddenly set upon by two policemen, who force her into a black maria.

LOUIS' VOICE continuing: *. . . with the inconvenient consequence that her public appearances were invariably made under the watchful eyes of the Metropolitan Police. When she was not making public appearances, she was in prison and still more inaccessible. In fact, before I could learn of a favourable opportunity, I had to join the movement myself.*

LOUIS is now marching along, rather furtively, in a procession of suffragettes holding one end of the banner which reads:

RELEASE
LADY AGATHA D'ASCOYNE

LOUIS' VOICE: *Secret plans had been made for Lady Agatha to celebrate her latest release from Holloway by a shower of leaflets over Whitehall and the West End.*

We are now in a park where a group of women surround LADY AGATHA, who stands shouting from within the basket of a tethered balloon. (*Still*) As the police rush forward, she releases it. The balloon rises into the sky, and she showers leaflets down upon the city. The poster on her balloon reads:

WOMEN OF BRITAIN
FIGHT FOR YOUR RIGHTS!

LADY AGATHA: *Anchor!*

LOUIS is at an open open window with a bow and arrow, he takes careful aim and lets fly.

LOUIS' VOICE: *I shot an arrow in the air . . . she fell to earth in*

Berkeley Square.

We now see part of a battle fleet on the high seas. Three ships are steaming along abreast. ADMIRAL LORD HORATIO D'ASCOYNE is standing on the deck of one, issuing orders to the CAPTAIN.

LOUIS' VOICE: *Admiral Lord Horatio D'Ascoyne presented a more difficult problem. He scarcely ever set foot ashore, and I was beginning to feel that this task was beyond even my ingenuity. . . .*

We see LOUIS looking puzzled as he studies a complicated print of a torpedo.

LOUIS' VOICE continuing: *. . . when he was conveniently involved in a naval disaster, which arose from a combination of natural obstinacy, and a certain confusion of mind, unfortunate in one of his rank.*

The ADMIRAL and the CAPTAIN stand side by side on the bridge of the ship.

ADMIRAL LORD HORATIO D'ASCOYNE: *Bring her to port!*

CAPTAIN: *Surely you mean starboard, sir.*

ADMIRAL LORD HORATIO D'ASCOYNE shouting: *Port!*

Two of the battleships steam steadily towards each other and collide.

LOUIS' VOICE: *Both ships sank almost immediately, though, fortunately, all hands were saved . . . save one! Admiral Lord Horatio, obstinate to the last, insisted on going down with his ship.*

The ADMIRAL stands like a rock on board his ship, and he is soon completely submerged. (*Still*) Only his hat remains floating on the surface of the water.

It is evening at the Cavalry Club. GENERAL LORD RUFUS D'ASCOYNE sits at a table, demonstrating his battles to some bored looking JUNIOR OFFICERS.

LOUIS' VOICE: *General Lord Rufus D'Ascoyne, on the other hand, who never tired of demonstrating how he had fought the most calamitous campaign of the South African War, was a fairly easy proposition.*

GENERAL LORD RUFUS: *At that moment, the concealed enemy emerged from behind the kopje. I held our guns' fire until we could see the whites of their eyes. . . . Then I gave the order — ' Fire '. . . . Boom! Boom! Boom!*

We are back in LOUIS' apartment. He is preparing a bomb to be hidden in a pot of caviare. (*Still*)

231

Louis' Voice: *It seemed appropriate that he who had lived amidst the cannons' roar, should die explosively. I therefore concealed in a pot of caviare a simple but powerful home-made bomb, and, through the post, I sent the caviare to the General.*

In the Cavalry Club, the waiter places the caviare pot on the table, in front of the General.

General Lord Rufus: *I pretended to be deceived by the feint, and sent our horse to meet it. At that moment, the concealed enemy emerged from behind the kopje. . . . I held our guns' fire till we could see the whites of their eyes. . . . Used to get a lot of this stuff in the Crimea — one thing the Russkies do really well.*

As the General puts his knife into the caviare pot, the bomb explodes.

Louis' Voice: *Not an atom of him was left.*

We are in the Banking House. Lord Ascoyne is sitting behind his desk in his office, Louis is seated opposite him.

Lord Ascoyne: *One could almost believe there was a curse on our unfortunate family, Mazzini.*

Louis: *Indeed, sir, one could.*

Lord Ascoyne: *I don't know if you realise how close this series of tragedies has brought you to the succession.*

Louis: *I had not actually given the matter any thought, sir.*

Lord Ascoyne: *Then it's time that you did. Do you not realise that you are heir presumptive to the Dukedom? That is to say, in the event of the present Duke dying without issue, I alone intervene between you and the title? And I am an old man. I've never really recovered from the first of these calamities.*

Louis: *You mean I might become Duke of Chalfont?*

Lord Ascoyne: *I mean that you almost certainly will. In view of that, I feel it would be more fitting that you should cease to be an employee here,* Louis' face falls . . . *and become instead my partner.*

Louis with obvious relief: *Ah! I'm most deeply grateful and honoured.*

Lord Ascoyne: *If you will come round here, I'll make everything very clear to you. Er — had she lived, your mother, of course, would have succeeded before you.*

Lord Ascoyne takes out a scroll and unrolls the family tree.

Later, we are again in the office of the Banking House. Louis is now sitting behind the desk in Lord Ascoyne's habitual place.

232

LIONEL comes in.

LOUIS' VOICE: *One of my first tasks as partner was to interview Lionel, who came cap, or rather, silk hat in hand. . . .*

LOUIS: *To save time, I presume you have called to ask for renewal of your bill?*

LIONEL: *The fact is, old boy, we sold short, and the market hasn't dropped as we expected.*

LOUIS: *I feel entitled to point out that we here regard our function as the encouragement of constructive investment, and not the financing of mere gambling transactions. Er. . . .*

LOUIS looks through some papers.

LOUIS' VOICE: *It would have delighted me to refuse him. However, a bankrupt Lionel could hardly have continued to support Sibella in her extravagances, and I had no wish to do so myself.*

LOUIS: *Very well. We will renew at three and a half per cent.*

In the gardens in front of HENRY's house, LOUIS and EDITH are taking a stroll.

LOUIS' VOICE: *I judged that the time was now ripe to make a move in the matter of Edith D'Ascoyne.*

EDITH: *It's coming cold. Shall we go in?*

In the sitting-room, LOUIS stands near EDITH, who is seated on the sofa.

LOUIS: *I know why you shivered just now. It was not because you were cold.*

EDITH: *No. I couldn't help remembering.*

LOUIS: *I know. But do you try to forget? Er — I may sound harsh, but believe me. . . .*

LOUIS is about to sit down in an armchair, but EDITH gestures to stop him.

EDITH: *Please — not there.*

LOUIS: *Because it was Henry's chair?*

EDITH: *It hasn't been used since that day. Nothing of his. Everything is just as he left it — his writing desk, his clothes. I cannot bear that it should be otherwise.*

LOUIS sitting down beside her on the couch: *You want this house to be a shrine. You are wrong. Shrines are not meant to house the living. I've always respected you — your principles, your courage, above any woman I've ever met. It is your duty to yourself and to others — to Henry even — to live again in the present — in the future!*

EDITH: *What future is there for me?*

LOUIS walks over to the window and turns to face EDITH.

LOUIS: *I am now going to say something presumptuous. You must order me from your house if you wish. It is this — If you should ever feel that the constant support of a — of a devoted admirer would be of assistance to you, I should be most honoured if you would permit me to offer you my hand in marriage.*

EDITH standing up: *Mr Mazzini! This is a shock. I'm most touched — most grateful, but I could not consider even the possibility of re-marrying.*

LOUIS: *I've spoken too boldly — and too soon. Please regard what I have said merely as something to draw upon should you ever feel so inclined.*

We return to LOUIS' apartment. SIBELLA is sitting in an arm-chair, gazing into the firelight.

LOUIS' VOICE: *Sibella was waiting for me when I got back. I was pleased to see her. For while I never admired Edith as much as when I was with Sibella, I never longed for Sibella as much as when I was with Edith.*

LOUIS coming into the room: *I'm afraid I'm late. Have you been bored?*

SIBELLA: *No. I've been looking into the fire and thinking.*

LOUIS: *What about?*

SIBELLA: *Oh, how we used to roast chestnuts round the other fire, and what a lot has happened since.*

LOUIS sitting down on the arm of the chair next to her: *Such as?*

SIBELLA: *How you told me not to marry Lionel because you might be a Duke one day. And how I laughed at you. And how I married Lionel, and now you very nearly are a Duke.*

LOUIS: *We're much better off as we are, you and I.*

He takes her hand and kisses it.

SIBELLA: *It's all very well for you to say that. You're not married to Lionel.*

LOIUS: *We see each other when we want to. . . .* He gets up and moves towards the sideboard. *We're not obliged to see each other when we don't want to.*

234

SIBELLA: *We don't see each other as often as I'd like to. You've been away the whole weekend.*

LOUIS pours some sherry.

LOUIS: *I had to go.*

SIBELLA: *Where?*

LOUIS: *To see Mrs D'Ascoyne, the widow of that cousin of mine who was killed.*

SIBELLA: *All your cousins seem to get killed. I really wouldn't be in the least surprised if you'd murdered them all. Oh!*

LOUIS stumbles with shock, and spills the sherry over SIBELLA's dress. He bends to wipe it off with a handkerchief. SIBELLA's eyes hold a glint of speculation.

LOUIS: *How clumsy of me! What ever made you say that!*

He rises and wipes his hands.

SIBELLA: *Just silliness.*

LOUIS: *Well, if you promise not to tell anyone, I'll let you into my guilty secret. I did murder them all.*

SIBELLA smiling: *Hm! Hm! I've suspected it for a long time. What's she like?*

LOUIS: *Who?*

SIBELLA: *Mrs D'Ascoyne.*

LOUIS: *Oh, she's — er — tall . . . slender. . . .*

SIBELLA: *Beautiful?*

LOUIS: *Yes, I suppose some people would call her beautiful.*

SIBELLA: *Would you?*

LOUIS: *I suppose so. I never really thought about that.*

SIBELLA: *What would you say if she asked you about me?*

LOUIS walks to the other side of the room and turns to face SIBELLA.

LOUIS: *I'd say that you were the perfect combination of imperfections. I'd say that your nose was just a little too short . . . your mouth just a little too wide . . . but that yours was a face that a man could see in his dreams for the whole of his life. I'd say that you were vain, selfish, cruel, deceitful. I'd say that you were adorable. I'd say that you were Sibella.*

He walks back across the room.

SIBELLA: *What a pretty speech!*

LOUIS: *I mean it.*

SIBELLA: *Come and say it to me again.*

235

Louis sits down beside her, on the arm of her chair. He touches her nose and mouth gently as he speaks.

Louis: *I'd say your nose was just a little too short. And your mouth — yes, your mouth just a little too wide.*

He kisses her.

Louis' Voice: *Shortly afterwards, my employer had a stroke.*

In the office, we see Lord Ascoyne lying on a couch. A Doctor is at his side. After a pause the Doctor leaves.

Louis' Voice continuing: *There was little that could be done, and the doctor gave him a month at the most to live. I was glad after all his kindness to me that I should not have to kill the old man. Soon, the only obstacle between me and my inheritance would be the Duke himself.*

Louis is walking thoughtfully up and down in front of the watercolour of the Castle.

Louis' Voice: *I could lay no plan for disposing of him, as the life he led within those great stone walls was a closed book to me. I was gloomily examining the problem for the hundredth time, as I awaited one day the expected arrival of Sibella at my apartments.*

The doorbell goes. Louis opens the door to reveal Edith looking very beautiful and dressed in half-mourning.

Edith: *Good afternoon, Mr Mazzini.*

Louis: *Mrs D'Ascoyne.*

Edith: *I was passing through St James', and thought I would take the opportunity to call on you.*

Edith comes in, Louis follows her looking rather concerned.

Louis: *Was that wise — er — discreet, I mean?*

Edith: *There are some conventions which must be governed by individual circumstance. Surely it is safe for a woman to visit a man of your reputation?*

Louis: *It is of your reputation that I'm thinking. Without being inhospitable, I would be happier if your visit were not a long one.*

Edith: *I appreciate the scrupulousness of your motives. I have anyhow only one important matter to speak of.*

Louis: *And that is?*

Edith: *I have thought a great deal about what you said at our last meeting, and I have tried to think what Henry's wishes would be. I remember he said to me once — 'You have too much good in you,*

Edith, for one man. I sometimes wish that others could have a share of it.' LOUIS *smiles and bows. I have reconsidered the offer you made to me — thank you again for it — and I accept it gladly.*

LOUIS: *Oh, you rob me of words.*

EDITH: *I think, however, we should make no announcement for three months at least.*

LOUIS: *Oh — as you think best. In these — er — new circumstances, I think it more than ever desirable that your unconventional, though in its purpose delightful, visit should be cut short.*

EDITH: *If your attention as a husband is the equal of your considera- tion as a friend, I shall have made a most fortunate decision.*

As he escorts her to the door, he glances at the picture of Chalfont.

LOUIS: *Do you not think, though, that perhaps Uncle Ethelred, as head of the family, should be told at once?*

EDITH: *Perhaps so. Yes, I'll write to him. Goodbye, Louis!*

LOUIS *kissing her hand: Goodbye, Edith! You leave behind you the happiest man in London.*

LOUIS opens the door for her to leave.

LOUIS' VOICE: *This was not a piece of news which I was looking for- ward to breaking to Sibella. She had no rights in the matter.* He wipes his brow and pours himself a sherry. *But women have a disconcerting ability to make scenes out of nothing, and to prove themselves injured when they themselves are at fault. Anyhow, I had three months' grace before I need face that storm.*

The doorbell rings and he goes to answer it.

SIBELLA appears wearing an enormous flowered hat. She comes in sniffing the air.

SIBELLA: *You've taken to using Attar of Roses?*

LOUIS: *No— why?*

SIBELLA: *Hm! I thought I could smell it. I met such a beautiful woman on the stairs just now.*

LOUIS: *I expect that would be Mrs D'Ascoyne.*

SIBELLA: *What was she doing here?*

LOUIS: *Oh, she called to see me.*

SIBELLA: *What about?*

LOUIS: *Business. Family business. Let me get you a glass of sherry.*

At the Banking House office, LOUIS is sitting behind his desk.

237

LOUIS' VOICE: *A day or so later, I received a letter from Lionel. He requested an interview with me at his house on a matter of some delicacy. I was somewhat perturbed, for nine times out of ten, what is referred to as a ' matter of some delicacy ', is, in point of fact, one of extreme indelicacy. Two days later, I made the tedious journey to Bayswater. It was typical of Lionel that he should live on the wrong side of the Park.*

LIONEL is standing in his drawing-room drinking; the maid lets LOUIS in. LIONEL's speech is very slurred.

LIONEL: *Hello, old boy. Have a drink.*

LOUIS: *No, thank you. Never during the day.*

LIONEL: *You don't mind if I do. Keep out the cold.*

LOUIS: *I was about to remark on the warmth of the day.*

LIONEL: *Just a joke, old boy.*

LOUIS: *Oh, yes.*

LIONEL: *Sit down, old boy.*

LOUIS: *No, thank you. I would rather stand.*

LIONEL: *A warm day, isn't it? For — the time of year, I mean.*

LOUIS: *Distinctly. It's also a very busy day. May we proceed to the matter about which you wished to see me?*

LIONEL: *Quite. Matter of some delicacy, actually, old boy.* He takes a gulp from his glass. *But I said to myself — ' Louis's a sport and a man of the world. Always been a sport.'*

LOUIS: *Thank you.*

LIONEL: *Always admired the sporting way in which you took Sibella marrying me, and not you. Some fellows would have taken it very differently. But, ' May the best man win,' you said. And when I won, you behaved like a gentleman.* He goes and pours himself another drink. *So I thought as you'd been keen on Sibella at one time, and you and I are old friends, I ... I'd ask you to help us.*

LOUIS: *Help you?*

LIONEL: *I told you some time back, business hasn't been going so well. Since then, it's gone worse. I'm bankrupt. So I said to myself — ' Why not talk to my old pal, Louis Mazzini, who we used to have such jolly times with round the old nursery fire, roasting chestnuts? '*

LOUIS: *I'm afraid your memory is deceiving you. By no stretch of imagination could you and I be described as ever having been ' pals '. If I remember correctly, we detested each other cordially from the first day we met, with a detestation which increased with our years.*

238

LIONEL slightly tearful now: *Always thought of you as a pal. Always have done. That's why I said to myself. . . .*

LOUIS: *It's only fair to warn you that any further expense of breath on this subject will be a waste.*

LIONEL: *You know what you're doing. . . . Condemning me to death!*

LOUIS: *What do you mean?*

LIONEL: *Only one way out for me. Do away with myself.*

LOUIS: *If you knew how absurd these histrionics sounded!*

LIONEL: *I'm insured. At least the little woman will be provided for.*

LOUIS: *Oh, don't be ridiculous!*

> LIONEL bursts into tears, falls on his knees in front of LOUIS, and grabs him by the waist.

LIONEL: *Louis, I appeal to you. Not for my sake. But for the sake of the little woman!*

LOUIS: *Please rise from that absurd position.*

> LIONEL rises and goes to pour another drink. He comes back and sits down.

LIONEL: *All I can say is I th-think you're a cad! A selfish cad!*

LOUIS: *Let me remind you of a little not so ancient history. When I was a draper's assistant, and you a rich father's son you showed me no kindness. Now our positions are reversed, and you come whining to me for favours.*

LIONEL: *Draper's assistant — that's right. Rotten little counter-jumper, that's all you are. Very high and mighty now, but your mother married an Italian organ-grinder.*

LOUIS icily: *Stand up.*

LIONEL: *Eh?*

LOUIS shouting: *I said — stand up!* LIONEL stands. *I will not tolerate hearing my mother's name on your coarse tongue.*

> LOUIS slaps LIONEL twice across the face, very hard. LIONEL falls back into a chair, then recovers himself enough to lurch forwards onto LOUIS in an attempt to fight back. (*Still*) LOUIS pushes him off and straightens his collar and tie. LIONEL staggers back against the wall, grabs an oriental dagger which is hanging there, and dashes at LOUIS with it. They grapple and LOUIS twists the dagger out of his hand, and hurls it across the room.

LOUIS: *If you take my advice, you'll go and put your head under a cold tap. I refuse to demean myself by fighting with a drunken oaf!*

> He pushes LIONEL over, who falls flat out on a bearskin rug on

the floor. He attempts to raise his head as Louis turns and leaves the room.

Louis' Voice: *There seemed no point in prolonging this vulgar brawl, so I returned to my apartment.*

Louis is sitting in his chambers. He is wearing a dressing-gown, and is sipping sherry.

Louis' Voice: *I took a bath and decided to relax for half an hour, and efface his disagreeable scene from my memory. I was not allowed to relax for long.*

A bell rings. He gets up and opens the front door. Sibella, dressed in a splendid feathered hat, comes inside.

Louis: *Sibella!*

Sibella: *Louis, I'm sorry to worry you when you must be so busy, but I have a piece of important news — bad news — I thought you ought to know at once.* She sits down and pauses for a minute. *Lionel has found out about us. About me coming here.*

Louis sardonically: *Really?*

Sibella: *Yes.*

Louis: *Oh!*

Sibella: *I had the most dreadful scene with him last night!*

Louis turns towards the mantelpiece.

Louis: *Well, I suppose even Lionel isn't stupid enough to be deceived for ever.*

Sibella: *You won't take it so calmly when you hear. He's going to start divorce proceedings.*

Louis: *How very unsophisticated of him!*

Sibella: *There's only one possible way out that I can see.*

Louis: *And that is?*

He takes a step towards her, enjoying the cat-and-mouse game.

Sibella: *Lionel is still in love with me. My happiness is all he cares about. He might do the gentlemanly thing and let me divorce him. . . .*

Louis: *If?*

Sibella: *If I were in a position to explain to him that otherwise he would be jeopardising the social position not only of the future Duke, but also of the future Duchess of Chalfont.*

Louis: *I see. You're a clever little thing, Sibella, but not quite clever enough.*

He moves behind her.

SIBELLA: *What do you mean?*

LOUIS: *I mean that not only do I know that you're blackmailing me — an ugly word, but the only appropriate one — but I also know that you're bluffing me!*

SIBELLA: *Call my bluff and see!*

He faces her and sits down.

LOUIS: *I will. Let me explain. It must have seemed to you that you hold a very strong hand. But — a very important ' but ' — it so happens that I hold a card which you did not even know to be in the pack.*

SIBELLA: *Who's bluffing now?*

LOUIS: *It so happens that I was with Lionel less than an hour ago, and it was transparently clear from his demeanour and conversation that he had not the faintest suspicion that you and I had any relationship other than that of — old pals who used to roast chestnuts together round the jolly old nursery fire.*

SIBELLA is in a state of controlled fury.

LOUIS continuing: *So, while thanking you for the honour that you've done me, I must decline your offer, because I have other arrangements which make it impossible for me to accept it.*

SIBELLA: *Namely?*

LOUIS: *I am shortly going to announce my engagement to Mrs D'Ascoyne.*

SIBELLA is speechless for a moment, then she rises, pulling on her gloves.

SIBELLA: *May I say that I think you've behaved despicably?*

LOUIS placing a finger on her chin: *Has it ever occurred to you, Sibella, that we serve each other right, you and I?*

SIBELLA in a dignified voice: *Would it be asking too much of your manners to escort me to the door?*

He does so silently.

A carriage, drawn by two white horses, is approaching Chalfont Castle.

LOUIS' VOICE: *I had suspected that to confide our secret to the Duke might be an adroit manoeuvre, and I was proved correct, for it produced an invitation for Edith and me to spend a few days at the Castle.*

The carriage, with EDITH and LOUIS inside it, drives over the bridge which crosses the moat to the castle.

LOUIS' VOICE continuing: *I must confess that I could not suppress an agreeable sensation of triumph as I approached the Castle gateway in circumstances so different from those in which I had last done so.*

In the dining-room of Chalfont Castle, ETHELRED and his guests are finishing a meal. LOUIS is sitting next to MAUD REDPOLE who is fat and ugly.

LOUIS' VOICE continuing: *It was just an informal little house party. Our fellow guests were Lady Redpole, and her daughter, Maud, who most suitably resembled nothing so much as a Red Poll cow, and had little more conversational ability.*

LOUIS to MAUD: *Did you go to the Opera this season?*

MAUD: *No!*

She stuffs her mouth full of food and chomps happily away.

Later LOUIS and ETHELRED are walking on the battlements of Chalfont Castle.

LOUIS' VOICE: *In the afternoon, Ethelred invited me to inspect the Castle. It was pleasant to stand on the battlements, and know that the acres, which stretched as far as the eye could see, would soon be mine.*

They pause as the DUKE points out features of the castle grounds. LOUIS and ETHELRED are now walking in the main hall. The DUKE points out family portraits.

LOUIS' VOICE continuing: *And it amused me to cover much of the same ground as that of my sixpenny tour.*

In another part of the hall there is a collection of old weapons hanging on the wall.

LOUIS' VOICE continuing: *I had never been in a building so lavishly equipped with the instruments of violent death.*

ETHELRED takes down a sword and hands it to LOUIS, who staggers under its weight.

ETHELRED: *Feel the weight of that! Our ancestors must have been fine men, Louis.*

LOUIS' VOICE: *They seemed, however, ill-adapted to the discreet requirements of twentieth century homicide. . . .*

The ladies are just leaving the dining-room. LOUIS and ETHELRED are left at the table to their port.

LOUIS' VOICE continuing: *And the end of the day found my host still*

intact, and myself still without a plan.
ETHELRED: *Beautiful woman, Edith. You're a lucky fellow, Louis.*
LOUIS: *I never cease to be conscious of that. Thank you.*
ETHELRED pouring the port: *What d'you think of Maud?*
LOUIS: *A charming girl — though perhaps at times her conversation is a little — er — lacking in sparkle.*
ETHELRED: *Dullest woman I've ever met in life. Plain, too, but good breeding stock.* LOUIS looks startled, while ETHELRED pauses to drink. *Good breeding stock, the Redpoles. And they litter a very high proportion of boys.*
LOUIS covers his alarm by taking a drink: *Do I gather you to mean . . .?*
ETHELRED: *Spoke to old Lady Redpole this afternoon. Only too glad to get the girl off her hands.*
LOUIS raising his glass: *My congratulations.*
ETHELRED: *Duty to the family, really.*
LOUIS: *And when does the — er — union take place?*
ETHELRED: *Very soon — I'm not growing any younger. Mightn't get a son first time. Quiet wedding, I thought. Maud's hardly the type for St Margaret's. We shall honeymoon on the Riviera, and then go on to Italy afterwards. No sense in inflicting her on one's friends. When she's got a family, that'll keep her out of the way.*

LOUIS takes another drink of port to steady himself.
LOUIS' VOICE: *This news threw me into such distress of mind that, had I had poison in my possession, I would probably have administered it to Ethelred there and then, and chanced the consequent enquiries. One thing was clear. . . . If I did not succeed in disposing of him during this present visit to the Castle, I was likely to see the ruin of my whole campaign.*

LOUIS raises his glass to the DUKE.
LOUIS: *My best wishes for a successful outcome.*

In the woods of Chalfont grounds it is early morning. LOUIS follows ETHELRED who carries a gun. They are accompanied by HOSKINS who is the game keeper.
LOUIS' VOICE: *Next morning, I went out shooting with Ethelred — or rather, to watch Ethelred shooting, for my principles will not allow me to take a direct part in blood sports.*

ETHELRED fires a shot into the air.

251

ETHELRED to HOSKINS: *Been round the traps this morning, Hoskins?*
HOSKINS: *Not yet, Your Grace.*
ETHELRED: *Sounds as if we've bagged one there. Ah!* To LOUIS. *Been losing so much game lately, we've started setting the man-traps again.*

They arrive at a clearing, to see a POACHER caught in a trap, hidden in the bracken. HOSKINS picks up a dead pheasant from the ground and frisks the POACHER.

ETHELRED to POACHER: *Hoskins is now going to thrash you. Then he'll let you go. Let this be a lesson to you not to poach on my land.*

HOSKINS raises his stick. As LOUIS and ETHELRED watch, we hear four whacks off screen.

ETHELRED to HOSKINS: *That'll do.*

HOSKINS releases the trap and the POACHER limps away.

ETHELRED raises his gun and fires into the air.

ETHELRED continuing: *Keep moving them around, Hoskins, or they'll tell each other where they are.*
HOSKINS: *Yes, Your Grace.*
LOUIS: *I thought man-traps were illegal.*
ETHELRED: *They are.*
LOUIS: *What happens if he tells the police?*
ETHELRED: *He comes up before the Bench for poaching, gets six months in jail. If he keeps his mouth shut, he just gets a few days in bed. Which would you choose? Only way to deal with these ruffians, I assure you.*

LOUIS is now in close-up. He has an idea. He pauses and ostentatiously pats his pocket.

LOUIS: *Oh, I must have dropped my cigarette case back there. I'll catch you up.*

He runs back into the clearing, pretending to search for something in the grass. As he does so, he watches HOSKINS setting up the man-trap. He turns back, catches up and falls into step with ETHELRED.

ETHELRED: *Find it?*
LOUIS: *Yes, thanks.*
ETHELRED: *Might have another walk round this afternoon, if you feel like it.*
LOUIS: *That would be most pleasant.*

Later that day LOUIS and ETHELRED are again walking towards

the wood.

LOUIS' VOICE: *After luncheon, we went out to massacre a few more unfortunate birds.*

At the edge of the clearing LOUIS stops suddenly.

LOUIS: *Listen!*

ETHELRED pausing: *What is it?*

LOUIS: *I thought I heard something — like someone running through the bracken.*

ETHELRED: *Another poaching ruffian. Come on!*

They run into the thicket. LOUIS points towards the trap.

LOUIS: *There was someone here. Look!*

ETHELRED steps forward and the trap springs. He falls on his hands, dropping his gun.

ETHELRED: *Blast! Louis, get me out of this.*

LOUIS saunters towards the trap and picks up the gun. He pauses and pulls out a cigarette from his case.

ETHELRED: *Hurry up, man! Have you gone mad?*

LOUIS: *Be quiet, Ethelred! I want to talk to you for a minute. If you make a noise, I shall blow your head off at once. By the time anyone has heard the shot, I shall be running back toward the Castle, shouting for help! I shall say that you — er — stepped on the trap, and that your gun went off accidently as it fell. So be quiet! To spare you as much pain as possible. . . .* He lights the cigarette. . . . *I'll be brief. When I've finished, I shall kill you.*

ETHELRED is trying to free himself.

LOUIS continuing: *You'll be the sixth D'Ascoyne that I've killed. You want to know why? In return for what the D'Ascoynes did to my mother. Because she married for love, instead of for rank, or money, or land, they condemned her to a life of poverty and slavery, in a world with which they had not equipped her to deal. You yourself refused to grant her dying wish, which was to be buried here at Chalfont. When I saw her poor little coffin slide underground, saw her exiled in death as she'd been in life, I swore to have my revenge on your intolerable pride. That revenge I am just about to complete.*

ETHELRED very agitated: *It is clear that you are insane. Give me that gun at once.*

LOUIS kneels down, then points the gun at ETHELRED.

LOUIS: *No. From here, I think, the wound should look consistent with the story that I shall tell.*

With a smile of achievement on his face, LOUIS pulls the trigger, watches for a moment, then drops the gun and runs off down the path.

LOUIS as he goes: *Help! Help! Help!*

The funeral bell tolls. ETHELRED's coffin is being carried into Chalfont Church. Family carriages are drawing up outside.

LOUIS' VOICE: *And so Ethelred, eighth Duke of Chalfont, duly came to his place in the family vault. There were few D'Ascoynes left to mourn him. My employer, who was ninth Duke of Chalfont for the shortest possible period, having expired of shock on hearing that he had succeeded to the title.*

A second coffin is borne into the church, in the wake of ETHELRED's.

LOUIS' VOICE continuing: *And so, I became the tenth Duke of Chalfont.*

LOUIS, dressed in black, is sitting at his desk in the D'ASCOYNE office.

LOUIS' VOICE: *Fortunately, the ninth Duke had found time before he expired, to make a will bequeathing to me his interests in the business.*

An obsequious SECRETARY stands beside his chair. LOUIS points to the photograph of young ASCOYNE D'ASCOYNE on the desk.

LOUIS: *You may remove that.*

The SECRETARY does so, while LOUIS pulls out his silk handkerchief and flicks the dust from where it stood.

In the main hall of Chalfont Castle, the tenants and farmers, wearing their Sunday best, are gathered to greet the new DUKE.

LOUIS and EDITH are on a dais, and he is making his speech.

LOUIS: *. . . And I promise you that my first consideration, and that of Mrs D'Ascoyne, who has done me the honour to consent to be my bride, will be the welfare of the Estate, and of the people who live on it. God bless you all!*

There is great cheering and cries of ' Long live His Grace ' from the crowd. LOUIS and EDITH descend the steps and begin to shake hands with the tenants who stand in a long line. The first is FARMER PENNYMAN, who lifts his cap and presents the rest of his family.

FARMER PENNYMAN: *Pennyman, Your Grace, from Sprockett's Farm.*
Mrs Pennyman. My son, Tom, from Sprockett's Farm. Mr Wyvold,
from Sprockett's Farm.

Next in lines is BURGOYNE, a solid looking man, wearing a heavy
tweed overcoat.

LOUIS: *Sprockett's Farm?*

BURGOYNE: *No, Your Grace. From Scotland Yard.*

LOUIS his smile fading: *Scotland Yard?*

BURGOYNE: *A matter of some delicacy.*

LOUIS pretends mild exasperation. He turns and whispers to
EDITH.

LOUIS to BURGOYNE: *Follow me, please.*

He conducts BURGOYNE towards the dining-room, still smiling
and bowing to the rest of the crowd.

LOUIS' VOICE: *The blow was so sudden that I found it hard to
collect my thoughts. Which of them could it be? Young Ascoyne?
Henry? Ethelred? The Parson? The General? Lady Agatha? Or
could it be all of them?*

LOUIS closes the door of the dining-room, and looks enquiringly
at BURGOYNE.

LOUIS: *Now!*

BURGOYNE: *You are, I take it, His Grace the Duke of Chalfont?*

LOUIS: *I am.*

BURGOYNE: *I am Detective-Inspector Burgoyne, of the Criminal
Investigation Department, and I hold a warrant for your arrest on
a charge of murder.*

LOUIS closing his eyes for a second: *Murder?*

BURGOYNE: *Of murdering Mr Lionel Holland at. . . .*

LOUIS frowning: *Murdering whom?*

BURGOYNE: *Mr Lionel Holland, at number two hundred and forty-
two, Connaught Square, Bayswater, on the seventeenth of October
last.*

A carriage drives across the bridge from the castle.

The TENANTS are still cheering and shouting ' Long live His
Grace '.

LOUIS and BURGOYNE are sitting inside the carriage. LOUIS
draws on his white gloves, while BURGOYNE lights a pipe.

LOUIS' VOICE: *Utterly bewildered, I tried to fathom what series
of events could conceivably have led to this not very amusing irony.*

I could only suppose that Lionel had actually carried out that drunken threat of suicide. But how then had the blame fallen on me? Time alone — and the trial — would reveal the answer.

We see the outside of the Houses of Parliament.

LOUIS' VOICE continuing: *Seeing no reason to forego any of the available privileges of my rank,*

We are now inside the Royal Gallery at the House of Lords. It is very ornate and splendid. At the far end sits the LORD HIGH STEWARD. In front of him are the advisory JUDGES, while down each side of the Gallery sit the PEERS. Beyond the Bar are the spectators' seats. LOUIS is in the prisoner's box.

LOUIS' VOICE continuing: *I exercised my right to be tried before the House of Lords.*

CLERK OF THE PARLIAMENTS to LOUIS: *Louis D'Ascoyne Mazzini, Duke of Chalfont. . . . You, as a Peer of England, are indicted for murder. How say you, Your Grace, are you guilty of the felony with which you are charged, or not guilty?*

LOUIS: *Not guilty!*

CLERK OF THE PARLIAMENTS: *How will you be tried?*

LOUIS: *By God and my Peers.*

CLERK OF THE PARLIAMENTS: *God send Your Grace a good deliverance!*

SIBELLA is now in the witness box. She is very demure and pathetic in widow's weeds.

SIBELLA taking oath: *. . . shall be the truth, the whole truth, and nothing but the truth, so help me God.*

CROWN COUNSEL to SIBELLA: *Mrs Holland, will you tell their Lordships in your own words the substance of the conversation you had with your husband the evening before his death?*

SIBELLA: *He told me that Louis — the prisoner — was coming to see him the next day on a rather delicate matter.*

CROWN COUNSEL: *Did he indicate what that matter was?*

SIBELLA: *He'd discovered that the prisoner and I had been. . . .*

CROWN COUNSEL: *Had been on terms of intimacy?*

SIBELLA: *Yes.*

There is a murmur through the crowd.

CROWN COUNSEL: *And what was his attitude?*

SIBELLA: *He felt that the correct thing to do was to tell him to his*

256

face that he intended to start proceedings for divorce.

Louis, appalled at her lies, cannot repress an admiration for her performance.

CROWN COUNSEL: *From your knowledge of the prisoner, how would you expect him to receive that news?*

SIBELLA: *I should expect him to be very angry. Now he was heir to a Dukedom, he had no more use for me.*

She looks down demurely, having gained the sympathy of her audiences.

CROWN COUNSEL: *I see. He was trying to discard you.*

SIBELLA: *Yes.*

CROWN COUNSEL: *Mrs Holland, I apologise for submitting you to this ordeal, but will you tell their Lordships how you found your husband's body?*

SIBELLA: *I came back about half-past four. . . .*

Her voice falters.

LORD HIGH STEWARD off: *Their Lordships have no objection to the witness being seated?*

SIBELLA gives a grateful and pathetic smile as a chair is brought.

CROWN COUNSEL: *Yes, Mrs Holland?*

SIBELLA resuming: *I came back about half-past four. I went into my husband's study. He was lying on the floor, with a dagger stuck in his chest.*

CROWN COUNSEL: *One last question, Mrs Holland. Had your husband ever at any time threatened suicide?*

SIBELLA: *Never!*

CROWN COUNSEL: *Thank you, Mrs Holland.*

CROWN COUNSEL sits down. LOUIS' COUNSEL rises.

LOUIS' COUNSEL to LORD HIGH STEWARD: *My client craves their Lordship's permission to cross-examine the witness himself.*

LORD HIGH STEWARD: *Their Lordships grant their permission.*

LOUIS rising: *Mrs Holland. You understand the meaning of being on oath?*

SIBELLA: *Of course.*

LOUIS: *You realise that a life may depend upon the truthfulness of your evidence?*

SIBELLA: *Yes.*

LOUIS: *I put it to you that the story of your conversation with your husband on the night before his death, is a complete fabrication.*

SIBELLA indignantly: *It is not.*

LOUIS: *I put it to you that your husband committed suicide.*

SIBELLA: *He would never have done that without leaving a message for me.*

LOUIS: *Can you swear that he did not?*

SIBELLA: *The police searched the room very thoroughly. They didn't find anything.*

LOUIS: *I suggest that your evidence is a tissue of lies, dictated by motives of revenge.*

SIBELLA crying: *It is not! It is not!*

LORD HIGH STEWARD to LOUIS: *I presume that the prisoner has some purpose in these submissions, other than that of distressing the witness!*

LOUIS: *My purpose, My Lord, is to determine the truth.*

LORD HIGH STEWARD sternly: *That, Your Grace, is the whole purpose of this assembly.*

> LOUIS sits down in a state of suppressed rage. SIBELLA, smiling faintly, leaves the witness box. There is a surprised murmur in the assembly as EDITH, a calm and dignified figure, is taking the oath.

EDITH: *. . . be the truth, the whole truth, and nothing but the truth, so help me God!*

LOUIS' COUNSEL to EDITH: *You are Edith D'Ascoyne Mazzini, Duchess of Chalfont?*

EDITH: *I am.*

> SIBELLA is looking at LOUIS, surprise and anger on her face.
> LOUIS' expression is smugly impassive.

LOUIS' COUNSEL: *When and where did you become the wife of the accused?*

EDITH: *Yesterday morning, in Pentonville Prison.* Another murmur in the assembly. *I wanted to publish irrevocably before the whole world my faith in his innocence. I wanted to show by my marriage, that though he was led astray, as I believe, by that innate kindliness and courtesy of his, which made it so hard for him to rebuff the advances of a woman. . . .* SIBELLA *look outraged. . . . I nevertheless regard him as a man to whom I can happily entrust the remainder of my life. I am not alone in these opinions of him. My late husband, Henry, and his late uncle, Ethelred, the eighth Duke, both, unfortunately, unable to testify today. . . .* LOUIS examines his fingernails . . . *these and other members of the D'Ascoyne family, had they been alive, would, I know, have echoed every word that I have said.*

The obvious sincerity of EDITH's words have created a strong impression. LOUIS looks at SIBELLA with faint triumph on his face.

A little later, LOUIS is in the witness box, being examined by CROWN COUNSEL. He looks very self assured.

CROWN COUNSEL: *The deceased was a client of the Banking House of which you are Chairman and Managing Director?*

LOUIS: *He was.*

CROWN COUNSEL: *In the normal course of business transactions, he would have come to see you at your office?*

LOUIS: *Yes.*

CROWN COUNSEL: *Instead of which, he asked you to go to his house?*

LOUIS: *Yes.*

CROWN COUNSEL: *He invited you to his house to discuss business?*

LOUIS: *Yes.*

CROWN COUNSEL: *And you ask Their Lordships to believe that?*

LOUIS: *Yes.*

CROWN COUNSEL: *In the course of this — er — business discussion, he burst into tears, fell on his knees, and threatened suicide?*

LOUIS: *Yes.*

CROWN COUNSEL: *Is that usual in business discussions?*

LOUIS: *Not usual, no.*

CROWN COUNSEL: *But it happened on this occasion?*

LOUIS: *Yes.*

CROWN COUNSEL: *And you ask Their Lordships to believe that?*

LOUIS: *Yes.*

CROWN COUNSEL: *Then this — er — business discussion became so heated that blows were exchanged, and he made a murderous attack on you?*

LOUIS: *Yes.*

CROWN COUNSEL: *Is that usual in business discussions?*

LOUIS: *No.*

CROWN COUNSEL: *But it happened on this occasion?*

LOUIS: *Yes.*

CROWN COUNSEL: *And you ask Their Lordships to believe that?*

Louis: *Yes.*

Crown Counsel: *Very well. You've heard of cases of a jealous husband and his wife's lover coming to blows?*

Louis: *Yes.*

Crown Counsel: *Frequently?*

Louis: *It is one of the clichés of the cheaper kind of fiction.*

There is laughter in the assembly.

Crown Counsel: *I put it to you that, in this case, it happened not in fiction, but in fact.*

Louis: *I put it to you that it did not.*

Crown Counsel: *I put it to you further that, being unaware at that time of your future wife's forgiving nature, you assumed that if you were cited in a divorce suit, it would ruin your chances of making this advantageous match with a wealthy and beautiful woman.*

Louis with conviction: *No, not at all!*

Crown Counsel: *Still, you were proposing to discard Mrs Holland?*

Louis: *No.*

Crown Counsel: *Even though you were about to be married to the other lady?*

Louis hesitates, perceiving the trap into which he has been led. Before he can make any answer, the Crown Counsel bows and sit down.

The Peers, Judge and the Lord High Steward have now retired to make their verdict.

Louis to His Counsel: *I must confess to feeling quite intrigued as to their decision.*

Everyone stands as the Peers enter in a procession.

Lord High Steward to Peers: *My Lords . . . the question for Your Lordships is this — Is the prisoner guilty of the felony whereof he stands indicted . . . or not guilty?* (Still)

The Peers rise in turn.

First Peer: *Guilty, upon mine honour.*

Second Peer: *Guilty . . . upon mine honour!*

Third Peer: *Guilty, upon mine honour!*

It is the interview room of the prison. Louis is brought in and he sits down. On the other side of the grille is Sibella. She looks demure and her eyes are cast down.

Louis: *I considered it both seemly and touching that my dear wife should visit me, as she did this morning, to make her farewells. Your arrival, on the other hand, appears to me unseemly and tasteless in the extreme!*

SIBELLA: *I couldn't bear my last sight of you to be that look of hatred you gave me as you went out from the trial.*

LOUIS: *In view of the fact that your evidence had put the rope round my neck, you could hardly expect a glance of warm affection.*

SIBELLA: *Isn't there any hope?*

LOUIS: *What hope could there be?*

SIBELLA looking into his eyes: *I was only thinking. . . . That question you asked at the trial — about Lionel leaving a suicide note. Suppose he did. Suppose that one were found — even now — this last evening!*

LOUIS: *It would savour of a miracle.*

SIBELLA: *Miracles can happen. Miracles could happen!*

LOUIS staring back at her: *I see.*

SIBELLA: *Oh, strange, isn't it, how things turn out? Now, if you had married me instead of Edith!*

LOUIS: *Or you had married me, instead of Lionel!*

SIBELLA: *He would still be alive, and you wouldn't be going to be hanged tomorrow morning. Hm! Hm! Unless, of course, you'd murdered somebody else!*

LOUIS: *All of which is rather beside the point, isn't it?*

SIBELLA: *Is it? Do you remember in the old days how we used to play ' eenie meenie minie mo'?*

LOUIS: *' Catch a nigger by his toe'. . . .*

SIBELLA: *' If he hollers, let him go. . . . Out goes he'! Quite a lot of little niggers have gone out, haven't they, one way or another? And every one of them a D'Ascoyne!*

She looks at him very directly, and it is clear to LOUIS that she has guessed the truth. He smiles:

LOUIS: *Hm, we do seem to be a very short-lived family.*

SIBELLA: *Of course, Edith is only a D'Ascoyne by marriage, so I suppose her prospects are better.* She pauses. *Except for a miracle. Like the other one we were talking about.*

LOUIS' VOICE: *So there it was. She would find the suicide note, if I, in return, would murder Edith.*

LOUIS: *So we now have two miracles in mind, do we?*

SIBELLA: *Yes.*

261

LOUIS: *I wonder if they are in any way dependent on each other!*
SIBELLA: *I suppose perhaps they might be. What do you think?*
　　She waits for his answer but before it comes, the WARDER steps
　　forward.
WARDER: *Time's up.*
SIBELLA: *What do you think?*
LOUIS: *Poor Edith! I'm afraid all this is going to take years off her
life.*
SIBELLA smiling triumphantly: *Au revoir, Louis.*
LOUIS: *Au revoir!*
　　LOUIS smiles back, and watches her leave.
LOUIS' VOICE: *What could I do but accept? After all, I could always
decide afterwards which of these two little niggers would finally have
to go.*
　　He examines his fingernails, smiling reminiscently.
LOUIS' VOICE continuing: *Dear Edith! Captivating Sibella! How
different they were — and how well I knew each of them.*

　　It is the following morning. LOUIS sits at the table in the
　　condemned cell, his memoirs are in front of him. Quill pen in
　　hand he stares moodily in front of him.
LOUIS' VOICE: *Or so I thought. But the night has gone by, and
nothing has happened. It is now but a few minutes to eight, and I
realise that Sibella came yesterday merely to tantalise — to raise
my hopes in order to dash them again. How unlike me not to have
guessed! But after all — how very like Sibella!*
　　He finishes writing and draws a line across the page with an
　　air of finality. There is the sound of approaching footsteps in
　　the background. They halt and the door opens. LOUIS stands
　　up, wiping his fingers delicately with his handkerchief. The
　　GOVERNOR comes into the cell.
GOVERNOR to ELLIOTT who is off: *Mr Elliott — His Grace the Duke
of Chalfont.*
ELLIOTT approaching: *Good morning, Your Grace! This won't take
a moment. First — if Your Grace will pardon the liberty, I should
like to read some verses, composed by myself for use on these
melancholy occasions. Your Grace permits?*
　　He produces a sheet of paper from behind his back. He is very
　　solemn.

262

LOUIS: *With pleasure.*

ELLIOTT reading: *Ahem! My friend, reflect — er — Oh. . . . Oh . . . pardon me!* He bows. *Your Grace, reflect. While yet of mortal breath some span, however short, is left to thee. . . . How brief the total span, 'twixt birth and death. . . . How long thy coming tenure of eternity! Your Grace, prepare!*

He breaks off as he hears the clatter of footsteps, running along the passage. A breathless WARDER appears in the doorway.

WARDER to GOVERNOR: *Colonel!*

GOVERNOR: *Yes?*

The GOVERNOR steps towards him and they talk in low tones. The GOVERNOR comes back to LOUIS.

GOVERNOR: *Your Grace, I am happy to inform you that a telephone communication has just been received from the Home Office. A note has been found — undoubtedly in Mr Holland's handwriting, expressing his intention to commit suicide! It is a miracle!*

LOUIS smiling: *Yes, it is like a miracle!*

GOVERNOR: *Pending receipt of further instructions, I'll try to make you reasonably comfortable in my quarters.*

He leads LOUIS towards the door. In passing, LOUIS turns to ELLIOTT who looks very disappointed indeed.

LOUIS: *Good morning!*

ELLIOTT: *Good morning, Your Grace, sir.*

Just inside the gates of the prison, the GOVERNOR is walking with LOUIS who is now in his outside clothes.

GOVERNOR: *I assure you that I have never been more happy to be relieved of an official duty.*

LOUIS: *Poor Elliott! If he had not insisted on reading that abominable poem, he would have had me neatly dangling at the end of his rope before the news arrived!*

GOVERNOR: *Hm!*

LOUIS: *He was so looking forward to it.*

GOVERNOR: *I understand, Your Grace, from the men on duty outside, that a large crowd awaits your leaving.*

LOUIS smiling: *Having robbed them of the pleasure of my death, the least I can do is to let them see me alive.*

GOVERNOR slightly embarrased: *Including, by the way, not only Her Grace, the Duchess, but also Mrs Holland.*

Louis amused: *Oh! How does the song go? 'How happy could I be with either, were t'other dear charmer away!'*

Governor: *Hm! Yes!*

They shake hands. A Warder opens the gate for Louis.

Louis: *Ha! Well, goodbye!*

Governor: *Er — goodbye, Your Grace!*

Outside the prison door Louis comes out and acknowledges the cheers of the crowd. On either side of the gateway are Edith and Sibella, each in a carriage. (*Still*) Louis looks speculatively from one to the other.

Louis' Voice: *'How happy could I be with either, were t'other dear charmer away!'*

A Little Man in a bowler hat approaches Louis.

Little Man: *Your Grace!*

Louis: *Yes?*

Little Man: *I represent the magazine 'Tit Bits', by whom I am commissioned to approach you for the publication rights of your memoirs.*

Louis vaguely: *My memoirs? Oh, my memoirs!* Faintly. *My memoirs!*

There is a look of consternation on his face, as he remembers.

Louis' Voice: *My memoirs!* (*Still*)

The music rises as we see the title page of his memoirs, which have been left inside the condemned cell.

Fade out.

CREDITS:

Produced by	Harry Saltzman
	Tony Richardson
Directed by	Karel Reisz
Screenplay adapted from his novel by	Alan Sillitoe
Director of Photography	Freddie Francis, B.S.C.
Film Editor	Seth Holt
Art Director	Ted Marshall
Production Manager	Jack Rix
Music composed and conducted by	Johnny Dankworth
Played by	Members of the Johnny Dankworth Orchestra
Special Lyrics by	David Dearlove
Camera Operator	Ron Taylor
Assistant Director	Tom Pevsner
Continuity	Pamela Mann
Sound Recordists	Peter Handford
	Bob Jones
Sound Editor	Chris Greenham
Make-up	Harold Fletcher
Hairdresser	Pearl Tipaldi
Wardrobe	Sophie Devine
	Barbara Gillett

CAST:

Arthur	Albert Finney
Doreen	Shirley Anne Field
Brenda	Rachel Roberts
Aunt Ada	Hylda Baker
Bert	Norman Rossington
Jack	Bryan Pringle
Robboe	Robert Cawdron
Mrs Bull	Edna Morris
Mrs Seaton	Elsie Wagstaffe
Mr Seaton	Frank Pettitt
Blousy Woman	Avis Bunnage
Loudmouth	Colin Blakeley
Doreen's Mother	Irene Richmond
Betty	Louise Dunn
Civil Defence Officer	Anne Blake
Drunken Man	Peter Madden
Mr Bull	Cameron Hall
Policeman	Alister Williamson

SATURDAY NIGHT AND SUNDAY MORNING

It is a huge factory workshop in Nottingham — the turnery, where small components for bicycles are made on lathes, crank-machines, drills, hand-presses and polishers. Men in overalls and women in turbans are at work by their machines. Some are sitting down to work, others standing. Some machines are worked by belts and pulleys twisting overhead. The noise is enough to make the brain reel. We move with the foreman ROBBOE as he hands out wage packets. As he moves off, we see ARTHUR SEATON busy at his lathe. He is an iron-faced, crop-haired young man. (*Still*)

His hand presses the control switch.

His hand turns a handle.

His hands put a piece of metal into position on the machine, which cuts it into shape.

ARTHUR takes out the component and puts it into a box.

ARTHUR: *Nine hundred and fifty-four. . . .*

He repeats all the actions on the lathe.

Again we see his hands as he finishes another component and puts it into the box.

ARTHUR: *Nine hundred and fifty bloody five. . . .*

Now ROBBOE approaches ARTHUR at work.

ARTHUR: *Another few more and that's the lot for a Friday.*

He takes his wage packet from ROBBOE, who then leaves.

ARTHUR: *Fourteen pounds three and tuppence for a thousand of these a day. No wonder I've allus got a bad back — though I'll soon be done. I'll have a fag in a bit. . . .*

We look down at the control button as ARTHUR presses it.

ARTHUR: *No use working every minute God sends.*

The machine works on.

ARTHUR stays at the lathe with the other men at their machines.

He lights a cigarette, then starts to work again.

ARTHUR: *I could get through it in half the time if I worked like a bore, but they'd only slash me wages, so they can get. . . .*

Now ARTHUR is washing his hands in the factory. He dries them.

Arthur: . . . *stuck! Don't let the bastards grind you down. That's one thing you learn.*

He looks over to his friend Jack who is still busy at his machine. All the other men are packing up to go.

Arthur: *Jack's one that ain't learnt. He wants to get on.*

A cleaner begins sweeping the factory floor. Robboe enters and talks with Jack.

Arthur: *Yes Mr Robboe, no Mr Robboe, I'll do it as soon as I can, Mr Robboe. And look where it got Robboe . . . a deadpan face and lots o' worry.*

Robboe goes off, as Arthur looks round the men among the factory. He sees Fred at his machine, while a black man loads it with raw material.

Arthur: *Fred's all right. Knows how to spend his money — like me. Enjoys himself. . . .*

Now Arthur sees three older men at their machines, working mechanically.

Arthur: *That's more than them poor beggars know. They got ground down before the war and never got over it. I'd like to see anybody try to grind me down. That'll be the day. What I am out for is a good time. All the rest is propaganda.*

He throws down the wash-cloth and goes out, as he hears the factory siren blow.

Now we look down into the factory yard as the men rush out from the buildings around it and come towards us. The titles of the film are shown over shots of the workers running towards their bicycles and streaming out of the factory. They bicycle away down the road outside the factory, Arthur in the lead. Jack on his motorbicycle rides away from the factory down the street, where children are playing.

Now Jack has reached his home. He leaves his motorbike in the yard. Two small boys run to meet him, as he goes to the back door. Brenda his wife comes out at the same time and empties a plate into the dustbin. She is a plumpish, easy-going, goodtime wife of about thirty. She follows Jack into the house. Arthur bicycles past children playing in the street, (*Still*) then turns down an alley, brushing past Mrs Bull who is standing at the end. She glares after him.

Inside the small Seaton house, Arthur's mother and father are seated, glued to the television set. Mrs Seaton rises and moves to the kitchen as Arthur comes in. He sits down at the table.

Arthur: *Hello, mum, do you want your money, mum?*

Mrs Seaton: *Okay.*

On the television, we hear a singing advertisement: 'Today's cigarette is a Bristol! Bristol is today's cigarette.'

Arthur has counted out his pay packet and now places a couple of pounds on the table.

Arthur: *There you are.*

Mrs Seaton comes from the kitchen and takes the money, then goes back again.

Arthur: *Everything go off all right at work, dad?*

Mr Seaton does not turn, but goes on staring at the television.

Mr Seaton: *Aye, all right.*

Arthur: *Did you hear about that accident in the three speed shop today, dad?*

Mr Seaton off: *No, not much. Another cup of tea, luv!*

Mrs Seaton comes in and places a plate in front of Arthur.

Mrs Seaton: *I got you somethin' good seeing it is Friday night.*

Arthur begins to eat.

Arthur: *Aye! This fellow got his hand caught in a press. He didn't look what he was doing. Of course he has only got one eye, he lost the sight of the other one looking at telly day in and day out.*

Mr Seaton goes on staring at the television set. (*Still*)

Mr Seaton: *Oh ay!*

Mrs Seaton hands him a cup of tea. He takes it without looking away from the television set.

Mr Seaton: *Thanks luv!*

She moves away, while Arthur goes on eating. He hears another singing advertisement. ' Silvikrin for lovely hair! '

He glares at his father.

Now we are in Arthur's bedroom at night. He is washed and dressed. He moves to his wardrobe, takes the paper off his jacket, then he comes forward and puts it on. He straightens his tie in the mirror, then goes to the door. He leaves the room, closing the door behind him.

In the alley outside the back gardens of the terraced houses,

Mrs Bull and Mrs Mackley are gossiping. Arthur knocks into them, then saunters on without apologizing. Mrs Bull glares after him.

Mrs Bull: *Mind what you're doing, can't you? That Arthur Seaton's going to get a good rucking one of these days.*

Arthur now runs along the pavement of the main road to catch a bus, which is just pulling away from the stop. He jumps on it, and it pulls away down the hill.

We are in a pub now, which is rocking with noise: the weekend has begun. A great row is going on. Near us two customers are at the bar, a large Blowsy Woman and a small inoffensive man, while a Barman gets their drinks.

Blowsy Woman: *Quiet tonight, isn't it?*

Barman: *You should see them next door though. There's a boozing match going on. Young chap, it is. He's down eight pints already.*

Blowsy Woman: *Eight pints already. He's having a good time, ain't he?*

Seated at a table by the window in the next room of the pub, Brenda watches Arthur slowly drinking his ninth pint. Also drinking his pint is a Sailor, who is taking on Arthur. People seethe around him.

Arthur finishes his pint and puts down his mug on the table.

Arthur: *Bring a couple o' more pints, 'ere, George.*

At the bar, the Barman turns and hands two more pints to the Waiter.

Barman: *Do you want any help down there?*

Waiter: *I'll let you know if I do. But they've just about had it, if you ask me.*

The Waiter goes back to the next room and places another pint in front of the Sailor, then moves to Arthur. Music and clapping sound from another part of the pub. Smoke has produced a deadly mist and the intensity of the noise varies.

Arthur: *Thanks, George. Take one for you'self.*

The Waiter puts Arthur's drink on the table.

Now we watch the small pub group with a heavy drummer and a loud Singer.

Singer: *What do you want if you don't want money?*
What do you want if you don't want gold?

Tell me what you want and I'll give it to you honey!
Wish you was my love, baby.

As he points off, we go back to BRENDA and ARTHUR, picking up his pint.

ARTHUR: *Come on then, sup up! I've lost count now.*

SINGER off: *What do you want if you don't want pearls.* . . .

The SAILOR is half-seas over, gazing at the pints of beer in front of him. People move about in front of the group and the SINGER.

SAILOR: *All right there's plenty of time.*

SINGER: *. . . Tell me what you want and I'll give it to you honey.*
Wish you was my love, baby.

The SAILOR starts to drink his pint slowly.

ARTHUR jeers at him.

ARTHUR: *Get the stuff down yer then. They'll be closed in a bit. Then you won't get any more till twelve tomorrow.*

SINGER off: *Because I am offering you this heart of mine,*
And all you do is turn me down
Oh boy. . . .

SAILOR: *Don't worry, I will.*

SINGER off: *. . . You're making a fool of me.*

A woman puts on her coat and goes out, as the SAILOR picks up his pint and starts to drink again.

SINGER off: *One of these days when you want me honey,*
One of these days when you want me too. . . .

BRENDA laughs by ARTHUR's side.

BRENDA: *Gee, Arthur.* . . .

SINGER off: *Don't turn around 'cause I'll be missing.* . . .

The SAILOR drinks on in front of the seething pub.

SINGER off: *Wish you wanna my love baby,*
What do you want if you don't want money,
What do you want if you don't want gold. . . .

The SAILOR puts down his pint and bends over the table.

ARTHUR and BRENDA watch him, smiling.

SINGER: *Tell me what you want and I'll give it to you honey,*
Wish you wanna my love, baby.

The SAILOR rises and goes out, walking like a ramrod and looking away.

BRENDA and ARTHUR laugh at the SAILOR.

BRENDA: *I don't know how he does it, I really don't. Not that it's anything to be proud of.*

ARTHUR: *You get thirsty working that machine all week. I'm going out to. . . .*

He rises.

BRENDA: *Well, hurry up then, duck, it will be closing time in a few minutes.*

SINGER off: *. . . One of these days when you want my kisses, One of these days when you want me too. . . .*

The BARMAN stands at the bar, as ARTHUR pushes his way through the crowd to where a group is singing.

GROUP: *She's my lady love. . . . She's the girl for sitting down and dream. . . .*

ARTHUR: *Pint, please.*

The BARMAN leans towards ARTHUR.

BARMAN: *Now then, what is it?*

ARTHUR: *A pint.*

GROUP: *I know she likes me, I know she likes me, Because she said so. . . .*

BARMAN: *Time now, ladies and gentlemen, please.*

The BARMAN hands a beer to ARTHUR who turns and moves off.

GROUP: *She is my Lily of Lagoona. . . .*

ARTHUR pushes his way through the crowd until he reaches the BLOWSY WOMAN and the SMALL MAN seated at a table.

ARTHUR trips, spilling some of his beer over the man, who jumps up quickly.

BLOWSY WOMAN: *Ooooh!*

ARTHUR looks round drunkenly.

SMALL MAN: *Would you believe it, it's me best suit.*

BLOWSY WOMAN: *Cheeky daft, in't 'e? Don't even apologize.*

The BLOWSY WOMAN gets up to confront ARTHUR.

BLOWSY WOMAN: *Go on, apologize. . . .*

ARTHUR sways and spills some beer down her blouse. (*Still*) She is outraged. The SMALL MAN stays seated where he is.

BLOWSY WOMAN: *Oh!*

ARTHUR moves off, while the people around comment.

The BLOWSY WOMAN rages at the SMALL MAN.

BLOWSY WOMAN: *Well, don't just sit there. Do something about it.*

ARTHUR is now at the top of the landing in the pub, near the stairs.

272

BARMAN: *Time, ladies and gentlemen, please.*

ARTHUR sways back and forth dangerously, while the chat and singing of the pub swells about him. He sways too much, treads on the top of the stairs and falls down them.

At the bottom of the stairs, ARTHUR lies unconscious. He opens his eyes and smiles stupidly.

Now we see ARTHUR in JACK and BRENDA's house. The scullery is in darkness and ARTHUR is bending over the sink and washing his face. He straightens up and begins to rub his face with a towel. BRENDA moves past the scullery window then, after a short pause, the door opens and she comes in.

BRENDA: *Did you come in through the scullery window?*

She moves to the window and pulls the curtains.

ARTHUR: *Yer!*

BRENDA: *You never think, do you! You'll have all the neighbours talking, you know.*

She takes off her coat.

ARTHUR: *I left the pub in a hurry, else I'd 'ave waited for yer!*

BRENDA: *Yes, I know all about it!*

He comes from the scullery into the kitchen, while she stands by the gas stove.

BRENDA: *Falling down stairs and spilling your beer all down that woman.*

ARTHUR: *Wasn't my fault. Somebody pushed me from behind. Then I tripped on the rail, coming down the stairs.*

She comes forward and switches on the light.

BRENDA: *I believe you, thousands wouldn't.*

She moves back to the scullery.

ARTHUR: *I'm not going in that pub again until they get that rail fixed.*

He turns and watches her as she bolts the window and the back door.

ARTHUR: *Hey, come here!*

BRENDA: *What for?*

She comes forward and he grabs her. BRENDA laughs with pleasure.

BRENDA: *You shouldn't have drunk all that beer with that loud-mouth, you know.*

ARTHUR: *You've had a drink as well. I can smell it a mile off.*

BRENDA: *You don't know what you're talking about. I've had two beers and a couple of orange squashes. You can't call that boozing, now can yer?*

They kiss.

BRENDA: *Arthur luv, don't let's stay down here too long. Let's go to bed, eh?*

They kiss again and turn to go.

BRENDA: *Come on!*

They move towards the door.

ARTHUR: *I wish Jack would bring your lad back from Skeggy every week.*

BRENDA: *I bet you do.*

They start climbing the stairs.

BRENDA: *He'll be home tomorrow, must make the most of it.*

ARTHUR: *Don't worry.*

BRENDA lets out a squeal of delight.

It is now early morning and the street is empty outside. ARTHUR is lying in BRENDA's bed. He looks up to see his trousers hanging over the back of a chair. His gaze travels round the room, past the dressing table to a chest-of-drawers, with a picture of JACK on it. ARTHUR's jacket is hanging on the wall.

ARTHUR is pleased with himself. He turns and looks down at BRENDA, smiling. She is asleep. He leans towards her and blows on her face. She stirs. (*Still*)

ARTHUR: *Come on, Brenda, wake up, duck.*

She smiles at him, then presses her face into his chest.

ARTHUR: *Oh, that's nice.*

BRENDA: *What's the time. luv?*

ARTHUR: *Ten past eleven.*

BRENDA sitting up: *What!*

ARTHUR roars with laughter.

BRENDA: *You're having me on again! Of all the liars, you're the biggest I have ever known.*

ARTHUR: *I always was a liar. A good'un and all.*

BRENDA: *Liars don't prosper.*

She leans over him and they kiss. A clock chimes.

ARTHUR: *It's only ten.*

BRENDA kissing him: *Good! Arthur?*

ARTHUR: *What!*

BRENDA: *What a time we had last night.*

ARTHUR: *It seems years. Oh you're lovely, Brenda.*

She kisses him, then he pushes her back onto the bed. Now in the living-room, ARTHUR sits at the table, eating hungrily. BRENDA comes out of the scullery.

ARTHUR: *Pour us some more tea, duck. It's thirsty work, falling down stairs.*

BRENDA laughs and pours him out some tea, then puts in some lumps of sugar.

BRENDA: *Two, ain't it?*

ARTHUR: *Ah, ah! Thanks!*

She takes the used dishes from the table into the scullery. The wireless is turned up.

ANNOUNCER: *Please make a soldier's life happy....*

ARTHUR: *You're good to me, Brenda luv. And don't think I don't appreciate it.*

She comes from the scullery and moves to the window behind him.

BRENDA: *It will be the last breakfast you'll have in this house, if you don't hurry.*

She looks out of the window anxiously.

BRENDA: *Jack'll be home soon.* She moves back to Arthur. *No more kiss and cuddle if he sees yer.*

ARTHUR: *When shall I see you again?*

BRENDA: *Not for a while. We don't want Jack catching on, now do we?*

She picks up the teapot and goes into the scullery.

ARTHUR: *What about the Welfare, can't we meet there for a change? Tell him you're in the darts team, he'll believe you. Work again next week. I don't know. I'll be hard at it, sweating me guts out at that lathe. It's a hard life if you don't weaken.*

BRENDA comes up and kisses him on the forehead.

BRENDA: *No peace for the wicked. Oh come on, luv, hurry up! Let me clear this.*

Back on the main street, JACK rides up on his motorbike. He turns into a side road, with his son on the pillion seat.

ARTHUR still sits at the table eating, while BRENDA stands watch-

275

ing at the window.

BRENDA: *Hey, he's coming on the bike, I think.*

ARTHUR gets up, finishing his cup of tea.

BRENDA: *Arthur, get a move on, luv.*

ARTHUR kissing her: *Tarr-ar!*

BRENDA: *Oh, babye!*

ARTHUR: *I'll see yer!*

BRENDA: *Go on, will yer!*

She quickly clears the table, as ARTHUR makes off.

JACK comes riding down the alley at the back of the house on his motorbike. He stops and the BOY jumps off the pillion seat. ARTHUR moves to the door of the living-room, opens it, then looks back.

Outside the back of the house, JACK and his son stand by the motorbike. The BOY runs over to the house.

Inside, ARTHUR moves from the doorway into the hall. As he gets to the front door. ARTHUR knocks over the BOY's bike, but he catches it before it falls to the ground.

BOY off: *Hello, mum!*

BRENDA comes into the empty living-room, followed by the BOY. She stubs out her cigarette, then turns on him.

BRENDA: *Come along now, let's get your clothes off.*

JACK comes in as she moves off with the BOY and sits down to help him with his clothes.

BRENDA: *Give me that! How did my little duck get on at the sea-side, eh!*

In the hall, ARTHUR slowly and quietly straightens the BOY's bike.

BRENDA off: *Have a nice time?*

BOY off: *Uhm!*

JACK off: *We had a good time, didn't we, Tommy!*

BOY off: *Smashing.*

BRENDA off: *I didn't expect you back so soon.*

JACK off: *Well, we had a clear run all the way down from Lincoln.*

ARTHUR quietly reaches the front door. BRENDA goes on fussing over the BOY, with JACK seated further back. She takes the BOY's coat off. There is a noise outside the room.

JACK: *Oh, who's in there?*

BRENDA: *Nobody as I know of, perhaps a cat got in.*
She hugs her son to her.

Now we are back in the pub, where the atmosphere is subdued and the lounge bar is nearly deserted on a Sunday morning. ARTHUR's aunt ADA is having a beer. She wears an open fur coat with a cheap cotton frock underneath. She is loud in her ways and voice, a rare person not broken by the 1930's. BERT, her unmarried son, is with her; a young man with a desperate look about him. As a boy, he has passed through approved schools and borstal, and because of this, his wildness is more controlled than his cousin ARTHUR's.

BERT: *Aye, he was on the run as well, mum, don't you remember?*

ADA: *He settled her though. Threatened to chuck her off Trent Bridge.*

BERT: *Aye, I forgot about that.*

ADA: *She thought it would be better to settle for a quid a week out of court than get a good wash.*
They both laugh loudly.

BERT: *Never heard a word after that, did we?*

ADA: *No!*
BERT looks up to see ARTHUR coming through the pub door.

BERT: *Hello, Arthur, you're out o' your way, ain't yer?*

ARTHUR: *Hello, auntie.*

ADA: *Hello, Arthur.*
ARTHUR comes over to his relations.

ARTHUR: *Your two young 'uns are outside up to their necks in ice cream.*

ADA: *No wonder they never eat their dinner.*

ARTHUR: *Did you go out last night?*

ADA: *Aye, we went to the Flying Fox . . . and oh dear! I had so many gins I thought I'd never get home.*

ARTHUR: *Oh, as long as you had a good time.* He talks to the barmaid. *A beer and stout, missus! What you having, auntie?*

BERT: *Beer!*

ADA: *I'll have a stout as well, Arthur luv! You should have been with us.*
ARTHUR puts a pound note on the bar counter. He notices a young girl DOREEN with her family.

ADA: *Our Ethel clicked with a bloke and he bought us drinks all round . . . the whole gang of us.*

BERT: *He must have got through a good five quid . . . the soft bastard. He had a car though, so I suppose he could afford it.*

ADA: *He thought he was on to a good thing wi' our Ethel. You should have seen his face drop when she came home with us instead of going off with him.*

The three of them laugh.

ARTHUR: *I wish I'd been there.*

He looks closer at DOREEN. She is about twenty, good-looking in a lively facetious way; a lithe-figured, sharp-mouthed factory girl. She is sitting with her friend BETTY and their two mothers, drinking.

ADA: *Yeah, you can't beat a bit of fun, can you, Arthur?*

ARTHUR goes on staring at DOREEN.

ADA: *How's your mum these days, Arthur?*

ARTHUR: *Oh, she's all right. She's got a lot to do though.* He lifts up his pint. *How's Johnny getting on in Australia?*

ADA: *Do you know, Arthur, I reckon Johnny is a lot better off out there. He never did well in this country, did he?*

ARTHUR: *He allus was a good worker, I know that.*

ADA: *He had to be, poor beggar. He had it hard when he was a kid, by God. Me and your mum had a struggle to bring you lot up, Arthur. Them were rotten days.*

She takes a drink.

ARTHUR: *It won't happen again, I can tell you that.*

BERT: *I was talking to a bloke the other day at the pit. He's always going on, you know. 'You can't beat the good old days'. So I got 'old of me pick and I said to him, 'You tell me owt else about them good old days as you call them and I'll cleave your stupid 'ead off'.* He laughs. *I would too!*

ARTHUR and ADA laugh as well. She turns and looks towards DOREEN's group.

ADA: *Look at 'im. Can't take his eyes off that girl over there.*

ARTHUR: *Not me. I'm courting already. I was looking at the calendar.*

ADA: *I believe you.*

The pub door opens and a boy peers round it.

BOY: *Mum!*

ADA turns to look at her child.

BOY off: *You coming, mum?*

ADA: *All right, I'm coming.* To ARTHUR and BERT. *I'll be going now. Are you coming, Bert? Or shall yer stay with Arthur?* She gets up. *If I don't get home, they'll come and fetch me for fear they'll starve.*

BERT begins to get up as well.

BERT: *Aye, I'm 'ungry meself, mum! Hey, how about a bit of fishing this afternoon up the canal?*

ARTHUR: *Okay! We'll get the bikes out.*

BERT: *All right.*

ARTHUR: *I'll meet you at Trowel Bridges.*

BERT goes off with ADA.

ADA off: *Tarr-ar, Arthur.*

ARTHUR: *Tarr-ar, auntie!*

BERT off: *I'll see you.*

ARTHUR: *Tarr-ar, Bert.*

ADA off: *Remember me to your mum.*

ARTHUR: *Tar!*

As ARTHUR begins to chat to the BARMAID, DOREEN leaves her group and comes forward to the bar.

ARTHUR: *Bit quiet today.*

BARMAID: *Isn't it.* She wipes the bar. *You ought to have seen it a couple of weeks back. Nearly lost our licences. Didn't you hear about it? Big fight! Took us a couple of days to clean up after that little lot.* To DOREEN. *Yes, my duck, what can I get for you?*

DOREEN: *Two packets of crisps, please.*

ARTHUR: *Are you sure you can afford it?*

ARTHUR knows he can hit it off with her because he is adept at manoeuvring within the limits of her somewhat narrow life.

ARTHUR: *What are you drinking?*

DOREEN takes the crisps and pays for them.

DOREEN: *Sharp, ain't yer!*

ARTHUR: *Is it somebody's birthday?*

DOREEN: *Mum's anniversary, if you want to know.*

ARTHUR: *I can't see your dad.*

DOREEN: *That's because he's not there.*

ARTHUR: *Is he coming?*

DOREEN: *I shouldn't think so. He left her fifteen years ago today, and she's just having a drink on it.*

ARTHUR finds this remark very funny.

279

DOREEN: *Well, I'm glad someone thinks it's funny.*

ARTHUR: *Well, have a drink then, while you're here.*

DOREEN: *All right, I'll have a small shandy.*

ARTHUR: *Small shandy, please.*

DOREEN: *What's that black stuff you're drinking? It looks like treacle.*

ARTHUR: *Beer and stout. Try some!*

DOREEN: *No, thank you. I think I tasted it once, but it was horrible.*

ARTHUR: *I'm not a boozer either, but I'm going fishing this afternoon and I like a drop beforehand.*

DOREEN: *Just a minute, I'll take these to mum.*

She picks up the crisps and moves to her group at its table.

ARTHUR stays at the bar, drinking his beer.

At the table, DOREEN's MOTHER has been watching her daughter, who comes back with the packets of crisps.

DOREEN's MOTHER: *You've been taking your time.*

ARTHUR finishes his drink, then sits on a bar stool.

DOREEN loudly off: *I've been waiting to get your packet of crisps for you.*

ARTHUR to barmaid: *Another beer and stout, missus.*

DOREEN's MOTHER off: *Oh, you have, 'ave yer!*

DOREEN is trying to get away from her MOTHER back to ARTHUR.

DOREEN loudly: *I won't be long. I'm just talking to this bloke I know.*

She walks back to ARTHUR at the bar.

ARTHUR: *Is your mum a bit deaf, then?*

DOREEN: *Yes, she is a bit.* Arthur offers her a packet of cigarettes. *No thanks, I don't smoke.*

ARTHUR: *What's your name then, duck?*

DOREEN: *Doreen! Rotten name, ain't it?*

ARTHUR: *What's wrong with it? My name's Arthur. Neither of them are up to much, but it ain't our fault, is it?* He lights a cigarette. *Where do you work then, Doreen?*

DOREEN: *Me! Harris's the hairnet factory. I've been there ever since I left school. All right, I will have a fag.*

ARTHUR hands her a cigarette.

ARTHUR: *I'm in the engineering trade myself.*

DOREEN taking the cigarette: *Ta!*

ARTHUR: *Come on, drink up! Have another shandy. It's your mother's anniversary.*

DOREEN: *No thanks.*

ARTHUR leans forward and lights her cigarette.

ARTHUR: *What do you do in the week, Doreen? Do you ever go to the pictures?*

DOREEN suspiciously: *Only on Wednesdays. Why?*

ARTHUR: *That's funny. I go Wednesday an' all. Which one do you go to?*

DOREEN: *The Granby as a rule.*

ARTHUR: *I'll see you next Wednesday then, at seven.*

DOREEN: *Fast worker, aren't yer! All right, but not in back row.*

ARTHUR: *I can't see unless I sit in back row. If I get any nearer the front, the picture gets so blurred.*

DOREEN: *You want glasses by the sound of it.*

ARTHUR: *Aye! I'll get some some day. But they make me look like a cock-eyed rent collector.*

DOREEN laughing: *I expect they do.*

ARTHUR: *I'll see you on Wednesday then.*

DOREEN: *All right.*

ARTHUR: *Well, don't be late then.*

DOREEN: *I won't be, but if I am, you'll just have to wait, won't yer?*

She turns and moves back to her mother's anniversary party. ARTHUR watches her go. (*Still*) Behind him, a darts game starts. The darts smack into the board behind his head.

Now we are with ARTHUR and BERT cycling down the main road with their fishing tackle. They turn off towards the canal and cycle along its bank.

Later, they sit on the bank by the canal, fishing idly. BERT takes a drink from a bottle, while ARTHUR sits beside him. It is a scene of utter tranquillity.

BERT: *I noticed that girl meself this morning. Smashing bit of stuff. Shouldn't think she'd want owt to do with a madhead like you, though.*

ARTHUR: *They all want a good time, you can bet.*

BERT: *That's what yer think. This one looks different. First kiss and she'll expect an engagement ring.*

ARTHUR now takes the bottle and drinks. Then he puts it down

281

behind him.

ARTHUR: *I take a tip from the fishes — never bite unless the bait's good. I won't get married until I'm good and ready.*

BERT: *You've got to get married sometime, ain't yer?*

ARTHUR: *Why don't you try then?*

BERT: *Ain't found anyone that'll have me yet.*

He gets up to move his fishing-line to a better bit of water.

ARTHUR: *It costs too much to get married. A lump sum down and your wages a week for life.*

BERT: *Most blokes ain't got owt else to work for, 'ave they?*

ARTHUR fixes his bait on his hook, his face grim as he sits on the grass of the canal bank.

ARTHUR: *I 'ave though. I work for the factory, income tax and insurance already. That's enough for a bit. They rob you right, left and centre. After they've skint you dry, you get called up in the army and get shot to death.*

BERT: *But that's how things are, Arthur. There's no use going crackers over it.* He sits on the grass. *All you can do is go on working and hope that some day somethin' good will turn up.*

ARTHUR: *Maybe. But you've got to be as cunning as them bastards. Take a few tips from the fishes. They all get caught in the end though, don't they? Can't keep their chops off the bait. Wasn't a bad-looking girl though, was she? Sharp an' all.*

He throws out his hook, bait and line into the canal water.

BERT: *Ar! Still going out with this married piece, aren't yer? It will be a good job when you're married. Her poor husband will be able to get a bit of rest then.*

ARTHUR: *Serves him right for being so slow. Should make her like being in bed with him. Then she won't come out with a bloke like me.*

He lights up a cigarette.

BERT: *You'll get your face bashed in one of these days.*

ARTHUR: *Don't worry, I can look after myself.*

BERT: *Just you be careful then and use a bit more sense.*

ARTHUR: *I'll watch it. I don't know, work tomorrow.*

He lies back at his ease on the grass by the water.

BERT: *Aye, me an' all.*

Now we see the black and smoky industrial town in the early

morning. It does not even have the charm of squalor. The houses are exactly uniform, the streets empty. The factory siren sounds.

Seen over the backyard fence, ARTHUR comes out of the Seaton house followed by his father. He sees MRS BULL standing at the end of the alley between the houses. She turns away as she sees ARTHUR. The father closes the back door and joins his son. Both are dressed for work.

ARTHUR: *Old Ma Bull's 'ere with her ha'penny.*

MR SEATON: *Aye, she's got nowt else to do, the nosey parker.*

ARTHUR unlocks the chain round his bicycle.

ARTHUR: *Spreading tales about me going with married women and boozing. It's all bloody lies.*

MR SEATON: *You want to make sure it is though, as well.*

He goes off to work as ARTHUR takes his bicycle and pushes it away into the alley. As he passes MRS BULL wheeling the bicycle, he glares at her. Then he mounts the bike and cycles down the road to work.

Inside the turnery department, the men work at their machines. ARTHUR works at his lathe. The siren sounds, so he stops his machine and wipes his hands.

A woman serves tea to the workers from an urn on a trolley. ARTHUR wipes his hands, then looks down at his feet. There, a cat lays a rat on the floor. ARTHUR bends down, strokes the cat and takes the rat from it. Then he rises and looks round, (*Still*) putting the rat under his shirt. He goes over to where clothes are hanging on pegs on the wall. He takes his lunch bag from a peg, then turns to look towards the women working at their machines. As he watches them, they knock off work. He waits for the women workers to pass him, then he moves across to put the dead rat on a woman's machine.

JACK is taking a cup of tea from the woman on the tea trolley, who smiles at him.

JACK: *Ta, luv!*

ARTHUR comes across to join him.

ARTHUR: *Any room for a rabbit arse, Jack? You've clicked by the look of it.*

The woman moves away with the tea trolley, while ARTHUR and JACK sit down.

ARTHUR: *I'll let Brenda know if you're not careful.*

JACK: *She wouldn't believe you, she can trust me.*

ARTHUR unwraps his sandwich lunch.

ARTHUR: *Can she though?*

He turns and looks round at the women workers moving back to their machines, while the men still sit reading the papers at their tea-break. He smiles to himself. As the woman with the dead rat on her machine sees it, she starts screaming.

ARTHUR smiles and turns away, while JACK looks over towards the screaming woman. She runs out, shouting, while some of the workers gather round her machine.

The smiling ARTHUR turns back to watch JACK drinking his tea.

ARTHUR: *That stuff will give you galloping dog rot — it's poison. A bloke in frame shop got laid up for six weeks for drinking firm's tea. Stomach trouble. You should bring your own flask.*

He drinks from his own flask and eats his sandwiches with JACK.

JACK: *If it's good enough for others, it's good enough for me.*

ARTHUR: *Don't be like that, Jack. Think of number one. Share and share alike's no good.*

JACK: *You wouldn't think like that if you won the pools though, would yer?*

ARTHUR: *Wouldn't I? I'd see the family all right, but nobody else. If I got a stack of begging letters like most blokes do, do you know what I'd do with them?*

ROBBOE the foreman comes up to stand above the seated pair.

JACK: *What?*

ARTHUR: *Make a bonfire.*

ROBBOE: *Ey! Have you had owt to do wi' putting a rat on that woman's bench?*

ARTHUR: *I don't know what you're talking about.*

ROBBOE: *I bet it was you, you young rogue.*

ARTHUR: *Me, Mr Robboe? I've got so much work to do I can't move from me lathe. I don't go around tormenting women. You know that.*

ROBBOE: *I don't know. Somebody did it and I reckon it's you. You're a bit of a red if you ask me, that's what you are.*

ARTHUR: *That's slander. I'll see me lawyers about that. I've got a witness, here.*

JACK turns away. He does not want to get mixed up in this.

ROBBOE: *I don't know, but I'll get the bloke that did it.*

ROBBOE goes away, dissatisfied.

ARTHUR: *I get the blame for everything.*

JACK: *He came up to me earlier on. Said I was to go on nights in frame shop.*

ARTHUR: *What?*

JACK: *In frame shop, on nights.*

ARTHUR: *Oh, I wouldn't fancy that.*

JACK and ARTHUR both drink their tea.

JACK: *I don't mind, it will be a change.*

ARTHUR: *It's not the first time that bastard's called me a red though. Not that I wouldn't vote communists if I thought I could get rid of blokes like 'im. I did vote for them in the last election. Did I tell you about that?*

JACK looks scandalized, although ARTHUR is laughing.

ARTHUR: *I shouldn't have voted at all because I was under twenty-one, but I used me dad's vote 'cause he was in bed with a bad back. Told 'em me name was 'Arold Spencer Seaton, just like that. Didn't believe it myself until I got outside again.*

JACK: *You could have got ten years for that if they'd 'ave caught yer. You were lucky.*

ARTHUR: *I told yer I was. That's what all these looney laws are for, to be broken by blokes like us.*

JACK: *You might cop it one of these days.*

The warning signal goes. Tea-break is over.

JACK: *Perhaps you won't be so cocky once you settle down.*

ARTHUR: *I shan't be doing that for a while.*

JACK: *There's nothing wrong with married life. I can tell yer. I'm married. Went into it with me eyes open. Married life's all right, if you're good to each other and you don't get too bossy.*

ARTHUR: *I believe yer then. Thousands wouldn't.*

He goes back to his lathe.

BRENDA is in her room, putting on her lipstick. As she leans back from the mirror, we see JACK seated behind her, reading the paper. He looks up.

JACK: *You off out again?*

BRENDA powdering her face: *Uhmm! I'm up to Winnie's for a bit. She's expecting her baby next week.*

285

JACK: *You've been seeing a lot of her lately. It's not much fun being on nights, we don't seem to get out together much these days.*

BRENDA: *Oh, how much longer is it going to go on for? You've only been on a fortnight.*

JACK: *I know. It might be another six months.*

BRENDA: *Still you don't mind it all that much, do you?*

JACK: *Well, it means more money and that's useful. We might even get a television set and you won't have to go out so much, will you?*

BRENDA: *No, I won't, will I? Won't be long, luv! Peggy will be here in a minute to look after Tommy.*

She rushes over to the door of the room.

JACK: *Right you are.*

He puts down the paper and stares after her.

Now we are in some trees by a club house. A motorbike roars nearby, as BRENDA follows ARTHUR walking through the trees.

BRENDA: *That sounds like Jack's bike.*

ARTHUR: *Can't be. Jack's not been at the club for weeks.*

ARTHUR stops and waits for BRENDA to catch him up. (*Still*)

ARTHUR: *Are you fit!*

BRENDA: *Yeah! You've got all lipstick on yer, luv! There!*

ARTHUR: *All right!*

They walk on.

BRENDA: *Yeah! I wonder if Jack does know anything.*

ARTHUR: *Course he don't.*

BRENDA: *Funny, ain't it? I tell him the same all the time.*

ARTHUR: *What?*

BRENDA: *That I go to the club to play darts. He said he'd come along one of these days to see if I really did.*

BRENDA laughs.

ARTHUR: *He'll believe all.*

BRENDA: *He never did come though. You sure he don't suspect anything. Do you think he does?*

ARTHUR: *No. We're too cunning.*

BRENDA laughing: *I wonder what he'd say if he did find out?*

ARTHUR: *We could always get married.*

BRENDA: *Oh, can't imagine that. He'd never make a divorce of it, anyway. I know Jack. As long as we go on loving each other, that's all that matters, ain't it?*

They stop for a moment and he kisses her. As they come forward, she is startled.

BRENDA: *That is Jack's bike, isn't it?*

ARTHUR: *What? Where?*

They come to the side of the club house with cars and bikes parked outside. BRENDA looks closely at one of the motorbikes.

BRENDA: *It is, you know.*

ARTHUR examines the motorbike, as BRENDA moves away uneasily.

BRENDA: *What shall we do, Arthur?*

ARTHUR: *Look, you told him you were going to yer sister's. You had better go there.*

BRENDA: *But will you come back to town with me?*

ARTHUR: *No, no, I'll show me face there and he won't suspect anything. All right luv, tarr-ar.*

He kisses her.

BRENDA: *Tarr-ar, luv!*

She moves off.

ARTHUR: *When will I see yer again?*

BRENDA stopping: *I don't know. You had better wait for a bit, hadn't yer, luv?*

ARTHUR: *I'll call round in a night or two.*

BRENDA: *All right! Babye!*

ARTHUR: *Tarr-ar. . . .*

She runs off. ARTHUR watches her, then moves to the club house.

He goes into the club room, where men are drinking or playing darts. He greets two of them, ALBERT and TOM, a union organizer.

ARTHUR: *Hey, Albert!*

ALBERT: *How do, Arthur.*

Arthur moves on to the bar to buy a beer from the barman, CHARLIE.

ARTHUR: *Hello, Tom. Come on, Charlie, give us a pint.*

JACK is sitting in the club room, alone at a table.

ARTHUR: *Hello, Jack.*

JACK: *Hello, Arthur.*

ARTHUR: *What are you drinking?*

JACK: *Oh ta, I'll have a mild.*

ARTHUR: *A mild. Another mild, please, Charlie. When's the next strike then, Tom?*

CHARLIE pulls two beers for ARTHUR.

TOM: *There's nothing to strike about yet, lad. I expect you're too busy with young women for that, anyway.*

ARTHUR: *No, not me. I spend my time with the bookies.*

He picks up the beers and goes over to JACK's table.

TOM: *I believe yer!*

ARTHUR: *How you getting on, Jack? How's Brenda these days?*

JACK: *All right! Can't grumble.*

ARTHUR sits and drinks his beer with JACK. (*Still*)

ARTHUR: *This ale tastes as if it has been pumped straight out of the Trent.*

JACK: *Mine's all right.*

He looks as if he has agreed to drink with ARTHUR against his grain.

ARTHUR: *I don't suppose you get out so much, now you are on nights. . . . It's a dog's life, if you ask me.*

JACK: *I wouldn't say that. I'm going out this weekend. Me brother's coming home for leave from Leicester.*

ARTHUR: *Doing his stretch in the service, is he?*

There is a hard edge between these two men.

JACK: *Oh no, he's a regular. In the Guards he is. Big broad lad, strong as a bull. You wouldn't think we were brothers. His pal's coming over as well. Expect we'll have a night out somewhere.*

ARTHUR: *It's good to get out a bit. I do a spot of fishing now and again. Your brother 'ome for long?*

JACK: *Fortnight!*

ARTHUR raises his glass to hide his expression.

JACK: *There's one thing about him, though, you know. He'll always help me if I am in any sort of trouble. If anybody does owt against me, I can always rely on him. I was with him and his pal once and we set on a bloke. . . . I never want to do owt like that again.*

ARTHUR: *Aye, but people like that should be careful. They might pick on the wrong bloke. I saw a fight like that once. . . .*

JACK looks back stonily at ARTHUR, as he picks up the challenge.

ARTHUR: *This was with two soldiers and all. They set on to a bloke and he wiped the floor with the both of them. It was 'orrible. Blood all over the place. I had to turn me 'ead away.*

JACK says nothing but stares at ARTHUR, who gets up.

ARTHUR: *Ah, this place is more dead than alive.*

JACK: *You want another?*

ARTHUR: *I've got a date. You'll have to go on soon, won't yer?*

JACK: *Yer!*

ARTHUR: *Tarr-ar! See yer!*

JACK: *Tarr-ar!*

ARTHUR turns and moves to the door of the club room, waving to the men at the bar on his way out.

ARTHUR: *Tarr-ar.*

TOM: *Tarr-ar!*

Now we see DOREEN with ARTHUR as they come down the steps into the foyer of the Granby cinema at night.

DOREEN: *That weren't a bad picture, but I knew it would end like that though.*

ARTHUR: *You could see it a mile off.* They stop. *Pictures allus make me thirsty. Fancy a drink?*

DOREEN: *No. Let's go straight home so you can meet mum. She'll get some supper for us.*

ARTHUR: *Will she mind you bringing me back?*

DOREEN: *No, she likes company.*

ARTHUR: *All right.*

He takes her arm and they go to the swing doors of the cinema and outside into the street. (*Still*)

Now we are on the porch of DOREEN's house, where she stands close to ARTHUR, but not too close.

DOREEN'S MOTHER off: *Don't be long there, Doreen.*

DOREEN loudly: *I shan't be, mum.*

ARTHUR: *How about tomorrow?*

DOREEN: *If you like.*

ARTHUR: *We can go to the White Horse for a drink.*

DOREEN: *I'm not all that keen on boozing.*

ARTHUR: *All right, I'll get somebody else then for tomorrow.*

DOREEN: *See if I care.*

ARTHUR moving close to her: *Don't be like that, duck.*

DOREEN'S MOTHER: *Come on in and shut that door.*

DOREEN loudly: *I shan't be a minute, mum.*

289

ARTHUR: *I'll see you next Wednesday then.*

DOREEN: *All right. See you next Wednesday.*

She goes in, closing the door in his face. He turns and moves away, then stops to listen to DOREEN in the house.

DOREEN'S MOTHER off: *I thought you were never going to come in.*

DOREEN off: *It's all right, mum.*

ARTHUR picks up a dustbin lid and slams it down. It echoes through the night street.

Back in the factory workshop, the men are working at their machines.

ARTHUR is also at his lathe. ROBBOE comes up with the pay packets. ARTHUR ignores him, working furiously.

ROBBOE: *Now then, if you'll spare a minute, I'll give you your wages.*

ARTHUR: *I shan't say no, Mr Robboe.*

ROBBOE: *You'd be the first one as ever did.*

ARTHUR: *How much this week?*

ROBBOE: *Fourteen pounds. It's more than the tool-setters get. When I started here, I took home seven bob a week.*

ARTHUR: *Aye, but in them days seven bob was worth summat. You could get a packet of fags for tuppence. You 'ad a marvellous time starving. But they've stopped me near three quid tax this week.*

ROBBOE: *Well, you can't blame the firm for that. You shouldn't grab so much.*

ARTHUR: *I don't grab, I earn every penny of it.*

ROBBOE: *I don't say you don't. But I wouldn't like anybody here to know how much you're taking 'ome. They'd all be at my throat asking for a raise.*

He goes off, disapproving.

ARTHUR: *Well, you could sack 'em then, couldn't yer? Just like them good old days you were just telling me about.*

He goes back to his lathe.

Back in the Seaton household later. ADA, ARTHUR and MR SEATON are sitting round, drinking tea. MRS SEATON is in the kitchen while ARTHUR counts out his money.

ARTHUR: *'Ere yer are, mum, me board. Six bob more this week. Go buy yourself some-fink!*

MRS SEATON comes from the kitchen, takes the money and moves off again.

MRS SEATON: *Thanks, Arthur, me old duck.*

ADA: *He's a good lad to you, ain't he?*

MRS SEATON off: *He is, an all.*

ADA: *Takes after his dad for 'ard work, don't he?*

ARTHUR looks up, hearing a small boy running in.

ARTHUR: *Ey, come here you!*

ADA also turns to see her son rush in.

MR SEATON looks back at his wife.

MR SEATON: *Got another cup of tea there, luv?*

ARTHUR grabs the boy.

ARTHUR: *Come 'ere!*

MRS SEATON moves to the kitchen. ARTHUR boxes with the boy.

ARTHUR: *Ol' blood-chop, that's what you are.*

ADA: *Don't be so rough with him, Arthur.*

ARTHUR swings the boy into the air.

ARTHUR: *He's all right. Hey, what do you feed 'im on, he's like a cannon ball.*

He holds the boy upside down.

ADA: *Oooo, 'e eats like a 'orse. Our Bert didn't want his dinner last night, so that little beggar scoffs every bit.*

The boy reaches for ARTHUR's money.

ARTHUR: *Get out of it . . . get away! Can't keep his 'ands off it. You better lock your hair grips up or he'll be at the gas meter.*

ADA: *Shut up, you daft nit, putting ideas in his 'ead!*

ARTHUR holds up a five-pound note while the boy dances round him, trying to get it.

ARTHUR: *Go up to shop and get yourself a fiver's worth of dolly mixtures.*

MRS SEATON comes back from the kitchen.

MRS SEATON: *Don't torment him, Arthur.*

ARTHUR: *Hey up! Oh he's all right . . . hey, come back here!*

The boy snatches the note and is away, with ARTHUR after him.

MR SEATON: *That was quick, eh!*

ARTHUR chases the boy out of the house and down the alley. They pelt into the main road, running past children playing. They rush past two women, with dogs barking around them.

ARTHUR: *Give me that fiver back or I'll give you a good tanning. Come 'ere.*

He catches the boy and they have a mock fight.

ARTHUR: *Give it 'ere! 'Ere! Aaah! Go on.*

He takes back the note, and then he pulls the boy with him towards the sweet shop on the corner. Inside the sweet-shop, the woman owner MRS ROE is serving MRS BULL.

MRS BULL: *Chalk it up, will yer, Mrs Roe?* She looks round. *Oh, there was something else I wanted, but I can't think what it was.*

The shop assistant puts down in the book what MRS BULL has bought. The shop door opens, and ARTHUR and the boy come in.

ARTHUR: *If you're good, I'll buy you some caramels.*

ARTHUR accidentally knocks into MRS BULL.

MRS BULL: *Oh! Look where you're going.*

ARTHUR: *Sorry I didn't see yer.* To the shop assistant. *Sixpen'th of caramels, please.*

MRS BULL: *You think you own the place, you young bleeder.*

ARTHUR: *Who, me? What are you talking about? You're daft.*

MRS BULL: *I'm not so daft that I don't know about your game. I've seen you going about as with them you shouldn't. Not the first time either.*

ARTHUR: *Oh, you have, 'ave yer?*

MRS BULL: *Aye, I have.*

ARTHUR: *Well, I know about you an' all. You're not past a bit o' rum stuff yourself. Are you?*

MRS BULL is outraged.

ARTHUR: *I bet your old man doesn't know about that.*

MRS BULL raises her hand to slap ARTHUR.

MRS BULL: *Go on you. . . .*

ARTHUR: *Yeah, go on! Come on, let's get out of here, we're not safe.*

ARTHUR goes through the shop door with the boy.

MRS BULL: *I'll clout you one of these days.*

ARTHUR: *Tarr-ar, fluffy!*

He closes the door behind him. MRS BULL comes forward to the counter, muttering below her breath.

Now we are inside the living-room of DOREEN's house at night.

All is prim and proper. BERT is there, looking over DOREEN's friend BETTY from the pub. ARTHUR is behind them. Some music plays from a radio.

BERT: *What's all the rush?*

BETTY coming forward: *I'm chef!*

BERT stops her passing him, while DOREEN joins ARTHUR.

DOREEN: *Will you help me with the tea in a minute, Betty?*

She turns and dances with ARTHUR.

BETTY: *I'm bringing it in, if some one will let me.*

BERT: *Come on, what you frightened of.* . . . He stands in her way. *. . . A kiss won't hurt yer.*

BETTY: *What do you think I am? I don't even know yer!*

BERT: *Give us a kiss, then you will.*

BETTY pushing him: *No, get off! Men are all the same.*

BERT: *But I'm different.*

BETTY: *You don't look like it to me.*

BERT: *But I am. I think you're a little cracker.*

BETTY is pleased, but pushes past him. He grabs her. ARTHUR and DOREEN are dancing. DOREEN's MOTHER suddenly comes in through the door.

DOREEN's MOTHER: *Well, looks as if you're having a birthday party or summat. I don't know. Look at the mess the house is in. I thought you was going to clear up for me today.*

She hangs her coat up in the hall.

DOREEN: *I was, mum. I just brought my pals in for a moment though. You know Arthur, me young man, don't yer?*

ARTHUR seems shocked, then pleased, to be called her young man. He tries to make an impression on DOREEN's battle-axe of a mother.

ARTHUR smiling: *How do, Mrs Greatton?*

DOREEN's MOTHER: *I don't know. You might help me at times, Doreen.*

As she switches off the music from the radio, BETTY and BERT come up to her.

DOREEN: *I was just going to clear up in a minute.*

BERT: *Hello, Mrs Greatton.*

BETTY: *Hello, Mrs Greatton.*

DOREEN's MOTHER talking at the same time: *I'm sure you were. People coming to supper and all.*

She moves off to the scullery. ARTHUR gives BERT the signal to go.

ARTHUR: *That's one way to make you feel at 'ome. We'll be going. Bert, are you fit?*

DOREEN: *I'm sorry about me mum.*

BERT: *If you've got company coming, we had better go.*

ARTHUR moves over to the door leading to the hall.

ARTHUR: *If you're ever round our way, drop into our house, you'll be welcome there.*

DOREEN following ARTHUR out: *It's not my fault. You know what she is.*

BERT to BETTY: *Tarr-ar, sweetheart.*

As the two young men leave, DOREEN'S MOTHER comes from the scullery into the living-room.

ARTHUR off: *Say goodnight to your mum for me.*

DOREEN comes back into the room.

DOREEN'S MOTHER: *Since when he's been your young man?*

DOREEN: *Not long.*

DOREEN'S MOTHER clearing the table: *He looks a bit wicked if you ask me.*

BETTY leaving: *Oh, he's all right.*

DOREEN: *You don't know him yet, do yer?*

DOREEN'S MOTHER: *Not like you know him, I don't suppose.*

She goes off with the plates from the table.

DOREEN: *Anyway, I like 'im.*

Now we are in the street with ARTHUR and BERT walking towards us.

BERT: *Did you get anywhere?*

ARTHUR: *No, did you?*

BERT: *No. That Betty's barmy. She wouldn't let me get near her. Telling yer, you've got to marry them these days before you get owt.*

ARTHUR: *Not if they are already married.*

Later we are on the main road at night, with a bus passing by. ARTHUR and BRENDA have just met each other and they move from the lights, down some steps. BRENDA is edgy and nervous.

ARTHUR: *What's up with yer?*

BRENDA: *Shut up! You make too much fuss.*

ARTHUR: *What's the matter with you tonight?*

BRENDA: *I'll tell you what's the matter with me, Arthur. I'm pregnant. Good and proper this time and it's your fault.*

ARTHUR: *Oh ay, it's bound to be my fault, ain't it?*

BRENDA: *I told you to be careful, but you don't bother. I allus said this would happen one day.*

ARTHUR: *What a wonderful Friday night. How do yer know?*

BRENDA: *You don't believe anything, do yer? I suppose you've got to see the kid before you believe me. I'm twelve days late. That means it's dead sure.*

ARTHUR: *Nothing's dead sure.*

BRENDA: *This is.*

ARTHUR: *All right.*

BRENDA: *Oh, don't.*

They stop by a dark wall.

ARTHUR: *How do you know it's mine?*

BRENDA: *Why don't you want to take the blame? You're backing out now.*

ARTHUR: *What blame? There's no blame on me. I just want to know whether it's mine or not. It's not bound to be.*

BRENDA: *It's your'n all right. I ain't done owt like that with Jack for a couple of months or more. And I don't want to have it, I can tell yer that now.*

ARTHUR: *Well, have yer tried owt? Took owt I mean?*

BRENDA: *Yes. Took pills but they didn't work. Thirty bob they cost me. Gone right down the drain.*

ARTHUR: *God Almighty!*

BRENDA: *He won't help yer. Now look, you've got to do something, yer know.*

ARTHUR: *Don't you want to have the kid?*

BRENDA: *I suppose you'd like me to have a kid by yer?*

ARTHUR: *Another one wouldn't make any difference, would it?*

BRENDA: *Don't talk so daft. What do you think having a kid means? You're doped and sick for nine months, your clothes don't fit and nobody will look at yer — one day you're yelling out and you've got a kid. Though that's not too bad. But you've got to look after it for the rest of its life. You want to try it sometime.*

ARTHUR: *Well, if that's how yer feel . . .*

BRENDA: *How do you expect me to feel?*

ARTHUR: *Look I'll go and see my Aunt Ada, she'll know what to do.*

295

She's had fourteen kids of her own and I'm sure she's got rid of as many others.

BRENDA: *I hope she knows something then, because if she don't there'll be a hell of a row, I can tell yer that.*

ARTHUR: *Don't worry, Brenda luv! You'll be as right as rain in a week or two. We'll go and see her about it tomorrow.*

BRENDA begins to cry, her anger dissolving.

BRENDA: *Okay!*

ARTHUR puts his arms round BRENDA to console her.

BRENDA: *Arthur . . .*

ARTHUR: *What?*

She kisses him.

Now we are in another street of the town with ARTHUR and BRENDA coming towards us. They reach ADA's front door. ARTHUR looks round, then knocks. He goes in while BRENDA is left waiting outside.

ADA is sitting in her living-room, reading. She turns to see who it is, as the door opens.

ARTHUR coming in: *Anybody in! Bring out your dead, Aunt Ada.*

ADA: *Oh, it's you, Arthur. Come on in, luv.*

ARTHUR: *Where's the tribe?*

ADA: *Gone to pictures. Sit yourself down and I'll give yer a cup o' tea.*

As he sits, she moves over to the cupboard for cups and saucers.

ARTHUR: *I can see Bert still works at pit.* He points to the fire.

ADA: *I'm glad you've come. Sunday afternoon is the only time I get a bit of peace and I like someone to talk to.*

ARTHUR: *I thought I'd come to see yer, I'm a bit worried about something.*

ADA comes up with the tea.

ADA: *Ay, and what would a good-looking chap like you have to worry about?*

ARTHUR gets up and moves over to the fireplace.

ARTHUR: *Not that I'm worried, Aunt Ada, I never worry. You know that. But it's this mate of mine at work. He's got this young girl into trouble and they don't know what to do about it.*

ADA: *That's a daft thing to do, couldn't he have been a bit more* careful? Well, he'll just have to face the music like our Dave did. Give me that kettle.

ARTHUR passing the kettle: But ain't there something that can be done? I mean, sometimes people get rid of it by taking things, don't they?

ADA prepares the tea.

ADA: How do you know about that?

ARTHUR: I read about it in the Sunday papers.

He sits down again, while ADA goes on making the tea.

ADA: You don't want to mess with such things.

She puts the kettle back on the fire.

ARTHUR: It's for me mate. He's in trouble. He's a good bloke and he'd do the same for me. You can't let your mate down at a time like this.

ADA comes back to the table, then sits down by ARTHUR.

ADA: It's you, ain't it? It's yo' as is in trouble.

ARTHUR: Well, it is, if you want to know.

ADA: I once knew a woman as got sent to prison for doing a thing like that. I'm sure I don't know what to tell yer.

ARTHUR: I thought you'd be able to help me.

ADA: Thought I'd be able to help yer. Just like that. You brainless loon! You ought to have more bloody sense. You can't expect to get out of fixes as easy as that.

ARTHUR: I've got nobody else to turn to.

ADA: Why don't you marry her if she's a nice girl?

ARTHUR: She's already married.

ADA: You are in a bloody fix, aren't yer?

ARTHUR: That's why I came to you.

ADA gets up and moves to the scullery.

ADA: I don't know! All right then, bring 'er to see me.

ARTHUR: Thanks. I can fetch her now, if you like.

ADA: The sooner the better, if you ask me. Let's get it over with.

ARTHUR moves towards the door.

ARTHUR: I'll be back then.

ADA: All right, get going.

ARTHUR leaves.

Outside in the street, BRENDA is still standing on the corner. She turns and walks towards us.

ARTHUR comes out of ADA's house.

297

BRENDA sees him and comes towards him. Outside the front door of the house, he begins explaining as he takes her arm. They go in through the front door to meet ADA.

BRENDA lags behind.

ADA: *You didn't take long, did yer?*

ARTHUR: *Come on, Brenda, duck!*

BRENDA: *Ta!*

ARTHUR: *This is me Aunt Ada.*

ADA: *Let's hope we can get yer out of it as quick as you got into it.*

BRENDA: *I don't expect it will be that easy either.*

ADA: *No, it won't. Come on in then.*

She goes out of the room and they follow her. All three come into the kitchen. ADA points to a chair.

ADA: *Sit yourselves down.*

BRENDA sitting: *Ta.*

ADA sitting: *How are you feeling now, then?*

BRENDA: *Well, you know how it is. I'm not too bad.*

ADA: *It ain't right, is it? I think men get away with murder.*

BRENDA: *They do, don't they?*

ARTHUR: *I don't know that much.*

ADA: *Don't be such a big 'ead. And get cracking so I can talk to her.*

ARTHUR pats her shoulder, then turns and leaves.

ADA: *What's your name, duck?*

BRENDA: *Brenda.*

ARTHUR comes out of ADA's house, looking rather low. He stops to light a cigarette. Then he moves to look through the window of the house.

He sees BRENDA seated in the kitchen, listening.

As he is looking through the window, he hears a door opening. It is BERT. ARTHUR goes over to him.

BERT: *Hello, Arthur, how are yer?*

ARTHUR: *All right!*

BERT: *Been to see me mum?*

ARTHUR: *Ah!*

BERT: *Well, don't tell us owt, will yer?*

ARTHUR: *There's nowt to tell.*

BERT: *Well, I'll go and get me tea then.*

ARTHUR: *Let's go for a walk.*

BERT: *What's up? You don't look too happy.*

ARTHUR: *I'm all right. Come on.*
BERT: *Okay!*

> They go out into the street. ARTHUR closes the back gate after them.
> As they walk along the street in silence, BERT looks at ARTHUR and shakes his head.

> Now we are outside a cinema, as ARTHUR and BERT leave it and walk off in silence through the night.
> Now we are in a deserted road late at night. A MAN comes out of a pub and goes across to the window of an undertaker's shop. ARTHUR and BERT pass him as they walk along. The MAN throws a brick through the shop window.

BERT: *What the devil? . . . It's that fella!*
ARTHUR: *Let's go and see what's happened.*

> The MAN just stands outside the broken shop window. A WOMAN in her Civil Defence uniform rushes on and grabs his arm.

WOMAN: *Hey you! I saw yer! I saw who did it.*

> The shop lights go on, and the owner and his wife come out into the street. Dogs bark, people gather.

WOMAN: *I should get down to that phone box and get the police. Here, take his other arm.*

> The MAN tries to run off, but the WOMAN catches him by one arm and some one holds onto the other one.
> ARTHUR and BERT come up to the group.

MAN WITH A PIPE: *What's he done then, missus?*
WOMAN: *Threw a brick through that window and smashed it.*

> The crowd mutters.

WOMAN: *Don't worry, we are holding 'im till they come.*

> ARTHUR cannot bear the sight of this.

ARTHUR: *Ratface, that's what she is.*
BERT to the WOMAN: *You'll get a stripe for this.*
ARTHUR: *Ah! Right across your back.*
CAUGHT MAN: *I only wanted flower vase for me mother.*
ARTHUR: *That window weren't worth breaking, mate.*
WOMAN: *Don't talk to him. He can do all his talking to the police.*

> In the crowd, there is a hard ELDERLY WOMAN standing by a man.

299

ELDERLY WOMAN: *Aye, he'll talk to them all right.*

CAUGHT MAN: *I only buried her three months ago. I wasn't doing any harm.*

ELDERLY WOMAN: *But you didn't have to do this, though, did yer?*

ARTHUR: *Why don't yer leave him alone, you old bag!*

ELDERLY WOMAN turning on ARTHUR: *Gercha! Yer cheeky young beggar!*

MAN IN THE CROWD: *You'll get six months in Lincoln.*

CAUGHT MAN: *Oh, let me go . . . come on . . . let me go . . .*

The crowd murmurs.

BERT: *Ark at 'er. . . . Talks to 'im as if 'e was dirt. . . .*

ARTHUR: *Walk off, mate, nobody will stop yer!*

The WOMAN holds on tighter to the MAN's arm.

WOMAN: *Don't put ideas in his head or you'll be in trouble.*

ARTHUR: *Shut yer bleeding rattle, ratface. What good is it going to do you, handing him over to the coppers?* To the CAUGHT MAN. *Go on, run! Get going!*

BERT: *Aye, 'op it!*

CROWD: *Aye! Go on!*

ARTHUR and BERT try to free the MAN from the WOMAN's clutch, with some of the crowd egging them on. Suddenly two POLICEMEN burst on the scene.

POLICEMAN: *All right! All right! What's the trouble?*

The crowd goes silent and begins to disperse. The WOMAN in uniform is still holding onto the MAN.

WOMAN: *This man here smashed that window. I saw him and this woman did.*

POLICEMAN off: *Any other witnesses?*

The CAUGHT MAN looks round, surprised as the crowd disappears.

ARTHUR and BERT hurry away down the street from the police and the MAN.

BERT: *I don't know how that ratface could do a thing like that.*

ARTHUR: *Because she's a bitch and a whore. She's got no heart in her. She's a swivel-eyed git.*

BERT: *She wants pole-axing.*

ARTHUR: *Some people would nark on their own mother. . . . We're living in a jungle, we are an' all. That bloke was a spineless bastard, though, he should have run.*

BERT: *Aye!*

ARTHUR: *I don't know. Still there's one thing I can do. . . .*
They walk off.

Now we are with ARTHUR in his bedroom at home, as he breaks
open his air-rifle, loads it, aims, and fires. The pellet hits the
ear of a china dog.

ARTHUR leans against the wall by his bed. He comes forward,
satisfied.

ARTHUR: *Right!*
He moves cautiously towards the window and looks out. MRS
BULL and MRS MACKLEY are standing on the corner of the
alley, gossiping.

MRS BULL: *We held him until police came. But that Arthur Seaton
were on him all time to tell him to run away.*

MRS MACKLEY: *Well, yer know, he never was any good, that boy.*

MRS BULL: *Coo, he went off as soon as police showed up.*
ARTHUR is looking out of window. He slowly opens it and
kneels down to take aim.

Unsuspecting, MRS BULL and MRS MACKLEY stand in the
alley, talking.

ARTHUR takes careful aim.

The two women go on talking.

MRS BULL: *Don't worry, he'll get checked one of these days. . . .*
Oooh!
She grabs her bottom as the pellet hits her.

MRS BULL: *Struff!*
ARTHUR smiles and leaves the window with his air-rifle.

MRS BULL is pained, while MRS MACKLEY stands behind her,
amazed. (*Still*)

MRS BULL: *God all bleedin' mighty, someone got me, that one.*

MRS MACKLEY: *Oooh! What's wrong? What happened?*
ARTHUR stands behind the curtains of his bedroom, watching
and laughing.

He breaks open his air-rifle.

MRS MACKLEY off: *I wonder who's gone and done that.*
The two women in the alley both look up towards the window.

MRS BULL: *I know who did it.*
They march down the alley towards the Seaton house.

301

A dog follows, barking. Suddenly another pellet lands in front of them. They stop.

MRS BULL: *Oooh! I'll wait until tonight when my old man comes 'ome. Come on!*

They run out.

ARTHUR now stands behind the curtains in the kitchen, watching and laughing.

ARTHUR: *Always gossiping about me so. . . .*

Now we see BERT sitting at the table with cards in front of him. ARTHUR moves over to sit by his cousin.

ARTHUR clapping his hands: *Smack! A pellet gets her right on the arse.*

He picks up a hand of cards.

BERT laughing: *I would like to have seen that.*

ARTHUR: *Didn't know what hit her.*

BERT: *Fat old cow! Serves her right! If you get put in clink, I'll send yer a file in a cake.*

He deals some more cards to ARTHUR, who arranges his poker hand.

ARTHUR: *She's got a bruise as big as a pancake.*

BERT: *Right.*

ARTHUR: *Tanner!*

BERT: *Tanner, I'm with yer!*

He puts his money on the table.

ARTHUR: *Two bob!*

BERT: *Two bob? In that case I'll see yer!*

ARTHUR puts down his cards.

ARTHUR: *Beat that!*

BERT: *Done!*

As he puts down his cards, there is a knock at the back door.

BERT: *I'll go.*

ARTHUR: *If it's anybody for money, tell 'em mum's out.*

BERT: *Right!*

Suddenly ARTHUR grabs BERT's arm.

ARTHUR: *'Ere, it's old Ma Bull. I thought she'd be back.*

BERT: *Shall I let her in?*

ARTHUR: *Yeah! I'll get me gun.*

He gets up and goes towards the door.

BERT: *Don't do that, Arthur, I'll bluff it out for yer! She won't twig owt.*

ARTHUR: *Go on!*

As he goes out of the room, BERT goes to open the back door to reveal the BULLS.

BERT: *What do yer want?*

MR BULL: *I 'ear you've been shooting at my missis.*

BERT: *Who, me, you've got the wrong bloke, I don't even live 'ere.*

MR BULL with relief: *Oh perhaps it weren't anybody at this 'ouse.*

BERT: *It couldn't have been. There ain't any guns here for a start.*

He starts to close the door, but he is forced back as MRS BULL pushes the door open and marches into the kitchen.

MRS BULL: *Arthur's got a gun. I know he 'as.*

BERT grabbing her: *'Ere, you've got the wrong 'ouse.*

MRS BULL: *You 'ave less o' yer cheek.*

She moves around the kitchen, looking for the gun with BERT following.

MRS BULL: *I got shot wi' an airgun today and I'm going to find out who did it.*

BERT: *Well, it weren't Arthur, he ain't home from work.*

MR BULL: *I didn't think it was anybody in this 'ouse.*

MRS BULL: *You shut your mouth. I ain't found 'em yet, and I won't rest till I do . . .*

ARTHUR comes through the door behind her with his gun.

ARTHUR: *Get out! Go on! Or you'll get another one.*

MRS BULL: *That's it. He's the one that shot me.*

BERT and ARTHUR face MRS BULL.

ARTHUR: *In your fat throat this time.*

MRS BULL runs to her husband for protection.

MRS BULL: *Well, what are you standing there for?*

ARTHUR: *Go on, and take laughing boy with yer.*

MRS BULL: *Hit 'im! Hit 'im!* They back out together. *We'll see about this!*

ARTHUR and BERT call after them, laughing.

MR and MRS BULL come out of the SEATON house, down the garden and alley. MR SEATON is watching them.

MRS BULL: *I'll settle that beggar once and for all.*

She goes off with her husband.

BERT and ARTHUR look out of the window.

BERT: *Did yer see her old man's face when she told him to 'it yer?*

They both laugh as Bert sits down to go on with the card game.

ARTHUR: *If she goes to coppers, she won't be able to show them the bruises.* He sits. *Who deals?*

MR SEATON comes down the alley. He turns off and goes into his garden.

ARTHUR is seated in the kitchen playing cards. MR SEATON comes in and moves to the dresser.

ARTHUR: *We'll have no cheating this time.*

MR SEATON: *That was the Bulls, weren't it?*

ARTHUR: *Yeah! They said I shot Mrs Bull with an airgun, but they are lying as usual.* To BERT. *Seven!*

MR SEATON: *I thought I told yer never to let them in this 'ouse. I 'ate nosey parkers like that.*

He takes off his coat, as ARTHUR and BERT smile at one another.

MR SEATON: *Wonder they didn't borrow a pound of sugar while they were at it.*

BERT: *They just barged in, couldn't stop 'em.*

MR SEATON: *I would have bloody well stopped them.*

ARTHUR: *What have you got?*

BERT: *A full house.*

ARTHUR: *What a twister!* Getting up at the sound of a knock on the door. *I'll go.*

MR SEATON: *Pack it up now, Bert, I'm making tea.*

ARTHUR opens the door to show DOREEN.

ARTHUR: *Doreen! Hello, duck, come on in.*

DOREEN: *A work friend of mine lives near here, so I thought I'd drop in to see yer.*

ARTHUR pulls her inside the room.

ARTHUR: *Take your coat off. Me mum's out but we'll have some supper.*

DOREEN: *I won't stay long.*

She looks as if she wished she hadn't come, although she doesn't show it more than she can help.

BERT: *How do, Doreen. How's Betty then?*

DOREEN: *She's all right, thanks. I thought it would be daft not to call being so near.*

ARTHUR helps her off with her coat.

ARTHUR: *I'm glad yer did. I'd 'ave been mad if yer ain't, and I'd 'ave found out. Was yer mum mad at us on Sunday?*

DOREEN: *No!*

There is another knock at the door. MR SEATON goes to answer it.

DOREEN: *Mum's all right, but she's a bit funny sometimes, being deaf as she is.*

POLICEMAN off: *This woman said you shot her with an airgun.*

MR SEATON: *Airgun! There's no airgun in this 'ouse.*

ARTHUR signals DOREEN to keep quiet, then moves away.

POLICEMAN off: *We'll have a look, shall we?*

MR SEATON: *What? Come in then, if yer like.*

MR SEATON comes into the kitchen followed by the POLICEMAN and then the BULLS.

MR SEATON: *Shut the door after yer, will yer?*

POLICEMAN: *Which one of them was it, you say?*

MRS BULL pointing at ARTHUR: *'Im.*

POLICEMAN: *She says yer threatened her with an airgun. Is that right?*

ARTHUR: *When was this then?*

MRS BULL: *You know when it were, just now.*

ARTHUR: *Dad, what have I been doing for the last hour?*

MR SEATON: *Don't be so bloody daft. What do you mean? 'What have I been doing?'*

ARTHUR: *Tell them, go on!*

MR SEATON: *You know what you've been doing. Playing cards with Bert 'ere.*

BERT: *Aye, and losing too.*

MRS BULL: *Oh, it's no use, they'll never own up to owt.*

MR SEATON: *You've got a bloody cheek coming in 'ere saying we've got an airgun. Some people would do owt to cause trouble.*

The POLICEMAN is getting fed up and sees it is no use pressing anything. Yet he suspects ARTHUR.

POLICEMAN: *Look then, I can't mess around here all night. But stop making trouble in the yard, that's all.*

ARTHUR looks smug.

POLICEMAN off: *If there's any more row. . . .*

DOREEN looks suspiciously at ARTHUR.

POLICEMAN off: *. . . I'll be down with the Inspector to sort you lot out.*

DOREEN, BERT and ARTHUR are seated facing MR SEATON, the

POLICEMAN and the BULLS.

POLICEMAN: *Just watch it. And I don't want to come back 'ere again.*

He goes out to the garden after the BULLS.

MRS BULL: *Well, that's telling them straight.*

MR BULL: *Aye, and about time too. I should say.*

The POLICEMAN goes down the garden path to the alley, followed by the BULLS. (*Still*)

MRS BULL: *Ta very much.*

POLICEMAN: *Just keep away for a bit, will yer?*

He goes off.

MRS BULL: *Did yer get a look at that kitchen?*

MR BULL: *Ah.*

Back in the kitchen, ARTHUR is very pleased with himself.

ARTHUR: *They didn't get much out of us.*

BERT: *They never would either.*

ARTHUR rises and turns on the radio. He goes across the kitchen and moves the table out of the way.

ARTHUR: *Come on, Bert, clear the floor.* He grabs hold of DOREEN. *Come on, Doreen, let's dance.*

MR SEATON leaves them to it.

DOREEN: *I can't stay. . . .*

ARTHUR dancing: *Don't look so sorry.*

DOREEN: *Do I?*

BERT: *Do you come here often?*

They all laugh. DOREEN and ARTHUR fall in each other's arms.

Now it is the slope leading up to the parapet of Nottingham Castle. BRENDA toils upwards to meet ARTHUR at the parapet, while children run past her. Beyond them is the Black Meadows district, with the grassy hills beyond the Trent.

ARTHUR: *Hello, duck.*

BRENDA: *Been 'ere long?*

ARTHUR: *Ten minutes. I was just looking at the lovely view.*

BRENDA: *Well, you'd better come down to earth then, hadn't yer?*

ARTHUR: *How did yer get on at Aunt Ada's? Did things go off all right?*

BRENDA: *No, it didn't. It was just one of them old wives' tricks. She made me sit in a hot bath for three hours and drink a pint of* gin. *I'll never go through that again. It was terrible. I thought I was going to die. And it didn't work.*

BRENDA and ARTHUR stand on the parapet in silence, listening to children's voices. Finally ARTHUR speaks.

ARTHUR: *How do yer feel now?*

BRENDA: *What do yer think? I got over it.*

ARTHUR: *I don't know. I can't think of owt else.*

BRENDA: *Somebody told me the other day they'd seen you come out of the pictures with a young girl.*

ARTHUR: *He was a bloody liar then.*

He walks away past some castle visitors towards an archway. BRENDA follows him and lights up a cigarette.

BRENDA: *Do yer think I'm daft, Arthur? I can tell yer don't think as much of me as yer used to.*

ARTHUR: *That ain't true, Brenda. You know I like yer a lot.*

BRENDA: *I know yer do. You can see it a mile off.*

ARTHUR: *It's not my fault if yer don't believe me, is it?*

BRENDA: *You know the trouble with you? You don't know the difference between right and wrong. And I don't think you ever will.*

ARTHUR: *Maybe I won't, but I don't want anyone to teach me either.*

BRENDA: *You'll learn, one day.*

ARTHUR: *We'll see. But it's now that matters, ain't it? We've still got to clear this mess up.*

BRENDA: *Look, I'll try just one last thing.*

ARTHUR: *What?*

BRENDA: *Well, a girl I know told me of a doctor that would do it.*

ARTHUR: *Where?*

BRENDA: *That doesn't matter, I've got the address.*

ARTHUR: *I don't know, all this mess.*

BRENDA: *Yeah, but who got me into it? Don't think yer backing out now.*

ARTHUR: *I'm not trying to. And I never would either.*

BRENDA: *I may as well tell yer, this doctor wants forty quid.*

ARTHUR: *I'll get that for yer.*

BRENDA: *When though?*

ARTHUR: *I'll have it for yer in a couple of days.*

BRENDA: *You're getting off light, aren't yer?*

ARTHUR makes a sign to BRENDA to follow him as he goes. She does so.

307

Now we see boys playing football in a Nottingham park. ARTHUR and DOREEN are sauntering by, arm in arm.

DOREEN: *You know the girl in our firm?*

ARTHUR: *Which one?*

DOREEN: *You know Tina, the one on the phone?*

ARTHUR: *Well, what about her?*

DOREEN: *She got married yesterday. She looked ever so nice.*

ARTHUR: *What was the bloke like, could yer smell the drink?* He moves away, losing DOREEN. *He must have been drunk to get married.*

DOREEN: *You're in a rotten mood today.*

ARTHUR: *I lost five quid at the races.*

DOREEN: *Serves yer right. Yer shouldn't waste yer money.*

ARTHUR: *It's not wasted. I enjoy betting.*

DOREEN: *I don't care what yer do with yer money. It's nothing to do with me.*

ARTHUR: *Well, stop telling me off then.*

DOREEN: *I'm not telling yer off. You don't think I'm bothered about yer like that, do yer?*

ARTHUR: *That's not what yer said in the pictures just now.*

DOREEN hitting him: *You're a pig throwing it up like that.*

She moves off to lean against a fence. ARTHUR joins her. (*Still*).

ARTHUR: *I like yer telling me off. I like it a lot, in fact.*

DOREEN: *You ought to show it then.*

ARTHUR: *I do.*

DOREEN: *No, you don't. Why don't you ever take me where it's lively and there's plenty of people? It's always the pictures or a walk at night.*

ARTHUR: *Now, that ain't true.*

DOREEN: *Anybody would think you were ashamed to be seen with me.*

ARTHUR: *Well, I'm not, I can tell yer that. I'll take yer to fair on Saturday night, all right?*

DOREEN: *All right, if yer like.*

Fairground music sounds, and we swing and swoop with BETTY, DOREEN, BERT and ARTHUR on a fairground car. Through the crowds at the fair, JACK and BRENDA come with their boy. They are followed by JACK's soldier brother and his friend. They go up to a stall to try their luck at shooting, while BRENDA looks around for ARTHUR.

ARTHUR and DOREEN are careering round in a dodgem car. They bump into BETTY and BERT. DOREEN laughs. ARTHUR bounces his dodgem off again.

At the shooting stall, BRENDA breaks away from JACK and his friends, and goes looking for ARTHUR.

On the dodgem track, ARTHUR and DOREEN in their car hunt BERT and BETTY in theirs.

The soldier friend of JACK's brother fires at the stall, while JACK and his brother show JACK's boy how to use a gun.

The dodgem attendant jumps onto the back of BERT's car, while ARTHUR careers on.

BRENDA passes a 'roll a penny' stall, looking for ARTHUR.

ARTHUR, DOREEN, BERT and BETTY are coming off the dodgems. ARTHUR kisses DOREEN, then suddenly sees BRENDA.

By the 'roll a penny' stall, BRENDA sees ARTHUR with his new girl.

ARTHUR looks across the stall to BRENDA and signals her to get to one side.

BRENDA looks back towards JACK at the shooting stall.

ARTHUR looks at BRENDA, then whispers to BERT to look after the two girls. He signals BRENDA to follow him, which she does. JACK finishes shooting with his son and the two soldiers. He comes up looking for BRENDA.

ARTHUR creeps between two tents, followed by BRENDA.

JACK's group all search for BRENDA.

ARTHUR makes room for BRENDA to squeeze between the two tents behind him. They face each other.

BRENDA: *Having a good time?*

ARTHUR: *Not bad, I'm with some pals from work. I had to come out or I'd go crackers. I've been worrying about yer all week.*

BRENDA: *You can stop worrying.*

ARTHUR: *Is everything all right then? You been to see that doctor?*

BRENDA: *I didn't wait. I didn't stay.*

ARTHUR: *Why?*

BRENDA: *I've decided to have it and face whatever comes of it.*

ARTHUR: *You want to have the kid now, then?*

BRENDA's face is working. She does not answer.

ARTHUR: *But I. . . .*

BRENDA: *Look, I must go. Jack will be wondering where I am.*

ARTHUR: *Look, I wanna help yer.*

BRENDA: *Do yer, Arthur?*

ARTHUR: *Yeah, what can I do?*

BRENDA: *There's nothing much yer can do, is there?*

ARTHUR is silent now.

BRENDA: *I must go now. . . .*

ARTHUR stops her from leaving him.

BRENDA: *Jack will be wondering. . . .*

ARTHUR still holds onto BRENDA.

BRENDA: *I must go.*

Now she looks frightened as she sees that JACK and his friends are looking for her.

ARTHUR pulls her out of sight. He grabs her hand, and they run off through the shadows at the back of the fair.

BRENDA: *Look, Arthur, I've got to get back.*

ARTHUR: *Wait a minute.*

BRENDA: *They mustn't see us together.*

She breaks away from him and mingles with the crowd. ARTHUR watches her, then races after her to the swings.

JACK and his friends look for BRENDA.

On the roundabout, BRENDA and ARTHUR whirl forward in a car. JACK and the two soldiers see them. The two soldiers move over to the roundabout, as the cars swing past.

In the car, BRENDA and ARTHUR see the waiting soldiers.

The soldiers watch.

The car swings past.

The soldiers watch and wait.

ARTHUR gets ready to jump out of the car.

He jumps and runs along the platform of the roundabout, and vaults over the rail.

He lands on the ground below and runs for it through the crowd.

JACK stands with his son and brother by the entrance to the roundabout. The other soldier runs in and takes the brother off with him.

BRENDA is alone in the roundabout car.

The soldiers come up onto the platform and they move round

looking for ARTHUR.

BRENDA watches them, scared.

The soldiers split up, looking for ARTHUR through the fairground.

JACK is standing at the bottom of the steps to the roundabout with his son. As BRENDA comes through to him, he grabs her and hits her across the face.

JACK: *Come 'ere! I'll murder yer!*

He seizes the boy and goes. BRENDA looks round at the crowd, then follows him, sobbing.

ARTHUR comes cautiously down a street, looking for danger. As he comes round a corner, he gets ambushed by the two soldiers, who are waiting for him. They force him onto some waste ground and beat him up.

ARTHUR is terribly beaten by the soldiers.

He passes out. They drop him and leave him.

As the fairground music blares again, ARTHUR wakes and staggers forward. His face is covered in blood. He reaches a tap and washes his face under it. (*Still*)

He staggers forward again, then collapses.

Fade to a scene of Nottingham, with the noise of the factory hooters summoning the workers from the houses.

Dissolve to the houses, row after row, all the same.

Now we see ARTHUR lying in bed. Slowly he gets out and moves around his room at home.

ARTHUR voice off: *They'd busted me right enough. Still, I'd had me bit of fun. It ain't the first time I've been in a losing fight. It won't be the last either, I don't suppose. How long have I been lying here, though? A week? I can't think. . . . Mum called me barmy when I told her I fell off a gasometer for a bet. But I'm not barmy. I'm a six foot prop that wants a pint of beer, that's what.* He looks at himself in his mirror. *But if any knowing bastard tells them that's me, I'll tell 'em I'm a dynamite dealer, waiting to blow the factory to Kingdom Come. I'm me and nobody else. Whatever people say I am, that's what I'm not. Because they don't know a bloody thing about me. God knows what I am.*

ARTHUR turns away from his reflection in the mirror to the window. He looks out.

Below him is the alley and the row of houses.

ARTHUR smiles as he sees DOREEN coming into the alley from the street. He closes the curtains.

ARTHUR is lying in bed again, when the knock on the door sounds.

ARTHUR: *Come in!*

The door opens and DOREEN comes into his bedroom.

ARTHUR sitting up: *Come on in, duck, this is a surprise.*

DOREEN: *I came to see how you were.*

ARTHUR: *I'm not bad. I'll be as right as rain in a day or two. Take your coat off and sit down.*

DOREEN moving round the bed: *This is a nice room. Are all them clo's yourn?*

She looks at ARTHUR's wardrobe.

ARTHUR: *Ah, just a few rags.*

DOREEN: *They must have cost yer a pretty penny.*

ARTHUR: *I earn good wages.*

DOREEN taking off her coat: *I've been worried about yer all week. Yer were in a state when we brought yer 'ome. What happened?*

ARTHUR: *Oh, I got knocked down with a 'orse and cart. Didn't see it 'till it was right on top of me. I thought I was a gonner.*

DOREEN: *You even told yer own mum yer fell off the gasworks for a bet. You won't tell anybody anything, will yer!*

ARTHUR: *Why should I? It pays to keep yer trap shut. Sit down.*

DOREEN: *No, it don't.*

ARTHUR: *I've just told yer, haven't I? I told yer I got run over with a 'orse and cart.*

DOREEN: *You are a liar.*

ARTHUR lying down: *You won't like it if I tell yer.*

DOREEN: *I won't mind.*

ARTHUR: *I got beat up with two soldiers.*

DOREEN: *What for?*

ARTHUR: *Well, I've been knocking around with a married woman, and her husband set them onto me. Two onto one. So they beat me. I'd have flattened them if it had been one at a time.*

DOREEN: *I suppose that's why you left us at the fair.*

ARTHUR: *Oh no, it wasn't. I saw a mate of mine on the dodgems, that owed me five quid and I went to collect it. I didn't see yer after that, what happened to yer?*

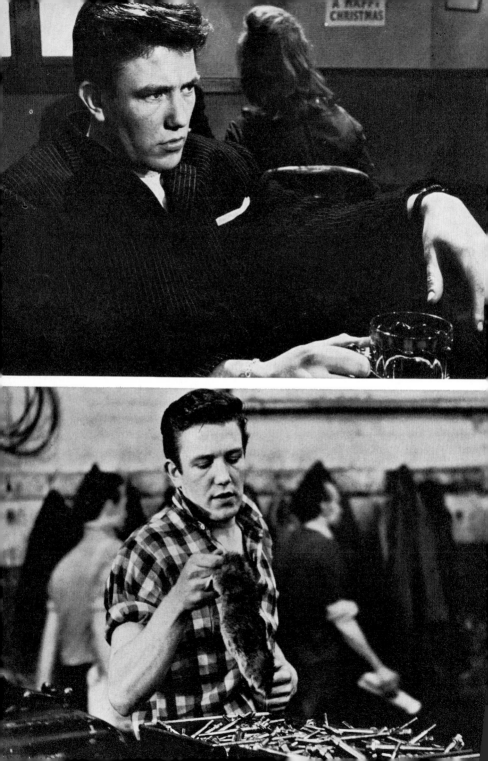

DOREEN: *You talk to me like I was a bit of muck.*
ARTHUR: *Look, don't be like that, duck, I'm sorry.*
DOREEN: *You look it.*

ARTHUR pats the bed.

ARTHUR: *Come 'ere.*

DOREEN looks suspiciously at him.

ARTHUR: *Come on, come 'ere.*

DOREEN pauses, then sits on the bed.

ARTHUR: *I'm glad you came to see me. I'd have stayed down in the dumps for good if you hadn't.*
DOREEN: *I wouldn't have known you were. Oh, I brought yer some fags.*

ARTHUR takes the cigarette packet.

ARTHUR: *Oh, thanks. What's it like outside?*
DOREEN: *It's a bit cold.*
ARTHUR: *Not in bed, it ain't. It's warm under all these blankets. Come and try.*
DOREEN: *What do yer take me for?*
ARTHUR: *We're courting, aren't we?*
DOREEN: *You might call it courting.*
ARTHUR: *You're a nice girl, Doreen. I like yer a lot. I'd like yer to stay with me for good so I don't get knocked down by any more 'orses. The trouble with me is I'm always bumping into things. It's not much of a paying game.*
DOREEN: *You'll have to watch where you're going, won't yer?*
ARTHUR: *I've never seen anybody look as nice as you do.*

DOREEN is very pleased.

ARTHUR: *I'll buy yer a ring next week if you're nice.*

DOREEN is very pleased.

ARTHUR: *Come on, give us a kiss then!*

DOREEN smiles and leans down.

In the scullery, MRS SEATON opens the back door to BERT, who comes in.

MRS SEATON: *Come on in, Bert.*
BERT: *Hello, Aunt Vera. All right, 'Arold?*

MR SEATON is sitting at the kitchen table, eating and watching television.

MR SEATON: *All right, Bert. How's things at the pit?*
BERT: *Black, but I can't grumble. How's the lad?*

321

MRS SEATON: *Still in bed. Take a clean shirt up while you are about it.*
BERT: *Right-o!*
MR SEATON: *Aye, it's about time he got up.*
BERT: *What's up, telly broke then?*
> He opens the door to go and see ARTHUR.
> Back in the bedroom, ARTHUR and DOREEN are on the bed, kissing. They break apart quickly as the door opens and BERT enters with the clean shirt.
BERT: *Here comes the world's delight.* He stops. *Oh, sorry, Doreen, I didn't know you were here.*
> DOREEN gets up from the bed shyly.
DOREEN: *Hello, Bert.*
BERT: *Okay, Arthur?*
ARTHUR: *I'm all right.*
BERT: *Oh, you' mum sent the shirt up.*
ARTHUR: *Oh, thanks. I suppose it is time I was getting up.*
DOREEN: *Well, I'll be going now, Arthur.*
BERT: *Oh, don't go, luv! I just popped up.*
DOREEN: *I'll have to go now, me mum's expecting me.*
BERT: *Oh, how's Betty these days?*
DOREEN: *She's all right, thanks.*
ARTHUR: *Okay, luv', I'll see yer later.*
DOREEN: *Okay. So long, Bert.*
BERT: *Tarr-ar, Doreen.*
ARTHUR: *Tarr-ar, luv. I'll see yer at your house. Good-bye.*
> She goes out.
BERT: *Smashing nurse. I'm sorry, I didn't know she was here.*
ARTHUR: *Come plodding in here.*
BERT: *Well, nobody told me downstairs. You two going steady then?*
ARTHUR: *What does it look like, eh? What do you think?*
> BERT sits down on the bed.
BERT: *Well, she's a lovely girl, I must say that. How are yer feeling?*
ARTHUR: *Oh, I feel fine now.*
BERT: *You fancy a bit of fishing this afternoon?*
ARTHUR: *Not this afternoon. I'll go tomorrow.*
BERT: *Why not this afternoon?*
> ARTHUR begins to put on his clean shirt.
ARTHUR: *I've got a date with Doreen!*

BERT: *You were born dead lucky, weren't yer?*

Dissolve to the living-room of DOREEN's house, where she and ARTHUR are seated at the dining-table. DOREEN's MOTHER is on the sofa, reading the paper. DOREEN looks from ARTHUR to her mother and smiles.

ARTHUR: *You' mother takes all night to read the paper. Does she read slow or is she looking at the adverts?*

A kettle begins to whistle off.

DOREEN: *She reads every word. She loves the newspaper more than a book.* She shouts. *Mum, your kettle's boiling.*

DOREEN's MOTHER: *I 'eard it.*

She gets up and goes into the scullery.

ARTHUR taking DOREEN's hand: *I thought she was never going to get out of that chair.*

DOREEN: *She won't be a minute. She's just filling her hot-water bottle.*

Her mother comes back from the scullery with a hot-water bottle.

DOREEN's MOTHER: *I'm off to bed. Don't be too long yourself, Doreen.*

DOREEN standing up: *I won't be. Arthur's just going in a minute. He's got ever such a long walk home.*

ARTHUR: *Aye, I have an all. I'll get cracking in a bit.*

DOREEN's MOTHER: *Well, don't be late. It's after eleven now.*

She goes out to the hall.

DOREEN: *I'll wash the cups up before I come, mum.*

DOREEN moves to the table, but ARTHUR stops her.

He is about to kiss her, but she breaks away.

DOREEN: *Let's make as if you're going first.*

They go to the door of the room. Out in the hall, the two lovers come to the front door. DOREEN opens it.

DOREEN: *Good night then, Arthur.*

ARTHUR: *Goodnight.*

DOREEN: *We'll have to do it a bit louder, you know she's deaf.*

DOREEN shouting: *Goodnight then, Arthur.*

ARTHUR loudly: *Goodnight, duck, see yer soon.*

DOREEN slams the door so that the whole house shakes, but

ARTHUR is still in the hall. The two lovers go back into the living-room. ARTHUR sits on the sofa. DOREEN closes the curtains, then comes over to ARTHUR, who takes her hand. She moves round the sofa to sit by him and he bears down on her in a long kiss.

Dissolve back to the factory floor, where ARTHUR is leaving his machine to come over to the first aid box. He puts a piece of plaster on his thumb.
Outside in the factory yard, a few men are busy working.
JACK passes them and goes into the main factory building. By the first aid kit, ARTHUR sees JACK come in. The two men stare at each other, then JACK starts to walk past.

ARTHUR: *What are you doing around here then?*

JACK: *I'm just going to faceshop. I'm on leave now.*

He steps forward.

ARTHUR: *I thought you might be coming to see me.*

JACK: *There's no good in that, is there?*

ARTHUR: *Isn't there? 'Appen you thought the swaddies had killed me?*

JACK: *I don't know what you're talking about.*

ARTHUR: *I didn't think you would. That's the sort of bloke you are, ain't it? Until yer get bashed in the face. Then yer squeal like a stuff pig.*

JACK turning on ARTHUR: *You caused a lot of trouble between me and Brenda. You can't deny it neither.*

ARTHUR gives nothing away.

JACK: *It weren't right.*

ARTHUR: *You don't have to tell me what's right and what's wrong. How is Brenda anyway?*

JACK wants to tell him nothing, and yet has to tell him something.

JACK: *She's okay. She'll be all right with me. I'll look after her. Keep that between you and me though. If you ever try and see her again, you'll get more trouble from swaddies.*

ARTHUR: *They won't find it so easy next time, whether I'm on me own or not.*

JACK: *You're too much of a trouble-maker, Arthur. You should take things as they come and enjoy life.*

ARTHUR: *I do enjoy life. Just because I'm not like you, don't think I don't.*

JACK: *I'll see yer sometime.*

ARTHUR: *Yeah!*

ARTHUR moves back to his lathe on the factory floor with all the other men working at their machines.

Dissolve to the canal, where we see ARTHUR and BERT on the far bank, fishing. ARTHUR is casting his line, while BERT starts to hum the wedding march.

ARTHUR: *Give over.*

BERT: *Thought you were the one that weren't going to get married till yer were good and ready.*

ARTHUR: *I hadn't met Doreen then.*

BERT: *Aye. What's the score with Brenda then?*

ARTHUR: *Finished. We packed it up.*

BERT: *It was about time. Don't you think?*

ARTHUR stands by a tree, considering.

ARTHUR: *I don't know. She was a good sort, though. I've given her lots to put up with.*

BERT: *What's her husband like?*

ARTHUR: *A bit of a dope. He's not a bad bloke really.*

BERT: *I told you to lay off weeks ago, not that yer took a blind bit of notice.*

ARTHUR: *Ah, you've got to enjoy yourself.*

BERT: *Right! But you've got to keep your feet on the ground as well.*

ARTHUR: *I can't see any use in that. You see people settle down and before they know where they are, they've kicked the bucket.*

BERT: *It ain't altogether like that.*

ARTHUR: *Yeah, I know, but it would be if yer didn't watch it.*

BERT: *There's an easier way of getting things than lashing out all the time.*

ARTHUR: *You think so? Listen! If I get mixed up in what goes on, that's my business.*

BERT: *I suppose it is.*

ARTHUR: *You bet it is. I've still got some fight left in me, not like most people.*

BERT: *I'm not saying you ain't. Where does all this fighting get yer?*

325

ARTHUR: *I don't see what not fighting gets yer . . . eh! Like mum and dad.*

BERT: *What do yer mean? They got all they want.*

ARTHUR: *Ar! They've got television set and a packet of fags, but they're both dead from the neck up. I'm not saying it's their fault, mind yer. They've had their hash settled for them, so that all the bloody gaffers can push them around like a lot of sheep.*

BERT: *I've seen you in some funny moods, Arthur, but I've never seen yer like this before.*

ARTHUR stops standing by the tree and comes to crouch beside BERT, his rod in his hand.

ARTHUR: *I want more in life, Bert, than me mum and dad have got.*

His rod gives a jerk.

ARTHUR: *Hey, I've got one!*

He starts to pull in the fish on the end of his line.

BERT: *Great.*

Now ARTHUR and DOREEN are coming across rough fields on a hill. They are happy. Beyond them is the devastation and hope of a half-built housing estate.

ARTHUR: *It's good to be out.*

DOREEN: *It's nice out here.*

ARTHUR: *Peaceful for a change.*

DOREEN: *I asked mum if we could live at home. She said it would be all right.*

ARTHUR: *Until we get a new house. I wouldn't mind living in an old one.*

DOREEN: *I would. I want a new home with a bathroom and everything.*

ARTHUR: *Me and Bert used to run all over these hills when we was kids. Blackberrying. There won't be blackberries or a blade of grass here much longer.*

He turns and throws stones towards the housing estate.

DOREEN sits on the grass.

DOREEN: *What did yer do that for?*

ARTHUR: *I don't know. Just felt like it, I suppose.*

DOREEN: *Maybe one of them houses will be for us.*

ARTHUR: *I know.*

DOREEN: *You shouldn't throw things, Arthur, like that.*

ARTHUR: *It won't be the last one I throw.*

> DOREEN looks at ARTHUR, and he gives up his mood and puts on his best smile.

ARTHUR: *Come on, duck, let's get down.*

> He pulls DOREEN to her feet, and they move away across the fields down the hill, towards the new houses.
>
> Fade out.

Brief Encounter (1945)

From *The Film and The Public* by Roger Manvell (Penguin Books, 1955)

Brief Encounter is one of those rare films for which one can never be sure to whom the real credit is due, one of those films one can offer to critics of the artistic integrity of the medium as an example of the unity achieved by the co-operation of many creative minds. That devoted care was given to this picture the result itself is evidence. I do not remember any more moving performance than that given by Celia Johnson. The theme and situation are perfect for so sensitive an actress, and these are the work of Noël Coward. The visual conception, the sympathetic eye that watches Miss Johnson, and relates her work to that of the other people, and to the environment of home, and street, and station which are so much part of her life, is the creative work of the director David Lean.

The theme and situation are universal. They belong to all human beings whether they have individually endured a similar love-tragedy or not. Laura Jesson is a kindly attractive woman with two children. She is married to a kindly, unimaginative husband and lives a contented, unawakened life. She visits the small town of Milford each Thursday, shops, goes to the pictures, and catches her evening train home from Milford Junction. She has a brief encounter in the station refreshment room with a doctor who removes some grit from her eye. He also visits Milford on Thursdays. A chance tea together follows. Then lunch. Then the pictures. Their acquaintance grows into an intense and passionate love. He also is married and has children. But unlike her husband he is a man with a genuine belief in his vocation, and the vital appreciation of life and need for love which go with it, and the sight of him stirs her to her depths and turns each Thursday into a vortex of emotional anticipation. They realize the dangers and difficulties of their situation. They experience the shame of domestic evasion, and lies, and subterfuge. They decide to part.

The film begins with their parting, mercilessly ravaged by an unsuspecting garrulous woman who is one of Laura's acquaintances. We ourselves know little more than this intruder. At home again, stricken with emotional sickness, Laura tells her story in imagination to her husband, who sits trite and dull over his crossword puzzle. The story takes us back and so leads through to their parting again, with our full realization of its pain and tension. It is a brilliant piece of structure and directing. We see the same final touch of his hand on her shoulder with new eyes.

I do not remember a moment when Celia Johnson's performance falters in a part where emotional over-playing or false intonations would have turned the film from a study of life itself into another piece of cinema fiction. It is a uniquely beautiful portrait; our sympathy grows with knowledge, and Laura's beauty grows with our sympathy. The movement of the film and our relation to the character develop with the same tempo of understanding with which we all live and meet and love. It is this quality which makes the film inescapably human, and whilst we watch it we are with this other human being as with a friend.

Celia Johnson has a small pointed face with wide emotional eyes. She looks quite ordinary until it is time for her to look like what she feels. Trevor Howard plays his first considerable part in this film: he does not look ordinary, but he is not required to do so. He has strength, ease, and charm; his performance is quiet and assured. The poetry of this film, its revealing study of a man and a woman almost out of control, reveals a fine balance of their strength and weakness, now one taking the lead, now the other. It would be difficult to find a more profound study of distressed love in the history of the cinema.

Into all this complexity, Milford Junction enters as a poetic image. Its passing express trains have the rush and power of passion, its platforms and subways the loneliness of waiting lovers. Its local trains jerk and shunt with their faithful service of routine domesticity. The imagery of trains has seldom been so finely used as in that last terrifying shot when the express screams by with its windows flashing a staccato rhythm of white lights across Laura's agonized face. It is hysteria visually and aurally personified. It is the image of a moment of intended but uncommitted suicide.

Each detail of background is authentic, the streets, shops, café, and cinema. To touch the film with humour Stanley Holloway and

Joyce Carey play out a grotesque love-affair in the station bar, and whilst this happens we can rest from the intense emotions of the main story in the comic casualness of their love-making. All the other characters, too, are exaggerations of reality. But this, strangely enough, does not matter, for they are all seen through the eyes of Laura, and in her suffering are as grotesquely different from herself as the close shots of Dolly Messiter's chattering lips are from Laura's pale face as she sits opposite her in the village train. The film always returns to Laura: it is her story told by herself and addressed without his knowledge to her husband. The main achievement is that of Celia Johnson, but supported throughout by the creative sympathy of her director, David Lean.

* * *

From *A Mirror for England* by Raymond Durgnat (Faber and Faber Ltd, 1970)
More representative of the range of middle-class loyalties is David Lean's *Brief Encounter* (1945). To see it again twenty years on, at the Baker Street Classic, is to see another film entirely. Not that it no longer rings true. But the lovers in the drab Milford Junction buffet seem so strained, guilty, cowed, and therefore cold, that in 1965 the audience in this usually polite and certainly middle-class hall couldn't restrain its derision and repeatedly burst into angry exasperated laughter. Infected by such reaction one could, with them, see how dismally Trevor Howard's cringing ' Please, please I humbly beg you . . .' suggested a little boy shame about anything so physical, while Celia Johnson's cold, pat, yap-yapping correctness taken at the time as the reactions of the nice Englishwoman, seemed to shriek the tensions of frigidity. The erstwhile ordinary housewife seemed another Bette Davis, with exotic-neurotic dark-ringed eyes, brittle voice and moral hypochondria. Not since *The Entertainer* on its general release have I known an audience so convulsed by loathing of a film. Even the name of the town enraged a well-spoken young lady who finally cried out, ' Where the hell is Milford Junction anyway? ' When the lovers were shamed out of consummation by the man's creepy smarmy friend (Valentine Dyall) — ' I'm not angry with you — just disappointed ', it seemed, suddenly, that these two had never been lovers at all; they were both too sick to be. Indeed *Brief Encounter* is the locus classicus of what is the renunciation

drama which in *Look Back in Anger* Claire Bloom tries to play so soulfully but which Jimmy Porter so scathingly disrupts. And that's what happened to Lean's film — Jimmy Porter came along. Much of Noël Coward's script was spotted as woman's magazine stuff anyway, but its subsequent collapse results, essentially, from the combination of proletarian energy and new morality eroding those conventions within which it had most meaning. The film, however, retains enough truth to win through to a new meaning, about utterly humiliated love. Perhaps audience derision is a defence against a tragedy far deeper than that of separation. This encounter reveals the externally decorous, concealed, internal destruction, by all the guilts in the decency code, of instinct and nerve; of which just enough remained for hope and pain. The last, ' happy ' scene thus becomes a nadir of abjectness. This isn't to deny that that code is defensible in many of its points of behaviour. If the old morality seems obnoxious to many now it's for the intensity of its guilts and complacencies, for its contempt for the libidinal even when that's perfectly compatible with social obligations, for the uniformity which it presupposes in human nature, for the reach-me-down crudity of its morality. ' Wives and husbands should put loyalty before joy. Never leave the plain old girl, however mean she always was, for a fresh young lady. Good time girls are cold hearted, and end strangled, or in the condemned cell, or racked by flames and typhus. Promiscuous people are stupid, vulgar and/or nasty. Men should quietly let woman nag them. True affection is restrained and asexual: ' Make tea not love '.

The Third Man (1949)

Graham Greene's description of his main characters

ROLLO (HOLLY) MARTINS:
> A Canadian, aged about 35. He has been invited to Vienna by his old friend, Harry Lime, to write propaganda for a volunteer medical unit Lime runs. A simple man who likes his drink and his girl, with more courage than discretion. He has a great sense of loyalty towards Lime whom he met first at school, and even his blunderings are conditioned by his loyalty.
> His love for Anna arises from the fact that she shares his

devotion to Lime. Unlike Lime he has never made much out of life. He is an unsuccessful writer of Westerns, who has never seen a cowboy, and he has no illusions about his own writing.

HARRY LIME:

Harry Lime has always found it possible to use his devoted friend. A light, amusing, ruthless character, he has always been able to find superficial excuses for his own behaviour. With wit and courage and immense geniality, he has inspired devotion both in Rollo Martins and the girl Anna, but he has never felt affection for anybody but himself. He has run his medical unit to help his racket in diluted penicillin.

ANNA SCHMIDT:

An Estonian (Czechoslovakian), and therefore officially a Russian citizen, she has been living in Vienna and working as a small part actress under the protection of forged Austrian papers procured for her by Harry Lime, whom she loves. Unlike Martins she has few illusions about Harry. She has loved him for what he is and not for what she imagined him to be, and his death leaves her completely indifferent as to her own fate.

COL. CALLOWAY:

In charge of the British Military Police in Vienna. A man with a background of Scotland Yard training; steady, patient and determined in his work — a man who is always kindly up to the point when it interferes with the job, who never gets angry (because it would be unprofessional) and regards Martins with amused tolerance.

SGT. PAINE:

An ex-London policeman whose spiritual home is the Tottenham Court Road and the streets around it. He has the same professional calm and patience as his Colonel, for they are both, as it were, from the same school — London and the Yard, the charge room and the Courts. He is the only man in Vienna who knows Martins' books, and he admires them greatly.

CAPT. CARTER (CRABBIT):

With his companion, Tombs, Carter has been shifted from regimental duties (for the good of the regiment) to the Cultural Re-education Section of G.H.Q. He is glad to be out of uniform (it enables him to eat in Austrian restaurants), and the only shadow on the new easy life of organising lectures, etc., at the Cultural Institute is the fear that some mistake may put him back in uniform again. In spite of this fear he is an ebullient, optimistic character.

CAPT. TOMBS (CRABBIT):

Unlike Carter, Tombs is saturnine. He has little hope that this culture racket will last, Needless to say that neither man has any idea of how the new job should be done, nor indeed of the meaning of culture.

DR. WINKEL:

Harry Lime's doctor and confederate. Very precise, very neat, very clean and unforthcoming. A collector of religious *objets d'art* without any belief in religion.

BARON KURTZ:

Harry Lime's chief confederate. An aristocrat who has come down in the world and now plays a violin at the Casanova night club. He manages to keep a certain faded elegance and charm, but like his *toupée* it doesn't quite ring true.

TYLER (POPESCU):

An American attached to an American cultural mission in Vienna, who has been enlisted by Lime, apparently very trustworthy, with tousled grey hair and kindly longsighted humanitarian eyes; one would have said a really good American type.

JOSEPH HARBIN:

A medical orderly at a military hospital who first acted as an agent for Lime in obtaining penicillin, but later became an informer used by the police to procure information against the racketeers. He has disappeared when the story opens.

PORTER:

An elderly man employed in the block where Lime lived; a cautious, nervous man who does not want to get involved in anything. He has heard the accident which so conveniently disposed of Lime and saw the body carried by three men. As only two men gave evidence at the inquest, his evidence would have been of great value, but he did not come forward.

Opening sequence of the film version

Credits roll out over a huge close-up of the strings of a zither.
Sound of the ' Harry Lime ' theme playing.

Many different shots of Vienna.

VOICE over: *I never knew the old Vienna before the war, with its
Strauss music, its glamour and easy charm — Constantinople suited
me better. I really got to know it in the classic period of the Black
Market —* Shot of boots and stockings changing hands — *We'd run
anything, if people wanted it enough and had the money to pay. Of
course, a situation like that does tend to amateurs —* Shot of a body
floating in an icy river — *but you know they can't stay the course
like a professional.* Shot of a poster: ' You are now entering the
American zone '. *Now the city is divided into four zones, each
occupied by a power —* Shots of British, Russian and French
posters — *the Americans, the British, the Russians and the French.
But the centre of the city — that's international, policed by an International Patrol.* Shot of guard duty being changed. *One member of
each of the four powers. What a hope they had, all strangers to the
place and none of them could speak the same language, except for a
sort of smattering of German.* Shot of jeep-load of mixed guards, all
silent. *Good fellows on the whole, even if Vienna doesn't look any
worse than a lot of other European cities, bombed about a bit. . . .
Oh wait, I was going to tell you —* Shots of bomb-sites — *I was
going to tell you about Holly Martins, an American — he came all
the way here to visit a friend of his —* Shot of soldiers standing on
parade in a square. *The name was Lime, Harry Lime.* Soldiers are
now seen marching. *Now Martins was broke and Lime had offered
him — I don't know — some sort of a job. Anyway, there he was,
poor chap, happy as a lark and without a cent.* Shot of a train pulling
into the station. The theme music swells with the train pulling in.
HOLLY MARTINS gets off the train and walks through the barrier,
looking for someone.

Guards from the four zones wait at the barrier.

AMERICAN GUARD: *Passports please. . . .*

[Continue as in the screenplay.]

*   *   *

335

From *The Theme of the Double in The Third Man* by Joseph A. Gomez (Film Heritage Vol 6; No 4; Summer 1971)

In *The American Cinema,* Andrew Sarris relegates Carol Reed to the ' less than meets the eye category ', and even dismisses his ' golden period ' with the remark that Reed never came to grips with the literary themes of Joseph Conrad or Graham Greene. One cannot attempt to rescue Reed from evaluations concerning the decline of his films since *Outcast of the Islands* (1952), but surely the fallacy of Sarris' generalization becomes evident to any sensitive reader of Greene's work who has seen Reed's *The Third Man* (1949). For it is in this film that Reed most brilliantly embodies the visual essence of Greene's literary conceptions.

The genesis of the film can be traced to producer Alexander Korda's desire for the successful continuation of the Greene-Reed collaboration which had begun with *The Fallen Idol* (1948). Korda requested Greene to write a screenplay ' about the four-power occupation of Vienna ', and Greene began his treatment of what was to become *The Third Man* with an old scrapped introductory paragraph about the funeral and later appearance of a supposedly dead man named Harry. His first draft was in the form of a short novel, but with Reed's assistance, it was then transformed into film script form.

Numerous changes were made during the shooting, and the post-production script differs somewhat from the shooting script as Greene conceived it. Problems with casting and setting necessitated many minor changes, and even actors contributed to the final script. Joseph Cotten objected to the name Rollo, which was changed to Holly, and Orson Welles (Harry) improvised the now famous Swiss cuckoo clock speech.

Both the first draft and the actual film script, however, harken back to one of Greene's obsessional motifs. The concept of the ' divided self ' or the double appeared in his first novel *The Man Within* (1929) and became the dominant theme of *Rumour at Nightfall* (1932). It is also found to some degree in such novels as *The Power and the Glory* (1940) and *The Heart of the Matter* (1948), but is perhaps most intriguingly presented in *The Third Man.*

Greene's exploration of the theme in his first treatment of the work is embryonic and offers little more than the employment of a hackneyed cliché in a ' pot-boiler ' story. The narrative presents the first person account of Major Calloway, who is quick to point out the warring elements in the character of the protagonist, Rollo Martins: ' There was always a conflict in Rollo Martins — between the absurd Christian name and the sturdy Dutch (for generations back) surname. Rollo looked at every woman that passed, and Martins renounced them for ever. I don't know which of them wrote the Westerns.' The tension in Martins' nature never reaches the simplistic profundities of the Jekyll and Hyde dichotomy; rather it is a division between a blundering, childish naive vision and the virtues of common sense, restraint, and intelligence.

Martins, a ' cheerful fool ', makes his meagre living by writing fourth-rate novels, and although he frequently suffers from poor judgment, at least, he has few illusions about his writing talents. He arrives in Vienna, with little money and a rather large appetite for women and liquor, to work for Harry Lime — only to find that his old school chum has just died.

Those warring factions which accentuate Martins' personality seem integrated in Lime, whom Greene himself describes as ' a light, amusing, ruthless character ' who possesses wit, courage and geniality. In the beginning, Martins refuses to accept a tarnished view of his friend and makes various connections between himself and Harry. ' Because if Harry was that kind of racketeer, I must be one too. We always worked together.' But what Lime really represents to the disintegrating Martins is something that he has never been — a success, and, at times, Greene even vaguely suggests that Lime is Martins' alter ego.

After his meddling uncovers the fact that Lime's death is merely a clever ruse and after his realization of the true nature of Lime's moral bankruptcy, Martins finally agrees to assist Calloway in Lime's capture. Moral integrity, however, plays little part in Martins' motivation in the betrayal of his friend. At least part of his reason stems from his attachment to Anna, Lime's girl friend, whom he finally wins in the first version of the story.

The idea of the ' divided self ' is still found in the shooting script, but the emphasis is distinctly altered. The split-personality of Martins is dropped, and instead the double relationship between Martins and Lime is expanded. In the short novel version, the device of the double seems to have little ulterior purpose, but in the shooting script, important moral aspects are involved. Martins and Lime are not exactly 'secret sharers', but it is through his confrontation with his alter ego in Vienna that 'happy as a lark' Martins finds a new maturity and a new moral centre.

Both characters are compared to children. Although Lime finds Nietzschen justifications for his actions, he is more frequently presented as the ego-centric, amoral child lost in a changing universe. 'He never grew up. The world grew up round him, that's all — and buried him.' Martins, however, grows from immature naivety to a sense of social and moral responsibility. This change is best suggested (albeit perhaps a bit too abruptly) in the sequence in which he visits the children's hospital, sees the victims of Lime's penicillin racket, and then again agrees to be Calloway's 'dumb decoy duck'.

Greene's shooting script is especially rich in verbal suggestions which link Rollo (Holly) Martins and Harry Lime. Early in the script, Holly makes a slip in talking about himself and Harry. 'I guess there's nobody knew Harry like he did . . . like I did.' The confusion of identity is later intensified when Holly comes to pick up Anna to visit the porter. He arrives at a time in early evening when Harry used to visit Anna, and for a moment, it seems that she thinks her visitor is Harry. She quickly recovers from her wish-fulfilling reverie and gets Holly to talk about his old friend, but before they leave, she calls him by Harry's name. Later at the train station, Anna questions Holly and again confuses his name with that of her lover.

Aside from these verbal suggestions, recurring patterns of imagery also define the particular relationship between Holly and Harry. There are comparisons throughout the script between the various characters and animals, and frequently this animal imagery is associated with the idea of betrayal. When Holly attempts to hide from Popescu's thugs at the Cultural Centre, his presence is revealed by the squawking parrot which nips his finger as he escapes through the window. Later, Harry's presence is made known, first to the audience and then to Holly, when Anna's cat reveals that he is standing in a doorway outside her apartment house. To some degree, these animals also serve as types of totem identification figures. The silly, loud, squawking parrot is like the blundering Holly, while Harry, the crafty silent cat, is capable of moving through the city like a demonic presence.

Imagery and verbal associations may present the theme of the double in the shooting script, but one must *see* the film in order to

338

be convinced of the brilliant, almost subliminal, suggestions that Carol Reed presents to the viewer.

Like Joseph Losey, Reed seems preoccupied with 'baroque construction' in his films, and through careful cinematic manipulation, he evokes a 'spirit of place' far beyond any usual preoccupation with setting. Thus, in *The Third Man*, the city of Vienna becomes intricately enmeshed in the continuity of the film. The city is a complex web of impressive beauty and utter ruin, and its sinister, labyrinthine qualities provide a perfect backdrop for the confrontation between Holly and Harry.

Holly, the visitor, the stranger in his own life, is frequently seen frustrated by the environment of this 'closed city'. Ladders, narrow alleys, barred windows, and winding staircases constantly hinder his physical movement, and these concrete objects mirror the maze of lies he encounters from Popescu and Kurtz and the confusion in his own mind. The cab sequence in which Holly believes he is being taken to his death is especially effective. Shots of the speeding car cross-cut with the close-ups of the bizarre, destitute, street people, and shots of Holly framed by the vertical bars which separate the driver from the passenger evoke this intense sense of entrapment, which will finally be shifted to Harry at the end of the film. Harry's mysterious appearances and departures give the film a gothic quality, which is enhanced by Orson Welles' sinister smile, but in the end, Harry is also trapped by the city he knows so well. After the astonishing chase sequences through the sewers, the haven of our demonic antagonist, the wounded Harry, his body entangled in a circular staircase, finally reaches the bars of a sewer grate. Without the strength to push open the grate, he slides his fingers through the bars in one last grasp for freedom.

Further visual parallels link Holly and Harry throughout the film. After the small child leads the suspicious neighbours in pursuit of Anna and Holly, they escape down a ruined staircase and take refuge in a theatre. Later, when Harry is pursued by the police after discovering the trap at the café, he descends the same staircase and flees into the sewers.

When Anna's cat betrays the presence of Harry outside her apartment house, Holly is stunned for a moment. He then rushes into the street and is nearly hit by a car. The incident is necessary in order for Harry to escape from the doorway unseen, but Reed presents the sequence in such a way that it closely resembles Harry's supposed death in front of his apartment.

Aside from establishing these visual relationships, Reed reinforces the literary theme of the double through ' space play '. To make effective use of ' space play ', the director first of all establishes certain areas of the screen (or frame) as appropriate to certain objects or characters, and maintains them in these areas from shot to shot. Of course, if the dramatic situation demands it, the character may be ' transposed ' to a different area of the screen within a single shot.

From the opening of the film, the screen right acting area is associated with Holly. That is until he begins to investigate the ' death ' of his friend. At that point, he assumes the area of screen left, especially when he appears with Anna. Holly's conscious attempt to make Anna forget Harry is underscored by this ' space play ', for Harry is seen exclusively in the screen left acting area. During the sequence on the great wheel, Holly assumes his old screen right position and remains in that area with Anna after she finds out that Harry is still alive. At the very end of the film, Holly again assumes his screen right area. He is simply silly Holly Martins to Anna, and she walks right past him without acknowledging his existence.

These details and visual parallels are not accidental; they are part of a pattern of visual rhythms which support the themes and the symmetrical structure of the film. Aside from the prologue, spoken by Reed himself, and forced on him by Korda in order to explain the location and situation to a mass audience, the film could be schematized in the form of a pyramid.

The film begins with Holly's arrival in Vienna and the ' burial ' of Harry. The rising action might be described as Holly's search for the truth about Harry's death. This culminates in the great wheel sequence, and the downward action, Holly's search for the moral centre of himself, begins shortly thereafter. The film ends with the burial of Harry and Holly's plans to leave Vienna.

The great wheel sequence, aside from being the most famous in the film, is the only intensely dramatic confrontation between Holly and Harry, and the sequence itself follows a pyramidal structure. The dramatic tension is reinforced by the very movement of the car on the wheel and by the numerous middle shots of both men together. As the closed car ascends, Harry and Holly probe each other. Holly finally realizes the depths of his friend's amorality, and Harry, in turn, finds out that the police 'know everything'.

As the car swings to a standstill at the top of the wheel, the dramatic tension reaches its high point. Harry debates the prospect of killing his old friend, but upon learning that the police have dug up his coffin and found Harbin, he turns to Holly. ' What fools we are . . . [Holly] talking like this, as if I'd do that to you — or you to me.' It is at this point that the car begins its downward movement and that Holly begins the difficult task of re-examining his own value structure.

The final confrontation between the two men takes place in the sewers below the city, and if one extends the symbolic ramifications of the setting in this film, one might suggest that the sewers represent the unconscious level of Holly's mind. In any event, it is here that the recently matured Holly Martins is forced to shoot his old friend, Harry Lime.

At present, it is not fashionable to sing the praises of collaboration in film making. Many critics see the ' true ' film artist as the man who both writes his own original scripts and directs his film. Quality film making in England and America, however, more often depends on collaboration and cooperation, and *The Third Man* is one of the many films which might be used to illustrate the fact that a sensitive director can transform literary conception into visual artistry.

Kind Hearts and Coronets (1949)

From *Kind Hearts and Coronets* by Alan Stanbrook (Films and Filming, April 1964)

Critical reception of *Kind Hearts and Coronets* was not unanimously favourable in 1949 but it found its most perceptive champion in the *Daily Telegraph* of 27/6/49. The critic writes: ' *Kind Hearts and Coronets*, following closely as it does on *Whisky Galore* and *Passport to Pimlico*, completes a remarkable trio of comedies from Ealing Studios. Quality it shares with its predecessors, a degree of fantasy too. There similarity ends, originality begins; the joke repeated with variations is an aspect of murder.

' A joke in bad taste? On the contrary, the taste is impeccable. Lamb, wishing to enjoy the wit of Restoration Comedy, excused its indecency on the grounds that the characters had no reality and their actions therefore needed no reprobation. It is a major achievement of this film that just such an atmosphere of artificiality, so necessary if death is to be humorous, is established from the start. . . .

' Style, not story, holds the key to this special store of humour. Text for the treatment is to be found in Lytton Strachey. " The characters in comedy are real, but they exist in vacuo. They are neither to instruct us nor exalt us, but simply to amuse us. And therefore the effects that would in reality follow from their conduct must not appear. By the magic of comedy, what is melancholy in the actual society of life is converted into charming laughter and glittering delight."

' This " magic of comedy " is present, the result of alchemy by the adapters, who appear to have transmuted a farthing into a £5 note. To glance at Roy Horniman's novel is to realize the achievement of Robert Hamer and John Dighton, authors of the screenplay. They have transformed an Edwardian melodrama, whose only humours are of the unconscious variety, into a high comedy that is enlivened with cynicism, loaded with dramatic irony and shot through with a suspicion of social satire.'

C. A. Lejeune, in the previous day's *Observer*, had similarly admired the film, stressing Alec Guinness' contribution to its success: ' This delightful burlesque of Victorian melodrama takes its gusto from the fact that Alec Guinness, an actor, I need hardly remind you, of parts, plays eight of them in it without flagging. He represents the entire membership of the ducal family of D'Ascoyne who must be eliminated before the latest upstart of D'Ascoyne can inherit the coronet. He plays an admiral, a general, a banker, a vicar (easily the best imitation), a hunting duke, an amateur photographer, a masher and even a suffragette with the ease of a Wimbledon champion at a suburban tennis-tea and such is his versatility that I was only sorry he didn't play, at least, every male role in the picture. In particular I should have liked him to have had a shot at the heir presumptive, the young man from the wrong branch of the family who goes to such vigorous lengths to secure the title. In this part Dennis Price is smooth enough — a good silk dressing gown type — but seems pitifully outclassed every time he comes up against a Guinness. Valerie Hobson and Joan Greenwood, as the two young ladies principally involved, do pretty work — although I preferred Miss Hobson's simulation of a slight lisp to Miss Greenwood's exaggeration of a wee catarrh — and Miles Malleson is splendid as a hangman who can never again be content with hemp after using the silken rope. This British version of *Arsenic and Old Lace*, however, remains predominantly a Guinness film.'

But if it pleased the newspapers, Hamer's film fared less well at the hands of the journals. Lindsay Anderson, for example, in *Sequence,* after complimenting it on its literacy, continues: 'It is not enough, however, for dialogue to be wittily phrased, playing finely timed; this is not after all a play but a film. And, excellently though some episodes are handled — the disintegration of Henry D'Ascoyne for instance, a happy plagarism (sic) from *M Verdoux* — the film in general lacks a visual style equal to its script. Not that it is often anything but attractive in appearance; the sets are mostly charming, the costumes exuberantly decorative and the photography delicately sensitive to the period elegances of each. But visual flow, expressiveness of cutting and set up seem largely absent. As a result certain dialogue sequences become tedious to watch; and the important trial scene in the House of Lords (prefaced by an inexcusable stock shot of the Houses of Parliament) is assembled without any particular visual logic or emphasis. *Kind Hearts and Coronets* is an enjoyable film and it gets away with a great deal. With so much in fact that its makers deserve salutation as pioneers in the little explored territory of adult British comedy.'

Kind Hearts and Coronets began its life when Robert Hamer decided that an indifferent Edwardian novel of 1910, called *Israel Rank* by Roy Horniman, contained an idea which could be profitably developed into a film. He spent seven weeks thinking about the project and then wrote a frenzied draft screenplay in a week. This was amended in later versions but the whole character of the film was established in the first version. Hamer calculated that sixty per cent of the original screenplay survives intact in the completed film.

Hamer's intentions were to make a film quite distinct in kind from anything hitherto seen in the English language, to use the latter in a more expressive way than he had previously had the opportunity to do and to break with the stereotyped characterization of British cinema by disregarding conventional morality. It was this last feature which compelled the producers to alter certain aspects of the script for American consumption because the censor disapproved of murder as material for comedy.

Alec Guinness' multiple roles presented fewer production difficulties than might be supposed — fewer, for example, than the dual roles of *The Prisoner of Zenda*. Though Guinness plays eight parts they are only seen together in one shot in the family church, where the surviving members foregather to inter the latest victim of Louis' vengeance. At first Hamer had thought of engaging eight actors of similar facial characteristics but when he realized that they were seen together only once he decided to cast the same actor for each role. In the required shot only six of the original eight remain and it was accordingly exposed six times, masking all except the particular D'Ascoyne in each case.

Kind Hearts and Coronets was the third of a tradition of comic film-making that rapidly acquired the distinguishing trademark of Ealing Comedies. Yet it is not typical of the genre. The Ealing Comedies were characterized by their quaintness and their respect for individualism. The theme was almost identical from film to film and only the protagonists changed. In each an individual or small unit is pitted against a bureaucracy and frequently triumphs. Thus in *Whisky Galore* we have spirit drinkers versus the Customs, in *The Lavender Hill Mob* a clerk versus the Bank of England, in *The Man in The White Suit* a scientist versus Big Business, in *The Titfield Thunderbolt* a village community versus British Railways and so on. It is a development of the 'little man' philosophy of Chaplin as applicable to peculiarly British institutions and anomolies. Anglo-Saxon platitudes were never so bitingly lampooned.

Against this mainstream of Ealing Comedies stand two works of a quite different order, which share a gallows humour not usually associated with the name of Ealing. These are *Kind Hearts and Coronets* and Mackendrick's *The Ladykillers*. There is a streak of viciousness in both these films which anticipates the sick humour of, say, a Jules Feiffer. Gallows humour is one of the most difficult of all genres to do well, which accounts for its rarity. One may think of Carné's *Drôle de Drame* or Hitchcock's *The Trouble With Harry* but this potentially rich field remains largely unexploited in cinema.

The social significance of *Kind Hearts and Coronets* is no less remarkable however. Hamer's Louis Mazzini is in effect Joe Lampton in drainpipe trousers. Both are obsessed by the injustices of class distinction and determined to force their way into a society to which they feel entitled. Both set their sights on marrying above their background and both have a mistress on the side. The differences between them lie in the half century that separates them in time. The class barriers are not quite so rigid and exclusive as they were for our fathers. To achieve his ends Louis Mazzini must polish off his competitors; Joe Lampton takes the simpler and less drastic expediency of putting Susan Brown in the family way.

The most controversial aspect of *Kind Hearts and Coronets* is the screenplay and the form it takes. No other English language film has relied so heavily on its dialogue and commentary. It has led purists to reject it as a valid contribution to motion pictures. But art is what works and not what theorists tell us ought to work. Those who insist on the supreme importance of the visual image are now thirty-four years behind the times. Film is now an audio-visual art and there is nothing reactionary about Hamer's adroit balance of visual and literary wit. In *Kind Hearts and Coronets* they are in fact complementary and critics who maintain that it is equivalent to filmed theatre have literally missed half the fun of the film. Curiously, the same year saw a similar experiment from America in Joseph L. Mankiewicz's *A Letter To Three Wives* which had the same urbane and caustic quality artfully established in the contrast between visuals and narration. Rules are made to be unlearnt and Robert Hamer has done so with consummate skill.

The mood of *Kind Hearts and Coronets* is confidently established with the credit titles — a series of Edwardian vignettes accompanied by the strains of *Don Giovanni*. Diabolism and elegance are to be the key tones of Hamer's direction, reflected in the machinations of Louis Mazzini and the period detail of the art direction and costumes. Sibella's monstrous hats, for example, are at once an ironic comment on her own extravagance and that of the era in general.

The prison scenes which frame the long flashback of Louis' career are purposely shot in a darker tone than the remainder of the film. They form a contrast to Louis' refined skulduggery, and help to accentuate the comic enormity of his crimes. These scenes are almost a parody of the German expressionist cinema of the 'twenties: the ominous music and the pools of spotlight promise melodrama but the atmosphere is instantly dispelled by the bumbling of Miles Malleson's earnest hangman. Similarly Dennis Price's emergence from Pentonville at the close, dwarfed as he is by acres of wall, echoes back to the portentousness of Fritz Lang's *Destiny*.

Hamer's title is taken from Tennyson's poem *Lady Clara Vere de Vere*:

> *Kind Hearts are more than coronets*
> *And simple faith than Norman blood.*

and this social antithesis epitomizes the conflict between Louis and the Chalfonts. The latter are shot through with aristocratic snobbery. Louis' mother, their own daughter, is to them ' some woman from Tooting or somewhere '; if they buried her in the family vault there would soon be no room for them. Louis, on the other hand, is really a very delicate and kindly man; his devotion to his mother is exemplary and his principles forbid him to join Ethelred in blood sports.

It is appropriate, therefore, that Hamer should have chosen contrast as the means of effecting his comedy. A simple dissolve underlines the gulf between the splendours of Chalfont Castle and the miseries of Balaclava Avenue. Louis' school lesson on the sixth commandment is cut back to a shot of the prison cell. A close-up juxtaposes Louis' small box of chocolates with the much bigger one that Lionel has just given Sibella. In a witty piece of dramatic doubling Hamer uses the phrase ' a matter of some delicacy ' as a motif in Lionel's self-pitying interview with Louis and the Scotland Yard Inspector's preamble to the arrest. And, best of all, Sibella's seduction at the hands of Louis precedes her immaculate white wedding to Lionel.

Though it was the verbal wit of the screenplay that attracted attention thirteen years ago, the visual wit is equally sardonic. The Chalfont title was earned for services rendered to Charles II during his exile and Hamer shows us a hand polishing the frame of a portrait of the king. A pan to the left reveals another hand polishing the picture of a woman and we learn that descent via the female line was earned for services rendered after his restoration. A close-up of the Ensign gradually sinking out of frame is used as a symbol of the sinking of Horatio D'Ascoyne, while Louis attaches a literal interpretation to the idiom ' caviare to the general ' to rid himself of Rufus. The huge dining hall at Chalfont Castle is filmed in long shot to reveal the circle of empty seats bearing witness to Louis' progress, and, during the trial scene, the absence of D'Ascoynes to testify to Louis' character is illustrated by a shot of Louis ruefully inspecting his nails.

346

Hamer is careful to make his points visually as well as verbally. Our introduction to Louis is effected by a track-in to the silken collar of his dressing gown as he sits in the cell. A ' Warning ' notice strategically placed left of the frame anticipates young Ascoyne D'Ascoyne's precipitant despatch over the weir. The director is also fully conversant with the possibilities of deep focus photography, such as Wyler and Gregg Toland perfected in the telephone scene of *The Best Years of Our Lives*. He shows us a medium close-up of Edith while smoke pours from the dark room in the background to verify her husband's inflammatory departure from life. Later he focuses simultaneously on the Rev. Henry D'Ascoyne searching for a cigar in the background while Louis administers poison to the port in the foreground. Sibella's suspicions of Louis are confirmed when she says: ' I wouldn't be surprised if you'd murdered them all ' and he drops a glass. A tilt of the camera as he bends to retrieve the fragments focuses on Sibella's accusing eyes.

The potentialities of music for ironic comment are ably exploited. The death of the tenor Mazzini is accompanied by a chorus signifying his transposition to the heavenly choir. A descending scale counterpoints the off-screen descent of Lady Agatha D'Ascoyne's punctured balloon and a rasping fanfare of trumpets the stock shot of the Houses of Parliament. Wit is Hamer's intention and he employs every means at his disposal to achieve it.

Lindsay Anderson accuses the film of lacking a visual style equal to its script. Certainly there are flaws like the studio tank shot of two miniature ships colliding. But there is more visual style in Hamer's film than Anderson suspected. What could be more stylish than the little scene that opens with Sibella waltzing alone and concludes with her spinning giddily in Louis' arms? It is a perfect illustration of Louis' remark: ' you were born to dance through life, Sibella.' Hamer's style is episodic but the cumulative effect is art. Frequently the visuals anticipate the narration: thus we see Louis' father keel over dead a second before the off-screen voice describes whose death we are watching. Cocteau and Resnais have later developed this device with remarkable effect. In the closing scene the director poses the problem facing the newly released Louis by intercutting shots of the two waiting women as our hero muses: ' How happy could I be with either. . . .' The awful realization of self incrimination is conveyed by two tracking shots, first into close-up of Louis and then into close-up of the memoirs still lying in the prison cell.

Finally there is the acting of this excellent comedy. Few directors have been so fortunate as Hamer in their casts, for each role is ideally filled. Alec Guinness received all the accolades when the film first appeared and undoubtedly his performances are a *tour de force*. One can scarcely imagine another actor extracting richer fun from the line: ' I always say that my West window has all the exuberance of Chaucer without any of the concomitant crudities.' But these are caricatures rather than fully rounded characterizations and retrospect is apt to throw a different light on comparative merits. It is Raymond Massey rather than the mannered James Dean who gives the better performance in *East of Eden* and so, here, it is Dennis Price who makes the greater impression. Price's gift for laconic humour has never been better displayed and this remains his finest, most expertly calculated performance. Joan Greenwood, too, is wickedly good as Sibella, a role tailor-made to suit her unique personality. *Kind Hearts and Coronets,* in short, is not a king size Guinness but a rare old port which deserves to be sipped and relished. And like port it matures with age.

Saturday Night and Sunday Morning (1961)

From *Saturday Night and Sunday Morning* by Boleslaw Sulik (Definition, No. 3; 1961)

I remember seeing Karel Reisz interviewed on television by Ricardo Arragno, soon after the premiere and initial success of *Saturday Night and Sunday Morning.* A moment before Karel Reisz came onto the screen the interviewer announced that he did not hold with those who regard a director as the film's author. Film, he argued, is a collective art, almost anonymous, like medieval gothic cathedrals. Mr Arragno's sense of timing — not to speak about his views on cinema — must be as disastrously bad as his tact.

Saturday Night and Sunday Morning is completely a director's film, yet few reviewers seemed to have realized this. Perhaps the fact that it was based on the best-selling novel, and the screenplay credited to the book's author, has misled them. But Alan Sillitoe's novel was not adapted — it was used, freely and creatively.

Even the plot was considerably changed. Sillitoe's rather rambling narrative makes only loose connections between various isolated incidents. Arthur Seaton's life is a shapeless mess; the events do not seem to lead one to the other. Arthur's association with Brenda, the married woman, never comes to any real climax: when she becomes pregnant the prescribed treatment works and they can resume their relationship on the same terms. Later, when the two 'swaddies' beat him up for playing around with married women, and Arthur comments that it was 'not the first time he had been in a losing fight', he is doing no more than stating a fact. Even his meetings with Doreen fail to build up a relationship convincing and strong enough to justify Arthur's sudden decision to marry and change his mode of life.

In the film the incidents are selected from the novel, modified and connected up in such a way that they form a continuous chain of cause and effect. Brenda's attempt at abortion fails and this of course breaks up her relationship with Arthur and leaves him with vague feelings of guilt (strangely enough the censor has played a material part in the successful adaptation of the novel's plot. The original intention was to leave the abortion sequence more or less as it stands in the book. Karel Reisz hoped to make it grotesque and ugly and powerful enough to suggest its lasting impact on Arthur's mind. But the Board of Censors objected to this treatment and the director and writer were forced to change the script. And yet Karel Reisz admits that he has never regretted making those changes. This must be the only case on record of BBFC making a really creative contribution to a film). The beating up comes as a real climax, Arthur's symbolic retribution. After this Arthur has to make a new start. The Sunday Morning part follows naturally, as a logical epilogue.

Even more striking than this rearrangement of the book's structure is the change in attitude. Alan Sillitoe's novel gives a powerful expression to a personal brand of romantic anarchism, destructive and passionate, but perhaps lacking a clear sense of direction in spite of its political implications. It is a first person novel, rather egotistic, with the outlines of all subsidiary characters, especially women, blurred or dissolved. Arthur and his personal rebellion envelop everything. The film, on the other hand, places Arthur at a certain distance and encircles him with sharply observed minor characters. It becomes a serious study in working-class manners and makes a political — or moral — statement only indirectly, through the quality of life described. The difference between the novel and the film amounts to no less than a difference between a romantic and a rational approach to a similar theme, between an excitable gesture of defiance and a controlled and logical construction.

It is in the cinema that we find this film's genuine artistic antecedents: Karel Reisz's own *Momma Don't Allow* and *We Are the Lambeth Boys*. In fact rarely do we find such a straight and consistent line of development. *Momma . . .*, an early ' free cinema ' documentary about jazz clubs, which Karel Reisz co-edited with Tony Richardson, seems now rather amateurish and clumsy, but even there one recognizes a genuine attempt to find a level where it would be possible to describe young working-class people without a superior, patronizing attitude, and an avoidance of all journalistic labels. *We Are the Lambeth Boys*, the peak of ' free cinema ', represents a fulfilment, in a documentary form, of this search, *Saturday Night and Sunday Morning* carries it into a field of fiction, observing the other, the private side of a young worker's life. In fact the two films together form a statement so complete that it is difficult to imagine what more can Karel Reisz achieve in this direction without repeating himself.

As a study in manners *Saturday Night and Sunday Morning* is undoubtedly successful. Amazingly so, when one considers that Karel Reisz had no tradition to draw from and many pitfalls to avoid. He started, it is true, with two advantages: Alan Sillitoe's excellent dialogue and several good and well cast actors. Against this one has to count his lack of experience in handling professional actors and the fact that he was leading his players into a territory which in British cinema is a virgin land. His achievement here is really tremendous. One says this not to belittle the creative contribution made by individual actors. There are some very good and some not-so-good performances, but there is not one that rings false; and for this the director must take the credit.

Albert Finney as Arthur Seaton is equal to the technical demands the part makes on him, and has just that touch of personal magnetism, ' star quality ' if you like, needed to establish Arthur as a focal point of the environment. Arthur's early undisciplined rebelliousness is conveyed beautifully, and his growing awareness, leading to the final acceptance of responsibility is equally well managed. This is, of course, of the greatest importance, because Arthur, perhaps with the exception of Brenda, is the only character conceived dynamically, changing, developing, gaining weight with each succeeding sequence. The others are merely stated and related to Arthur so as to create a firm frame of social reference around him. Brenda, Arthur's married mistress, extremely well played by Rachel Roberts, supplies a note of real human tragedy, necessary, I think, to give the film true stature. Shirley Anne Field is surprisingly effective as Doreen. Her great beauty, which one was afraid might seem out of place in this story, is turned into an asset. Physical attractiveness, coupled with a pleasant manner, goes some way towards explaining Arthur's infatuation for such an essentially conventional girl. Hylda Baker as Aunt Ada, wise and cynical, conveying richness of experience in every word and gesture, completes a trio of successful female characters. Among the men, Norman Rossington is excellent as Bert. Quiet and authentic, he gives great solidity to Bert's friendship with Arthur.

What one remembers about *Saturday Night and Sunday Morning* apart from Arthur's character study, is a rich texture of minutely observed human behaviour, rather than any ' cinematic style '. The film is shot in a quiet, self-effacing manner, the camera being usually placed at a distance making possible an intimate and yet detached observation. Karel Reisz avoids big close-ups, anything smacking of melodrama, sensationalism or artificial ' hotting up ' of the story. Thus the fight scene is filmed entirely in a long shot, and only after it is finished are we taken closer to inspect the damage: Arthur's smashed, swollen, ugly face. The only departure from it and, it seems to me, the director's only false step, is a fairground sequence. There Karel Reisz falls into an obvious temptation of constructing a virtuoso passage. In a resulting mechanical excitement the motivation of Arthur's actions becomes blurred: the camera is taken for a breathless ride. Curiously, in the context of this film the bravura passage seems unoriginal, conventional. Fortunately, it does not last long. We are soon to the wonderful sanity of the rest of *Saturday Night and Sunday Morning*. But within this controlled and uniform style, the use of camera movements, editing and lighting is considerably varied. One has only to compare the love-making with Brenda, which has a certain documentary objectivity about it, with a lyrical quality the director gets into a similar scene between Arthur and Doreen.

The film is also strikingly successful as a piece of narrative. This is all the more note-worthy because the plot is rather feeble. Little really happens. Karel Reisz overcomes this by shrewd and daring pacing, and overlapping sequences, sometimes not obviously connected. Of course, the richness of sympathetic observation also helps. The bare plot could not sustain the interest in this way. As it is, Karel Reisz does almost too well. The narrative becomes so brisk, so smooth and self-contained, that one could almost wish for some frayed edges. But this is, perhaps, carrying criticism too far.

Karel Reisz has made a film which one can respond to and enjoy on several levels at once. It is a popular film, obviously seriously intentioned, entertaining, but not distracting. I think it will be enjoyed by a working-class audience and related by them to their own experience. It is, almost ideally, exactly a kind of film that is needed at this particular time.

Where now? One should perhaps sound a word of warning. This careful avoidance of sensationalism, fear of overstatement, may yet develop into an inhibition and restrict Karel Reisz's great potential. Whatever theme he tackles next, one hopes that having now mastered the techniques, he will let himself go.

Saturday Night and Sunday Morning ends with a beautiful scene, where the director perhaps for a moment identifies himself with his central character. Arthur throws stones at the new housing estate where he may soon live. Reprimanded by Doreen, he answers: ' these won't be the last stones I will throw, either.' Let's hope that this applies to Karel Reisz, too. In a dreary British cinema these stones are precious.